LITURGICAL
Spirituality

✠

LITURGICAL
Spirituality

Philip H. Pfatteicher

TRINITY PRESS INTERNATIONAL
Valley Forge, Pennsylvania

Trinity Press International, P.O. Box 851, Valley Forge, PA 19482-0851
Trinity Press International is a division of
the Morehouse Publishing Group

Library of Congress Cataloging-in-Publication Data

Pfatteicher, Philip H.
    Liturgical spirituality / Philip H. Pfatteicher.
    p.   cm.
    Includes bibliographical references and index.
    ISBN 1-56338-194-X (pbk. : alk. paper)
    1. Liturgics.   2. Spirituality.   I. Title.
BV178.P44 1997
264'.001–dc21   97-7376
                                        CIP

Printed in the United States of America

97   98   99   00   01   02   10   9 . 8   7   6   5   4   3   2   1

To Lois
and
to three exemplary priests and pastors
Andrew Mead
Jürgen Liias
Martin Hauser
all of whom have influenced these pages
in more ways than they can know

CONTENTS

✠

PREFACE

✠

In 1955 Louis Bouyer published his admirable study, *Liturgical Piety*. Bouyer, however, wrote before the far-reaching reforms of the Second Vatican Council, and that Council has fundamentally changed the whole Western church. Moreover, the word "piety" has long ceased to be a complimentary word, and even if one sets aside its derogatory connotation, "piety" may suggest merely an attitude, an approach rather than a way of praying and living.

"Spirituality" is currently a popular word. That very popularity makes one suspicious of its use and perhaps suspicious too of those who use it. The virtue of the word, however, is that it may suggest a process, a development, and so, at the risk of adopting a fad word of transitory interest, the present book bears the title *Liturgical Spirituality*.

The title, it should be noted, is not *Liturgy and Spirituality*. Such a title would seem to suggest a study of those places where two essentially separate disciplines and interests intersect as each moves along its particular axis. The title *Liturgical Spirituality* is meant to refer to that distinctive interior life of the spirit that is formed and nurtured by the church's liturgy. There are other kinds of spirituality that at least seem to flourish apart from or in addition to the liturgy: the spirituality of the desert ascetics of the early centuries of Christianity, the devotion of the Religious Society of Friends, many forms of meditation and spiritual discipline such as the Spiritual *Exercises* of Ignatius Loyola. The focus of this book, however, is on the spiritual life as formed by the liturgy.

"Liturgy" here is broadly understood as the basic ordered form of Christian worship, Eastern and Western, Catholic and Protestant, for I know of no other satisfactory way of considering worship except with a broad and inclusive view. Liturgy indeed may be said to be the fundamental source of Christian spirituality because liturgy is essentially prayer, and prayer is at its heart the work of the Holy Spirit. Systematic theology, biblical study, church history, pastoral theology — all, at least indirectly, deal with spirituality, that is, how one is to experience and live the Scriptures and their message as they have been received and interpreted and proclaimed and celebrated by the church. All the disciplines of divinity are drawn together by the liturgy of the church into an effective and evocative unity.

In considering the liturgy of the church we are not examining the work of a single independent artist but rather a work of centuries shaped by countless hands, some known, most unknown to us. We ought, therefore, to approach the liturgy as we approach a great medieval cathedral on which many generations have labored. The liturgy, like the great buildings in which it may be celebrated, is an imaginative construction that is still in progress, the creation of a living symbolic world by which we may order our lives and interpret our experience in continuity with the generations that have gone before us. Especially in chaotic and tumultuous times in which we reform and revolt and reshape, we need to attend closely to the church's liturgy that stands as a great achievement of the human imagination, a vision of rhythm and order, diverse and satisfying. And what it once was it can still be for those willing to give themselves to its stirring and noble action.

We must resist the temptation to warp and falsify the old to make it palatable to our own time. Such efforts at being current close off the possibility of learning from an unsettling confrontation with the old. Without a sense of a living past, we are corrupted, in whatever time we live, and we share unwittingly in the era's characteristic blindness. The only palliative for such inescapable distortion is to attend to old, apparently even alien ideas and actions. They can help free our minds from slavery to current fashion, sharpen our awareness of mistakes and half-truths, and correct our peculiar errors. Religion at its authentic best preserves the deep complexity of human experience.

A worthy liturgical spirituality involves the integration of objective and subjective piety, a balance between the communal and the personal maintained in such a way that each enriches the other. It is most of all through the experience provided by the liturgy, rather than by doctrine and discipline, that the church — particularly the Eastern church — has developed its people in Christian faith and life. This book then is an explication of the principal symbols of Christian worship, an essay on spirituality as experienced by a congregation, an expression of what a Christian assembly might feel as it goes about its characteristic and essential activity of worshiping God, for rituals reveal the deep convictions and experiences of a community. As the abbreviated summary of a dictum attributed to Prosper of Aquitaine has it, *lex orandi, lex credendi,* the rule of praying shapes the rule of believing. In anthropological terms, creed follows cult. The Christian liturgy is a most effective means of preserving and interpreting the faith.

The liturgy must be seen for its uniqueness, its inherent character, lying wrapped in its own ambience like the butterfly in the cocoon; and it must also be seen in its other capacity, as a vital germ that incites the spirit to make connections. The transition from the embryonic to the fuller world suggests, as Northrop Frye notes in *Words with Power,* a transition from the visible to the spiritual, reached by taking a second breath, an inspiration, in a higher kind of air. The spiritual, Frye suggests, may thus be defined as the highest intensity of consciousness.

Liturgy must be rooted in the "real world," but its flower is in another realm. Thus liturgy joins hope to everyday life and vision to reality. Liturgical spirituality seeks an ever closer correspondence between the two by deepening and correcting our understanding of reality and by expanding the clarity and conviction of our vision.

I must record my gratitude to the first national Liturgical Conference of the Evangelical Lutheran Church in Canada held on the campus of the University of Manitoba in Winnipeg in July 1982. The Canadian church honored me with an invitation to serve as both keynote and closing speaker at the conference. Their theme, "Praise Throughout the Land," encouraged my reflection on the subject of this book. I am also grateful to the Lutheran Theological Seminary at Philadelphia and Muhlenberg College, which in 1992 jointly sponsored a course they asked me to teach on worship and spirituality. I could find no suitable text for that course and thus was encouraged to begin work on this book. Philip Gehring, the editor of *Cross-Accent: The Journal of the Association of Lutheran Church Musicians,* asked me to contribute to the second issue of the journal an essay on the subject of hymns in the life of the church; significant portions of that essay form the basis for chapter eight of this book. Despite the denominational source of the prodding to write this book, the ideas set forth in the following pages will, I trust, be of interest and even perhaps of some use to the ecumenical church as it seeks to keep faith with its long history even while moving into a new millennium.

Those to whom this book is dedicated include the rector of St. Thomas Church in New York City, the assistant to the rector of the Church of the Advent in Boston, and the pastor of Grace and St. Paul's Church in New York City. To them and to their parishes, my deepest thanks. All those to whom the book is dedicated exemplify what this book attempts to describe: Christian faith that is both evangelical and catholic. As Andrew Mead has said, "It does not matter how high a liturgy is but how deep."

Chapter One

TOWARD A DEFINITION
OF SPIRITUALITY

An ancient collect from the Leonine sacramentary, the earliest sur-
viving collection of prayers from the Roman rite (fifth and sixth
centuries) and included also in the later Gelasian and Gregorian
sacramentaries, sets forth in a terse and memorable way the essence
of the spiritual life.

> Almighty and everlasting God, increase in us the gifts of faith,
> hope, and charity; and, that we may obtain what you prom-
> ise, make us love what you command; through Jesus Christ
> our Lord, who lives and reigns with you and the Holy Spirit,
> one God, for ever and ever.[1]

The highly concentrated language of the prayer gathers into one
the past, the present, and the future. By faith we appropriate and
keep alive the past; by hope we anticipate and already live in the
future; by acts of charity we make concrete and tangible the objects of faith and hope. All three — faith, hope, and love — are not
human achievements but the gifts of God. In the vision of this ancient prayer, what may appear to be opposites are understood to
be one: promise and possession are joined and made one, as are
obedience and love.

Spirituality is properly a dialogue, but it is a dialogue in which
God must speak first; otherwise there can be no conversation. God
opens the mystery of divinity and opens up the human heart to receive that revelation.[2] The ancient collect asks, therefore, for three
gifts. The gift of faith is the means by which we receive what is
offered; faith is our yes to the saving yes spoken to us and for us
by Christ. The gift of hope is not finally our longing for what we
do not have but our confidence that God's will and intention for us
is unwaveringly good. Our hope is our grateful yes to the present

moment in which salvation resides but may not yet be apparent. The gift of charity or love (the Episcopal and Lutheran translation of the prayer retains the old word "charity," familiar to many from the Authorized Version of 1 Corinthians 13:13, to distinguish it from the thin and airy associations of the word "love") is nothing less than the gift of the very being of God, who is love. The increase of the three theological virtues is sought so that we may learn not only to obey God's commandments but indeed to come to love them, finding there the loving will of God who desires our welfare and happiness. By such loving and glad obedience, God's promises may become a reality for us, our possession.

These general truths presented in the Leonine collect have been given a more pointed statement in the concatenation of New Testament passages that Lutherans in North America for more than a century have used as the formula to accompany the laying-on of hands at confirmation.

> The Father in heaven, for Jesus' sake, renew and increase in thee the gift of the Holy Ghost to thy strengthening in faith, to thy growth in grace, to thy patience in suffering, and to the blessed hope of everlasting life.[3]

It is a memorable summary of the Christian life and a concise statement of what biblically rooted spirituality is all about. The spiritual life originates with God's gift of the Holy Spirit, who proceeds from the Father, and entails the response of deepening commitment, growth in the knowledge and love of God, and acceptance of suffering as a mark of the true faith, all informed by the expectant hope of eternal life. The formula is a summary of the work of salvation in each believer, the goal of which is communion with the living God, an intimate participation in the divine life that is the source and the goal of human life.[4]

Spirituality: A Provisional Definition

One must consider at the outset what exactly is meant by spirituality. Dictionary definitions ("of, concerned with, affecting, relating to the soul or the spirit") are not helpful. Synonyms are only somewhat less unsatisfactory. "Devotion" has to do with "acts of prayer," and that may be too external. "Piety" has to do with "religious fervor," and that may be too internal, too emotional. A traditional name for the study of devotion is ascetic or ascetical theology; it is used by many Anglicans and by the Quaker scholar Rufus Jones in his *Studies in Mystical Religion*. The word "ascetic" has its origin in the Greek *asketes*, one who exercises or trains (from *askein*, "to work"), a hermit, one who practices spiritual discipline. But the preponderant connotations of austerity and renunciation of the world and society make the word of little help in commending to people of the twenty-first century the work of discipline, training, and exercise.

Louis Bouyer in his *Introduction to Spirituality* (1961) carefully distinguishes between the religious life, the interior life, and the spiritual life. As Bouyer understands it, the religious life need not involve any interior life or spiritual life, for the religious life can mean nothing more than correctly performing certain rites, fulfilling ritual obligations, receiving the sacraments, reading the Bible.

The interior life, as Bouyer defines it, can be carried on apart from religion and spirituality. Poets, composers, artists of all sorts who may be utter unbelievers nevertheless exhibit a rich and deep interior life "of imagination, of thought, of emotion, which is all their own."[5]

The spiritual life as Bouyer defines it incorporates both the religious life and the interior life and goes beyond them. The religious life must be joined to the interior life to give it depth and substance. The spiritual life is not attained until the interior life "develops, not in isolation, but in the awareness of a spiritual reality, however this be understood, a reality that goes beyond the consciousness of the individual."[6] When the spirit known in the spiritual life is recognized not as some *thing* but as someone, then the spiritual life will be a religious life as well. Throughout human history, Bouyer asserts, the interior life of its own accord tends to develop into the spiritual life, which, in turn, orients itself no less spontaneously toward some form of religious life.

Characteristics of Spirituality

Biblically rooted spirituality may be said to have several defining characteristics, given focus by the traditional Lutheran confirmation formula cited above.

Spirituality is, first of all, always a response.[7] We have been created by God for ultimate union with our maker, as St. Augustine declared in the memorable opening of his *Confessions:* "You have made us for yourself, and our hearts are restless until they find rest in you." We love because God first loved us, St. John wrote (1 John 4:19), and Bouyer comments, "It is not primarily the love with which God is loved, but the love with which God loves us."[8] Such is the basic characteristic of *agape*, God's generous and costly love for us, which we are invited to reflect and to emulate. There is thus built into us a longing to draw near to God, returning to the one from whom and through whom and to whom are all things (Romans 11:36), our "Source, Guide, and Goal" (NEB).

Our love of God, our spiritual life, therefore, is not of our own doing. It is the Holy Spirit at work within us, that Spirit who "calls, gathers, enlightens, and sanctifies" each of us together with the whole Christian church on earth and preserves us in union with Christ in the one true faith.[9] Even when, having heard the invitation, we cry out in belief and faith, it is not our own achievement. "When we cry 'Abba! Father!' it is that very Spirit bearing witness with our spirit that we are children of God" (Romans 8:15–16). "No one can say 'Jesus is Lord' except by the Holy Spirit" (1 Corinthians 12:3). The spiritual life is our response to the work of the life- and faith-giving Holy Spirit within us[10] (2 Corinthians 3:18). So the confirmation prayer is that "the Father in heaven, for Jesus' sake renew and increase" in each confirmand "the gift of the Holy Spirit." Our faith, like our life, is a gift from God. Spirituality is always a response to what God has done.

This leads to a second characteristic. Spirituality is essentially God dwelling within us. It is our most personal, most interiorized relationship with God, fully recognized, realized, and cultivated within us. Theologians sometimes speak of immanence, the doctrine that complements the transcendence of God. Immanence asserts that the transcendent God is also close at hand, within the universe, within each created being.

If our response to God's initiative is itself God's doing, then our faith is not our own intellectual achievement or decision for Christ; it is the work of the Spirit within us. So, appropriately, the first result of the working of the gift of the Holy Spirit for which the confirmation formula asks is "strengthening in faith." This, in fact, is the confirmation: God confirms, that is, strengthens, God's own work of faith begun in us at our baptism. We pray that this will continue throughout the life of each confirmand.

Such strengthening of faith expands our understanding of what is ours and what is best for us. The wise Rabbi Abraham Heschel observed, "To be sensitive to the ultimate question one must have the ability to surpass the self, the ability to know that the self is more than the self; that our highest concern is not our own concern."[11] Knowing that God dwells within us, we redirect our lives and our energies from our selfish preoccupation with ourselves and our own needs and desires toward what is truly best for us. In other words, spirituality encourages us to overthrow the idols that command our attention and to install in their place the living God. That is the work of faith. In *The Large Catechism* Luther speaks eloquently of the meaning of the First Commandment:

> To have a god is nothing else than to trust and believe him with our whole heart. As I have often said, the trust and faith of the heart alone make both God and an idol. If your faith and trust are right, then your God is the true God. On the other hand, if your trust is false and wrong, then you have not the true God. For these two belong together, faith and God. That to which your heart clings and entrusts itself is, I say, really your God.[12]

Salvation is nothing else than communion with God, union between Christ and the believer, their mutual indwelling.[13]

Such intense intimacy is, however, not the whole of the spiritual life. A third characteristic of Christian spirituality is an awareness of other believers, for Christian spirituality is cultivated within the church, the community of believers, "the blessed company of all faithful people."[14] Indeed, there is no fully authentic Christian spirituality without the realization of an equal presence of other believers with Christ and ourselves in the church. Such a communal sense not only provides the necessary means for spirituality; it is in fact, Bouyer claims, "essential to the very goal of the spiritual life."[15] Spirituality as it is known and practiced within Christianity is intensely personal, but it is not individual. We are saved not alone but with other people, and together we comprise a vast and diverse body of believers from all times and all places.

The life of the spirit is not a kind of pure subjectivity, untouched by social location and by all the particularities of experience that create one's own perspective. Rather, subjectivity itself is a social construct, a cultural artifact.[16] The spiritual life is social. The love of God and the love of one's neighbor are inseparable.

> God calls us to love Him. But we cannot love Him as He loves us, with the love with which He loves us, without loving inseparably from Him all those whom He loves inseparably

from us. We are not only to love our neighbor *after* having loved God. We are to love God *in loving* our neighbor. The experience of life in the Church is, finally, the experience of the inseparability of these two loves.[17]

And so it is that the second work of the Holy Spirit sought in the Lutheran confirmation formula is "growth in grace." As faith may be understood as God working within us, so grace may be understood as God working in and beyond each believer and throughout the universe to create and sustain and nourish the goodness that is the divine intention for all that has been made. Growth in grace involves the increasing awareness of the breadth of God's love and the corresponding breadth of the love that is expected of each of us, for the love of God and the love of one's neighbor cannot be separated. The realization that God is to be found within ourselves leads us inevitably to identify with the love of God for the world, with Christ, the One for others, who gave his life for the life of the world.

The history of salvation is the history of God calling people into community. The creator found that it was not good for the man even in the garden of paradise to be alone and so made a companion suitable for him. Community was established from the very beginning. Sin continually breaks the divinely intended community and isolates individuals in barren solitude. But the continuing story is the account of God's unwearied work to reestablish the ruptured society and to reincorporate the fragmented community of humanity. In the First Testament, God calls a people to be a blessing to the nations, and in the New Testament God calls together the church as the people with a mission to the whole world. The story of salvation is, in Dante's title, a "divine comedy." The movement of classic tragedy is from wholeness to brokenness and isolation, but the movement of a comedy is the opposite: from a broken and fragmented society to a restored society of unity and harmony in which those who had been excluded are finally restored to the community. The work of salvation cannot be individualistic. The growth of each one is dependent upon the growth of all.[18]

A fourth characteristic to be noted in authentic biblical spirituality is that growth and development mark the normal state of a healthy life in Christ. Too often we are satisfied with stunted and underdeveloped lives because of a lack of vision and hope. Many devout people remain for a lifetime at the beginning of the way,[19] content to be like children, blind to possibility and promise.

The biblical image of such growth is a pilgrimage, and the model is Abraham and Sarah, who in faith left their familiar surroundings to make an epic and archetypal journey in search of spiritual truth, not knowing where they were going but only that God's hand was leading them and divine love supporting them as the writer to the Hebrews noted (Hebrews 11:8–16).[20] God's people since Abraham have been a pilgrim people, nomads on the move through what was ultimately understood to be alien territory. They trod the desert with Moses in search of the promised land. Even when they were returned to their land, they were still in search of something more, and they learned that the promised land and its splendid capital Jerusalem were but promises of a yet greater future that God had in store for them and for all the world. The imagery passed into Christianity. For all the grand claims that Christianity has fulfilled the promise of Israel, Christians too still look beyond the present to what is real and abiding. A ninth-century Latin hymn, *Christe cunctorum dominator alme,* sings of the church building,

> Hallowed this dwelling where the Lord abideth,
> This is none other than the gate of heaven;
> Strangers and pilgrims, seeking homes eternal,
>   Pass through its portals.[21]

Christians too embraced the image of pilgrimage and applied it to themselves.

That richly suggestive picture of a pilgrimage implies change, growth, and development. Indeed, the whole message of the Bible is a restless, probing message. The archaic torso in Rilke's poem *Archäischer Torso Apollos* ("Archaic Torso of Apollo") says to us, *Du musst dein Leben ändern,* "Change your life." The same command, George Steiner observes, is given by any poem, novel, play, painting, or musical composition worth encountering. Serious art in all of its variety as visual art and literature and music "queries the last privacies of our existence."[22] And the task of art here is at least a partial expression of what the Word of God is constantly doing, opening the final curtain, lifting our last veil, refusing to allow us any secret recesses that can remain unlighted by the Sun of Righteousness, requiring of us sustained, relentless examination.

The Lutheran confirmation prayer asks for "patience in suffering." It is a remarkable prayer for those who are being confirmed, mostly young people, acknowledging the tragic nature of human life, especially the life of the servants of God. Throughout the Bible those who are summoned particularly by God would rather have no part of the summons; indeed many, like Jeremiah and Jonah, would rather be dead. The call of God is a call to a life of suffering. But the pattern and model for those who are singled out for this odd blessing is the Suffering Servant. In their suffering Christians emulate the suffering of Christ, "patient, meek, though guiltless,"[23] and share his redemptive life. Patience in suffering may appear to mean passively accepting the cross and quietly bearing burdens heaped upon one. But if one is to follow Christ, one must actively, willingly embrace suffering and even death, knowing that one suffers not alone but with Christ and, like Christ, on behalf of others.

An understanding of the inescapability of suffering is deeply embedded in all the peoples of the earth. Margaret Miles has shown[24] that in epics such as the *Iliad* and the *Odyssey*, the development of the hero entails a journey to self-knowledge achieved through physical struggle, labor, and pain. The hero's self-knowledge is carnal knowledge, awareness recorded in the body. Those who have not experienced limitation and suffering cannot recognize the suffering of others and cannot locate themselves in a human community shaped by awareness of limitation and mortality. The consanguinity of human beings depends on mutual recognition of the common bond of a sentient body, whose most vivid experiences create consciousness. Such is "carnal knowing," embodied self-understanding, the intimate interdependence and irreducible cooperation of thinking, feeling, sensing, and understanding. As Tertullian recognized, the soul is always dependent on the body.[25]

To many, spirituality suggests a separation of spirit from body and the placement of higher value on the spirit. This seems an obvious approach, for the body inevitably must age and wither and decay, but the spirit may be understood to endure unchanged by time. There is, however, in biblical religion a clear sense of the importance of the body, the flesh. Indeed, in the Hebrew understanding, the spirit cannot be understood without the body in which it dwells. The death, burial, and decomposition of the body does not signify the end of it, for the Apostles' Creed boldly and baldly asserts "the resurrection of the flesh" (*carnis resurrectionem*, usually translated "the resurrection of the body.") The prototype is the risen Christ. The empty tomb declares that the body apparently participated in the resurrection. In St. Luke's Gospel the risen Christ eats, consuming fish (an ancient symbol of reproduction and life) in the presence of the frightened disciples. In St. John's Gospel, Thomas is given the opportunity to touch and finger the wounds in

Christ's body. Representations of the Ascension show Christ taking his wounded body into the heavenly realm. An authentic biblical spirituality must be embodied, and the liturgy will not allow us to forget that. The liturgy requires the participation of the body in worship: standing, sitting, kneeling; seeing color and movement; smelling the aromas of incense and candle wax and wine; hearing words and songs and melodies; touching and tasting consecrated bread and wine. Such participation of the body in worship must inevitably lead to concern for the plight of the needy who suffer physically and mentally as well as spiritually.

A fifth characteristic of spirituality is the goal of the process of growth, and this brings us to treacherous ground. The Lutheran confirmation formula concludes with "the blessed hope of everlasting life." This hope is easily and often misunderstood. The work of the Holy Spirit in each believer is more than simply spiritual growth, and the goal of life is not merely more of the same, without the pain, in heaven forever, as if the change were only from the temporal to the eternal. The Orthodox Church insists, with St. Paul, that the goal of the Christian life is nothing less than the total transformation of the human person by the grace and glory of God. St. Paul wrote to the Corinthians that "all of us, with unveiled faces, seeing the glory of the Lord as though reflected in a mirror, are being transformed into the same image from one degree of glory to another" (2 Corinthians 3:18). Charles Wesley in the final stanza of his hymn "Love Divine, All Loves Excelling" has impressed St. Paul's vision upon the hearts of generations of worshipers:

> Finish then thy new creation,
>   Pure and spotless let us be;
> Let us see thy great salvation
>   Perfectly restored in thee!
> Changed from glory into glory,
>   Till in heaven we take our place,
> Till we cast our crowns before thee,
>   Lost in wonder, love, and praise.

Each believer is being changed, in the language of the Authorized Version, "from glory to glory" into the image of God that we both see and reflect, namely, Christ. We are being elevated in ever more splendid stages until we are at last totally transformed into God's glorious image. In Second Peter the picture is still more striking: "He has given us...his precious and very great promises, so that through them you may escape from the corruption that is in the world because of lust, and may become participants of the divine nature" (2 Peter 1:4). Orthodoxy calls this process of transformation *theosis*, "divinization." Many Western Christians almost automatically react negatively to such language with a forceful assertion of human sinfulness. St. Athanasius put it clearly and, to Western Christians, shockingly, "God was humanized so that we might be divinized."[26] This teaching of *theosis* is, upon examination, not so foreign to Western Christianity as it may at first seem.

We are "God's beloved, called to be saints" (Romans 1:7). We have not yet completed the journey just because we have heard the Gospel and made some response. We are pilgrims on the way toward our final destination. Before we arrive safely there, we will need to grow through grace and suffering until we learn to find grace in the way of the cross and learn that grace and suffering are one. A saint is simply one in whom God has more and more undivided sway.[27] The costly redemptive process is still going on; grace is continually laying siege to every life and every corner of every life, and is forever drawing at our hearts for our healing, for our reconciliation with God and with each other. The aim of the nurture of prayer is a condition of prayerfulness, a constant sensitivity to what is really going on.[28] And what is really going on is an overwhelmingly grand refashioning and purification and transformation of each believer until the divinization is complete and we reflect perfectly the glory of God.

Such a sense of the unity of prayer and life and an awareness of the restorative work that is taking place can and ought to have its focus on the ordinary work that one does. Mary Ward (1585–1645), founder of a Roman Catholic religious order for women, declared,

> This is verity: to do what we have to do well. Many think it nothing to do ordinary things. But for us it is. To do ordinary things well, to keep our Constitutions, and all other things that be ordinary in every office or employment whatsoever it be. To do it well: this is for us, and this by God's grace will maintain fervor.[29]

Spirituality then is prayer plus love plus devotedness. It is, in the words of Brother Lawrence, "the practice of the presence of God," the way one does one's religion. It is interpreting the world according to one's innermost life and intimate and ultimate concern. It is an everyday activity, the way one goes about daily life — and a discussion of that requires a library of books — but that is rooted and focused in the intersection of time and eternity that we call worship, or better, in the German *Gottesdienst,* "divine service," which is both, equally important, God's service of us and our response in our service of God.

Such a wide and inclusive understanding of worship suggests that it is not possible to reduce worship or spirituality to one simple proposition. The fundamental pattern of Christian spirituality is the paschal mystery, the unitive event of the sacred triduum: the passion, death, and resurrection of Christ celebrated in the great Three Days from Maundy Thursday evening through Easter Day. The culmination of that manifold activity is the sending of the Spirit on Pentecost, the fiftieth day of Easter. That Spirit, working within us, urges us to put to death the disordered desires of our selfish nature, to die with Christ, and thus to know the promise of new life, a life that begins now. As Christ came to do the will of God by giving himself into human hands for our sake, so we, redeemed by that offering, are also to do the will of God, giving ourselves to others. Spirituality is therefore an act of loving adoration of God and simultaneously an act of loving service of those in need. Thus our ingrown nature is redirected to God and neighbor so that paradoxically in this service we may enjoy the freedom of the children of God. "My will is not mine own / Till thou hast made it thine," wrote George Matheson in 1890 in a hymn packed with paradoxes:

> Make me a captive, Lord,
> And then I shall be free;
> Force me to render up my sword,
> And I shall conqueror be.
> I sink in life's alarms
> When by myself I stand;
> Imprison me within thine arms,
> And strong shall be my hand.[30]

The religious heart renounces its self-centeredness, and with a joyful and uninhibited abandon finds its deepest meaning in service of Another and therefore in service of others. Therefore, Christians pray earnestly to God in the words of the Leonine collect, "Make us love what you command."

Chapter Two

THE SOURCE AND SUMMIT
OF FAITH

The church exists to worship God. That basic fact needs to be asserted clearly and unambiguously again and again, for it is not at all obvious to many members of the church who assert that the church exists to evangelize the world ("the church is mission") or to serve people's needs (the clergy are thought of as members of the "helping professions.") The church, in its grandest view of itself and its most basic view of its purpose, exists to give God what is due, to acknowledge God as God. The one who is the creator and preserver of the whole universe is, as the Te Deum sings, "worthy of all worship." The purpose of the church is to focus and render that worship.

The church finally has no other purpose than to respond to the mighty acts of God with a corresponding selfless offering of praise. This offering may appropriately, even inevitably, involve service to those in need, particularly if no other agency is rendering that service, but always and forever the primary and eternal purpose is to give glory to the one who is worthy of all worship.

It is a thoroughly impractical purpose. By worshiping God, the church expects no reward, no special blessings or graces, no benefits. The church worships God simply because the church cannot do otherwise. Given what God has done in the life, death, and resurrection of Jesus Christ, the church can only respond in grateful praise. Frederick W. Robertson preached to his congregation at Trinity Chapel, Brighton, in the middle of the nineteenth century on the text from Philippians 3:14, "I press toward the mark for the prize of the high calling of God in Christ Jesus":

> They who seek knowledge for the sake of a prize are not
> genuine lovers of knowledge — they only love the reward of
> knowledge.

I say this is a spurious goodness which is good for the sake of reward. The child that speaks truth for the sake of the praise of truth, is not truthful. The man who is honest because honesty is the best policy, has not integrity in his heart. He who endeavors to be humble, and holy, and perfect, in order to win heaven, has only a counterfeit religion. God for His own sake — Goodness because it is good — Truth because it is lovely — this is the Christian's aim.[1]

Worship is the admission of our creatureliness, the confession of our utter and complete dependence on God for life and being. It teaches us a selflessness that is unnatural to us, a generosity that we must learn to make our own. The liturgy requires a radical reordering of our view of the world, more and more shifting the focus from ourselves and even from humanity and its often desperate needs to God until God becomes the only focus and center of our attention. Calvinism has always been characterized by its clear understanding of and insistence upon the absolute sovereignty of God. The first question of the Westminster Catechism, "What is the chief end of man?" is answered, "Man's chief end is to glorify God and to enjoy him forever." Noble hymns inspired by this unyielding view of God make clear the proper condition of sinful mortals before the holiness of the eternal. Isaac Watts's words (1719) combine with the slow and solemnly majestic tune *Old Hundredth*.

> Before Jehovah's awful throne
> Ye nations bow with sacred joy:
> Know that the Lord is God alone,
> He can create and He destroy.

William Kethe's versification of Psalm 100 (1561) invites,

> O enter then his gates with praise;
> Approach with joy his courts unto;
> Praise, laud, and bless his name always,
> For it is seemly so to do.

> For why? The Lord our God is good:
> His mercy is forever sure;
> His truth at all times firmly stood,
> And shall from age to age endure.

The language seems quaint now, but because of their age such hymns are venerable and still compelling. Such an awareness of

the sovereign majesty of God is not limited to Calvinism of course.
It is found in the Lutheran Gerhard Tersteegen's hymn:

> God himself is present,
>   Let us now adore him,
>   And with awe appear before him!
> God is in his temple,
>   All within keep silence,
>   Prostrate lie with deepest reverence.[2]

The Roman Catholic hymn writer Frederick William Faber expresses similar holy fear:

> My God, how wonderful thou art,
>   Thy majesty how bright;
> How beautiful thy mercy seat,
>   In depths of burning light.
>
> How dread are thine eternal years,
>   O everlasting Lord,
> By prostrate spirits day and night
>   Incessantly adored.

Swedish Christianity has retained this sense of awe in the daunting
presence of the Holy One, especially as it is expressed in the thrice-
holy hymn of the seraphim in Isaiah's vision: "Holy, holy, holy is
the Lord of Hosts. The whole earth is full of his glory." The Sanctus of the Eucharist, echoing Isaiah, acclaims with holy fear the one
who descends to us from the throne of God.

   With such a view of the glorious majesty, selfishness has no
place. A learned bishop created a stir when he declared some
years ago that our personal eternal life is of little importance.
Our concern should not be, What is going to happen to *me?*
but rather a confidence that God's purpose will at last be vindi-
cated. We as individuals may be incidental to that purpose, and
the assurance of the ultimate triumph of God should be enough
for us to know. Still more pointedly, in the old ordination service
when double predestination was still widely taught and believed, a
Calvinist ordinand was required to answer affirmatively the shattering question, "Are you willing to be damned for the glory of
God?" One cannot answer yes to that question and retain a shred
of self-importance.

   Worship is the response of the church to what God has done,
just as the church itself is a response to what God the Holy Spirit

has done to summon it into existence, gathering it "from the ends of the earth"[3] and bringing unity out of diversity. We worship because it is God who is God: "We praise you for your glory." Worship is the source and the summit of faith. A pair of visual images may help our consideration of that declaration.

Above the plain of ancient Mesopotamia rose a great mound of bricks, a veritable mountain. It was a pyramid shape but made in a series of great steps, five in all. On the very top of this immense pyramid was the shrine of the chief deity of the city-state. A visitor's gaze was lifted up to that high shrine, far above, soaring in the sky. The eye after a time descended the stairs of that mud brick mountain, and at the base one saw another shrine, similar to one at the top of the pyramid but much smaller. The traveller pondered the meaning of the mountain with its two shrines and then, we may imagine, the traveller understood. The mountain was like the world. The large shrine at the summit was reflected in the small shrine below. Such is the relationship between heaven and earth. The real home of the gods is in the sky, beyond the vault of heaven, itself far above us, and the shrines and temples that mortals build here are but tiny, indeed puny imitations of the true palace of the deity. More than that, the mountain was made in a series of great steps, far too large to serve any human use but designed to serve rather as a staircase for the god to come down from the shrine above to visit the people below, and to return home above when the visit was finished.

We have testimony to the impressive size of these mountains. Some say it was such ziggurats (for so they were called) that so impressed the early Hebrew nomads in their wanderings and that it was such a mountain that they had in mind when they told the story of the tower of Babel. The settlers on the plain in the land of Shinar said to one another,

> "Come, let us make bricks, and burn them thoroughly." And they had brick for stone, and bitumen for mortar. Then they said, "Come, let us build ourselves a city, and a tower with its top in the heavens, and let us make a name for ourselves...." The Lord came down to see the city and the tower, which mortals had built.... So the Lord scattered them abroad from there over the face of all the earth, and they left off building the city. Therefore it was called Babel, because there the Lord confused the language of all the earth. (Genesis 11:3–5, 8, 9)

The name Babel seems to have meant "gate of God," but in the story it is connected to the Hebrew verb *balal,* "to confuse." The ziggurat image therefore became the evidence of human pride, a Promethean quest for fame and security.

> The huge building, raised to establish a bond with the power upon which the city depended, proclaimed not only the ineffable majesty of the gods but also the might of the community which had been capable of such an effort. The great temples were witnesses to piety, but also objects of civic pride. Built to ensure divine protection for the city, they also enhanced the significance of citizenship. Outlasting the generation of their builders, they were true monuments of the cities' greatness.[4]

Thus, in the biblical story of the tower of Babel we are warned against idolatry and pride, which some say was and remains the original sin.

There is another memorable biblical image that deals with similar understandings of God's relationship to the earth, but this time there is no reference to a mountain. The image is Jacob's ladder. The fugitive Jacob, who had just stolen the blessing his father had reserved for the elder brother, Esau, was on the run. He came to "a certain place," which in the morning he was to call *Bethel,* "house of God." It was an ancient holy place but at this time apparently uninhabited. (According to an old belief, oracles could be received by sleeping in a holy place; the boy Samuel heard God's call as he slept in the temple.) As Jacob slept, he dreamed of a ladder, or as E. A. Speiser calls it in his commentary on Genesis, a staircase, because angels (or at least humans) cannot pass one another conveniently on a ladder. The staircase was "set up on the earth, the top of it reaching to heaven; and the angels of God were ascending and descending on it" (Genesis 28:12). Jacob saw a visible connection between heaven and earth. Separation was temporarily overcome and communication and commerce between them was possible. The Lord stood above the stairs and addressed Jacob.

> I am the Lord, the God of Abraham your father and the God of Isaac; the land on which you lie I will give to you and to your offspring; and your offspring shall be like the dust of the earth, and you shall spread abroad to the west and to the east and to the north and to the south; and all the families of the earth shall be blessed in you and in your offspring. Know that I am with you and will keep you wherever you go, and will bring you back to this land. (vv. 13–15)

Jacob arose early in the morning with that vision still fresh in his mind, took the stone that had been under his head and set it up as a memorial pillar, anointed it with oil, and gave the place a name: Bethel, house of God. He exclaimed in words that have echoed down through the centuries, "How awesome is this place! This is none other than the house of God, and this is the gate of heaven" (v. 17). A fugitive thief found in the wilderness a place filled with the presence of God. The desert was not deserted after all, and there in that place he discovered a gate through which God came to him and by which he could enter the presence of the God of Abraham and Isaac.

The story of Jacob's dream is particularly congenial to evangelicals. It tells of a sinner who is clearly unworthy of God's attention, surely undeserving of divine care, a sinner caught and trapped in sin, unable and even unwilling to escape. The story also tells of God coming to that sinner out of pure, free, unmerited grace — solely because God wants to. God comes to give the sinner the gift of a divine promise. There is no contract, no bargain here, no contractual arrangement that "if you will serve me, I will be good to you." The Holy One of Israel says to the sinner, "I am the Lord.... I am with you and will keep you...." That encounter with God is a powerful dramatization of grace, God's undeserved, unexpected favor to one who is unworthy, who in fact deserves only condemnation and destruction.

The biblical ladder teaches more clearly than the Mesopotamian ziggurat that our prayer is a response to what God has done. In the image of Jacob's ladder, God first comes down and then the movement can go upward. As St. John wrote, "We love because he first loved us" (1 John 4:19). That is the order authentic evangelicals insist upon: God comes first, and we respond.

Jacob's response is cautious, befitting a thief, one who knows from his own behavior that people cannot be trusted. Not wanting to be deceived himself, he offers God a test.

> If God will be with me, and will keep me in this way that I go, and will give me bread to eat and clothing to wear, so that I come again to my father's house in peace, then the Lord shall be my God, and this stone, which I have set up for a pillar, shall be God's house; and of all that you give me I will surely give one tenth to you. (vv. 20–22)

(That's not as generous as it may sound: one tenth for God, but nine tenths for Jacob.) Jacob acts here as if he were controlling the situation, even to the extent of suggesting a kind of bribe of God; but the story makes it clear that God has already spoken and acted and that the outcome of the matter is already settled. God can wait for Jacob.

So the action in this story reverses that of the Mesopotamian ziggurat and of Babel. In Mesopotamia mortals built great mountains by which God could come down. (So did the Maya in Central America.) They built a staircase for God. That is a pious work, but it is fundamentally and dangerously misleading. It suggests a yearning for communion with the divine and an invitation for the gods to come down, but it also suggests that this encounter cannot occur unless mortals provide a means by which it can happen. More daringly, the more obviously wrong-headed mortals at Babel began in their pride to build their great tower to achieve more than fame and security. It is perhaps not reading too much into the text to suggest that they built their tower so they could climb up to heaven. That is the way God seems to have understood what they were doing. The people wanted to construct their own gate (*Bab-el* means "gate of God") by which they could enter God's presence. They wanted to cut their own door in the heavens and look in upon God.

Set against that gate of God on the plain of Shinar and its ziggurat models is a staircase erected by God's initiative and design. Bethel, called by Jacob "the gate of heaven," is a holy place because there God came down, not because the people asked for the visit but because God chose to come down. Thus the ladder or the staircase is a useful and instructive symbol of God's interaction with his people. God sets up the ladder, God builds the stairs. At last God comes down bearing a child, so that we children may come up. God descends to us in order to help us do what we cannot do on our own: ascend to our true home. It is a sacramental sign: God condescends to come down to bestow gifts, and one of those gifts is to raise us by the very means God used to come down to us. In the words of Jesus, the one who came down, "I, when I am lifted up from the earth, will draw all people to myself" (John 12:32).

Worship, and the Holy Communion most of all, is God's way of descending to us. God comes to speak to us in the proclamation of Scripture and in the sermon, and God comes to feed us in the sharing of the holy meal. In the dazzling vision of the ancient liturgy of St. James, which many modern Western Christians know in Gerard Moultrie's translation, we find the hushed stanzas,

> Let all mortal flesh keep silence,
>   And with fear and trembling stand;
> Ponder nothing earthly-minded,
>   For with blessing in his hand
> Christ our God to earth descendeth,
>   Our full homage to demand. . . .
>
> Rank on rank the host of heaven
>   Spreads its vanguard on the way,
> As the Light of light descendeth
>   From the realms of endless day,
> That the powers of hell may vanish
>   As the darkness clears away.

In the most holy sacrament is found the gate of heaven by which Christ our God, Light from Light, descends to earth and by which we are able to enter the presence of the One before whom the cherubim veil their faces. Worship, especially eucharistic worship, is God's way of descending to us "with blessing in his hand." Worship is "divine service," *Gottesdienst,* first of all in the sense of God's service to us. Worship is God's coming to serve the gifts of God to the people of God. Worship is thus the source of the faith, for worship — especially eucharistic worship, but all worship — sets before us God's mighty acts on our behalf. But worship is more than a lesson or a review or a mere reminder; and the church is more than a classroom. In worship God is active, God does things. God reaches out and gives us gifts of life and salvation. God puts a claim on us, and while we pray God comes to us to teach us and to show us and to transform us and to strengthen us.

Worship directs our attention to the top of the staircase down which the angels descend. Worship is our way of raising our eyes to the mountain of God whence our help will come. Worship is the spring on the height of Zion from which descends a stream that as it flows down the hillside gathers into a mighty river that refreshes and renews all the earth. Worship is the source of faith.

Worship is also the summit of faith. It is the place from which our salvation comes, and it is the place to which our salvation lifts us. God comes to give us faith, and that faith leads us back to God. The staircase that descends to us from God's dwelling place also ascends from this world to the One who comes down to us through the gate of heaven and who leads us back though it to our true and abiding home. Worship, therefore, is divine service in a double sense. It is God's service of us, and it is our service of God

in response to the divine initiative. Worship is our response to what
God has done. It begins with God's service to us and it continues
with our response. It is the honor and adoration we pay to God
for what has been done for us by none other than our Maker and
Redeemer.

Through the centuries the Christian church has maintained that
although God comes to us in many ways, the place that God has
chosen to meet us most fully is in the fellowship of faith, that is,
in the church, the assembly and congregation of believers. God
comes to us not as individuals but as members of the fellowship
of the body of Christ, the church. The social dimension of our encounter with God is important, although it is often ignored. God
meets us through other people and with other people. Privatized religion, as if all that mattered were "me and God," is excluded. The
gospel is experienced in and through other people. When the gospel
comes to us when we are alone, it drives us to seek the company
of others so that we might share the good news and find others
to rejoice with us. The woman in Jesus' parable who found her
lost coin, like the shepherd who found the lost sheep, called in the
neighbors to rejoice with her (Luke 15:1–10). The evangelical faith
leads us always out of ourselves toward God and toward other
people. It leads from our selfish pride to God's prior grace. It leads
us from private religious experience to the fellowship of the faith.
It leads us from our own interests to the service of others. From
ourselves to God, from ourselves to the church, from ourselves to
the neighbor in need: that is the movement of the evangelical faith.

There is still more, for worship reminds us of all that is happening here. We are saved not alone but with others. We are saved
not out of the world but with the world. We are not lifted up and
taken away from all this, for we are part of all this. We are not
separate from the natural world; we are part of it, and it is by
that natural world that God raises us: by water and by bread and
wine. We dare not despise or ignore that natural world, because
God does not despise or ignore it. God made it, preserves it, and is
redeeming it. So the good news of redemption is for us and for all
creation. Romans 8 is the classic text:

> The creation waits with eager longing for the revealing of the
> children of God; for the creation was subjected to futility,
> not of its own will but by the will of the one who subjected
> it, in hope that the creation itself will be set free from its
> bondage to decay and will obtain the freedom of the glory

of the children of God. We know that the whole creation has
been groaning in labor pains until now; and not only the creation, but we ourselves, who have the first fruits of the Spirit,
groan inwardly while we wait for adoption, the redemption
of our bodies. (vv. 19–23)

When our first parents sinned, all creation fell. Everything was distorted (Genesis 3:14–19). Men and women were no longer thought
of as equals, but instead a hierarchy emerged in which the man
ruled the woman, who, verse 16 suggests, enjoyed being dominated. The relation between humans and animals was corrupted,
and the serpent became the venomous enemy. Childbearing became a painful burden. The relation between the man and the soil
was corrupted: "Cursed be the ground because of you; in toil you
shall eat of it all the days of your life." Humans, made "in the
image of God," became mortal: "You are dust, and to dust you
shall return." When the human race fell into rebellion and death,
we took the whole of creation with us into decay and destruction.
And when Christ's redeeming work was done, all creation was redeemed. As the sixth-century hymn by Venantius Fortunatus puts
it, perhaps drawing its imagery in part from Jude 12–13,

> He endures the nails, the spitting,
>   Vinegar, and spear, and reed;
> From that holy body broken
>   Blood and water forth proceed:
> Earth, and stars, and sky, and ocean,
>   By that flood from stain are freed.[5]

In those marvelous lines is a powerful reminder of how profoundly
the early church understood the depth of sin and the height of
grace. It is a meditation on the vision of St. John the Divine: "I
saw a new heaven and a new earth" (Revelation 21:1).

In our service of worship, therefore, we are encouraged to see
beyond the immediate assembly. We see others, not yet of this fold
(John 10:16), joining in the praise of God. By that vision we are
driven so to purify what we do that these others will want to come
in and share what we enjoy. We join our songs with the praise offered by all creation: the cycle of night followed by day, the return
of the seasons, the voices of the birds, the splendor of the flowers
and trees, the sweep of the wind, the song of the rivers, and the
thunder of the sea. The rousing canticle *Benedicite, omnia opera*
from the apocryphal/deuterocanonical Song of the Three invites all
creation, all the creatures of nature, to bless the Lord.

All you works of the Lord, bless the Lord —
praise him and magnify him forever.

The heavenly beings (angels, heavens, powers of the Lord) are invited to praise God. Then the creatures of the heavens and air are commanded to join the chorus (sun and moon, stars, showers and dew, winds, fire and heat, winter and summer, dews and frost and cold, ice and snow, nights and days, light and darkness, lightnings and clouds). The earth and its inhabitants are urged to take up the song (the earth, mountains and hills, green things that grow on the earth, wells and springs, rivers and seas, whales and all who move in the waters, birds, beasts, and cattle, all children of mortals). Finally, in the most intimate circle of all, God's own people are included in the grand song of the universe (people of God, priests and servants of the Lord, spirits and souls of the righteous, the pure and humble of heart). In the stirring song we see beyond the bounds of earth to the church triumphant, and we join the angels and all the company of heaven in their praise.

All this is the chief purpose of Daily Prayer: to give voice to the praise of creation and to join our songs with the songs of the whole company of heaven. We join with the natural world, seen and unseen, and with the saints and angels. We do not go our own way in isolation, insulated from everyone and everything around us. Daily Prayer puts us in touch with what is happening around us, to expand our vision and awareness, to make us more consciously part of a grand chorus of praise. Daily Prayer lifts us out of our selfish concerns to a grander view of the purpose and will and work of God. It invites us to let God work in us as God wills. As we offer our praise and prayer, we glimpse the conclusion to which all of our struggle is tending, and our strength is revived and our resolve renewed.

The liturgy of the church provides a framework within which the deepest mysteries of Christianity await discovery. With the Holy Communion and the Daily Prayer of the church, one has all one needs to know about Christianity. All the essentials are there to be pondered, explored, and acted upon.

The church in its long experience has found that the careful ordering of its grateful response contributes to the preservation of the fullness and variety of that response. For most of Christianity, a liturgy, a relatively fixed and predictable order, is the means of ensuring the fullness and variety. Indeed, those denominations and congregations that pride themselves on not adhering to "formal" worship are even more bound to their order of items in the service than are the "formal" churches whose liturgy changes from season to season and from week to week as the variable propers enliven the invariable ordinary of the liturgy.

The testimony of the free churches in their rejection of symbolism and ornaments is a valuable reminder to those denominations that revel in the richness of worship. We might well learn from the Society of Friends an uneasy feeling that to pray through a liturgy is to approach God secondhand.[6] Scripture is more important than the prayers we compose, and listening to the voice of God is more important than listening to our own voice, no matter how cultivated and elegant our expression. The answer of the liturgical churches has been that it is better to pray with consideration than without it and that the congregation cannot give their amen of assent to a prayer that they have not had time to consider, for to venture to address God is a most daring and dangerous enterprise. Carefully drafted forms guard against the mental laziness of ex tempore prayer, for not many have the gift of fluency.

The liturgy that has grown through the centuries, rooted in the Bible, is a marvelous work of the human imagination. The resulting creation is a wonderfully rich assembly of human arts. It is founded on the biblical myths, for myth expresses in story what can be expressed in no other way, touching the deepest springs of human nature and telling a story of continued interaction and response. The liturgy is drama, for it employs movement and gesture as well as carefully arranged words. It is barren without the gifts of music that lift us to a realm beyond words, those areas of meaning and understanding that words cannot enter. John Keats lamented the cold touch of natural science that he included in his understanding of the word "philosophy":

> Do not all charms fly
> At the mere touch of cold philosophy?
> There was an awful rainbow once in heaven:
> We know her woof, her texture; she is given
> In the dull catalogue of common things.
> Philosophy will clip an Angel's wings,
> Conquer all mysteries by rule and line,
> Empty the haunted air, and gnomed mine....
> Unweave a rainbow....[7]

Explanations of ritual can often perform the same chilling work, as necessary as it is, as helpful as it can be in some ways. The theologian without a sense of poetry and art can become a mortician. Scholarship is knowledge and knowledge is power, but such control can flatten a diverse terrain, and empty and trivialize that which is full of surprise. Artists can encourage a confining control to yield to an awareness and acceptance of mystery, heights of hope, flights of daring, opening on a life finally beyond our control. J. B. Priestly declared,

> I would rather believe too much — so long as I can do it without bigotry and intolerance — than to believe too little. If mistakes are to be made, I prefer to make the mistake of thinking this life too large, complicated, mysterious, wonderful, than to fall into the opposing error and see it smaller and simpler than my own imagination, tidy, and all known, tedious. It is better to risk being taken in than to be shut out: Too much credulity can be foolish, too much incredulity may be death.[8]

The purpose of liturgy is to stretch our imagination, to test the limits, to call us to larger and more inclusive ideas and views — all this while preserving the fullness of the Christian experience.

Art intensifies our sense of the world around us and of our place in that world by working at the limits of human understanding, unveiling what lies beyond discursive language and thought. Art provides a way of approaching the deepest and finally inexplicable enigmas of existence, our own nature and our own death. What is "out there," George Steiner has argued, is a "real presence" that forever eludes our complete grasp. Well done, art is fresh, daring, and disturbing, a contrary occupation showing new modes of knowing. At its best, art can summon or at least reveal the dangerous holy among us. The text, the work, the musical structure

> has entered into us. We have given it, it has taken, "the run of the house." It has gained the freedom of our inner city.[9]

This otherness that enters into us makes us other.[10]

The Christian liturgy joins imagination to faith, and, according to Kant, imagination is that human faculty that strives to unify our knowledge. It connects one area of experience with another, relating disparate realms, making all experience one. In his *Defense of Poetry* Shelley spoke of the relation of reason to imagination.

> Reason is the enumeration of qualities already known; imagination is the perception of the values of those quantities, both

separately and as a whole. Reason respects the difference and
imagination the similitudes of things.[11]

In so unifying experience, art does not gloss over troublesome and
enigmatic experiences any more than the Bible does, for the wel-
ter of the world cannot be made simple. A Bible that presents
God's motiveless attempt on Moses' life (Exodus 4:24–25) and
that records Jeremiah's anguished howl at his seduction and (sexual) assault by the same God (Jeremiah 20:7) cannot, when heard
in its depth, give rise to easy generalizations about a God whose
love and forgiveness are entirely predictable.

Art and the liturgy provide us with a vision of the completeness
and beauty of the whole. Existence is all of a piece, intricately inter-
related, finally inseparable. In such a vision of a harmonious whole,
everything has significance. Everything counts. Liturgical custom
has therefore decreed that when a series of collects are prayed, as at
the conclusion of Morning Prayer (Matins), there should be an odd
number of such prayers, odd numbers being of greater significance
than even numbers: three for the Holy Trinity; five for the wounds
of Christ in hands, feet, and side; seven, the holy number of perfection, as in the Revelation of St. John the Divine; nine, triply holy,
being three times three.[12] Custom has decreed that an altar be elevated on an odd number of steps, especially three or five, not only
because of the numerical symbolism but also so that the minister,
who would always take the first step with the right foot, the left
since ancient times being the less honorable side, would also arrive
at the top step on the right foot. Christian custom has devised reg-
ulations governing the ringing of church bells. It is not enough that
the bells should sound for a while to announce the approach of
service time and to summon those of the faithful who are within
hearing. The number of strokes given a single bell is regulated so
that not only the sound of the bell would speak but the number too
would offer additional testimony to the Triune God. Thus every
action, every object (fake organ pipes are out of place in a building dedicated to the worship of the God of searching truth), every
Scripture passage in interlocking patterns of types and antitypes,
foreshadowing and fulfillment, all together form one harmonious
whole, a grand and overpowering work of art inexhaustible in its
treasures and discoveries.

The Jewish liturgy addresses God, "Our God and God of our fathers, God of Abraham, Isaac, and Jacob." The appeal to the God
of the ancestors of the people implies the dominance of tradition

and requires faithful transmission of that tradition down through the succeeding generations. Such transmittal, however, need not imply a constricting and deadening repetition. The God of the Bible, the God of the ancestors and forebears is a subverter of predictability. The God who is Most High, who knew Moses face to face, is the Other who cannot be described apart from paradoxes. William Blake observed, "Without contraries there is no progression."[13] Such is the manner and the language of the liturgy, juxtaposing contrary pictures and images. A liturgy that provides "a foretaste of the feast to come" at the triumphant messianic banquet in heaven concludes with a dismissal that sends worshipers, with the taste of the bread of heaven still in their mouths, out into the mundane world: "Go in peace to love and serve the Lord." The Lutheran baptismal rite declares confidently, "In Holy Baptism God liberates us from sin and death," and yet the confession used weekly in most congregations acknowledges that "we are in bondage to sin." A minister announces, "I baptize you," yet the baptism is not the minister's doing but the work of the Holy Trinity in whose name the minister functions and to whose work the minister is but the principal witness. The word of God proclaimed in readings and sermon and sacrament consists of Law and Gospel, command and promise, condemnation and hope; and the mark of the competent theologian is the ability to distinguish between them. Gifts of bread and wine are presented to God in the offering as if they were the congregation's own, and yet offertory prayers acknowledge that we but return what God has first given to us, as does the popular offertory hymn, "We Give Thee but Thine Own." The eucharistic preface invites the congregation, "Lift up your hearts," yet those who "lift them to the Lord" do not leave the world and its needs behind when they enter the nearest presence of the Holy One, and some eucharistic prayers conclude their praise with intercessions for the needs of the world. The eternal and transcendent God inhabits bread and wine to live within those who consume them, so in the womb of the virgin mother mortality contains eternity. The miracle of the God-bearer, *Theotokos,* is extended to and in each communicant. The paradoxes of Scripture and the liturgy are fundamental to the spiritual life, for when devotion is allowed no contact with actual experience that has the power to shake it, there is little chance to avoid the pious, the esoteric, the dogmatic.

The Christian church understands itself to be the continuation of Israel, a people called to be separate from those around them.

God's people form a community with a different story, vision, and way of life, an outpost of the new creation in the midst of the old.[14] They are to be in this world, as Augustine described them, a community of resident aliens whose homeland is elsewhere. Christians reside in this passing world, take an active interest in it, and take active care of it, as Jeremiah urged the exiles in Babylon: "Seek the welfare of the city where I have sent you into exile, and pray to the Lord on its behalf, for in its welfare you will find your welfare" (Jeremiah 29:7). But the Christians' home and citizenship are elsewhere in another age and another place. It is therefore the calling and task of the church to be other, like the God who calls it into existence: "You shall be holy, for I am holy" (Leviticus 19:2). Instead of adjusting to the times and making the message suit us, the church is called to transform its members and the world in the light of the gospel.

Such is not a welcome message. Preachers commonly assert with St. Paul that the gospel is a stumbling block and a scandal. If that is in fact so, then the church ought not expect growth and popularity. Indeed, the church ought to be suspicious of what is popular and attractive. (Dante in the *Inferno* has the heretics, those who pick and choose among the doctrines of the church to select what is congenial, punished by emtombing "like with like" [*Simile qui con simile è sepolto, Inferno* IX.130], stuffing like-minded heretics into iron chests heated by great fires — an appropriately diabolical torture.) The church's contrary message upsets the way of the world and counters its natural course. But because it is not what is expected, the gospel has the potential of answering the deepest human need.

The liturgy, the church's primary expression of its response to the word of God it finds in the Scripture, is necessarily rooted in the Bible and shot through with Scripture. It therefore confronts us as a sometimes alien voice, challenging our notions of what we have come to church for and of what we should expect when we arrive there.

In the wastes of our own making through war and pollution and greed, heaping desolation upon desolation, we are easily lost. We find ourselves without any sense of direction. We need a landmark. Our attention needs to be fixed somewhere if we are to make sense of the world and find our way safely through it. Our eye needs some object around which to organize what we see. Wallace Stevens wrote a poem called "The Anecdote of the Jar." It is not an easy poem, but the point is, at least in part, that even an ordinary jar placed on a hill in Tennessee gave order to "the slovenly wilderness" and organized it so that the wilderness rose up to the jar and sprawled lazily around, "no longer wild." A gray and bare jar tamed and ordered the wildness of nature, taking dominion everywhere. It became the center of that world.

For most of us a jar will not do. We need a common symbol to focus and order our minds and spirits. All of us need such a center to make experience intelligible. Devotion needs such a focus to give center and coherence, and it is worship that can give that center and that coherence to our lives. Throughout the world there is a deeply ingrained need for mountains. Travellers describe the heightened color contrasts and the apparent eradication of distance in the rarefied air.[15] The deep silences of mountains invite reflection on the passages of one's life. People in cultures around the world tell tales of mythical mountains that are far grander than any seen in the natural world. Cosmic mountains give focus to our minds and spirits, providing a symbol of strength and permanence that calls us to a strenuous life of ascent.

The mountain of God gave ancient Israel such a focus, and by metaphorical extension it gives focus to our devotion still. John Campbell's paraphrase of Psalm 121 is a favorite in Canada.

> Unto the hills around do I lift up
>   My longing eyes;
> O whence for me shall my salvation come,
>   From whence arise?
> From God the Lord doth come my certain aid,
> From God the Lord, who heaven and earth hath made.[16]

Of all the hills, only one is the source of abiding strength: Mount Zion, the city of the living God. In past generations, one of the most popular names for Lutheran and Reformed churches was "Zion," an enormously rich and suggestive name that invites us to

> Make the circuit of Zion;
> walk round about her;
>   count the number of her towers.
> Consider well her bulwarks;
> examine her strongholds;
>   that you may tell those who come after.
>   (Psalm 48:11÷12 BCP)

There is a great mountain from which our help comes and to which our life and hope are directed. This mountain, both source and

summit of faith, governs our lives and is "the place of the name
of the Lord of hosts" (Isaiah 18:7). For much of the Old Testament, the God of Israel lived on a mountain. God's own city
Jerusalem was built on the mountain called Zion, that mystical
and magic place.

> For the Lord has chosen Zion;
> he has desired her for his habitation.
> (Psalm 132:14 BCP)

The Lord of hosts "dwells on Mount Zion" (Isaiah 8:18); that is
where he may be found.

> You are to be praised, O God, in Zion;
> to you shall vows be performed in Jerusalem.
> (Psalm 65:1 BCP)

That holy site became the beloved center of faith and the inexhaustible source of hope.

> Shout aloud and sing for joy, O royal Zion,
> for great in your midst is the Holy One of Israel.
> (Isaiah 12:6)

> On the holy mountain
> stands the city he has founded;
> the Lord loves the gates of Zion
> more than all the dwellings of Jacob.
> Glorious things are spoken of you,
> O city of our God.
> (Psalm 87:1–2 BCP)

The holy mountain was where the Messiah was enthroned:

> I myself have set my king
> upon my holy hill of Zion.
> (Psalm 2:6 BCP)

It was therefore a place of promise.

> So you shall know that I, the Lord your God,
> dwell in Zion, my holy mountain.
> And Jerusalem shall be holy,
> and strangers shall never again pass through it.
> (Joel 3:17)

Mount Zion and her daughter Jerusalem became the place from
which in later generations deliverance would come.

> Get you up to a high mountain,
>   O Zion, herald of good tidings;
> lift up your voice with strength,
>   O Jerusalem, herald of good tidings,
>   lift it up, do not fear;
> say to the cities of Judah,
>   "Here is your God!"
>
>   (Isaiah 40:9)

> The Lord shall reign forever,
>   your God, O Zion, throughout all generations.
>   (Psalm 146:9 BCP)

Then I looked, and there was the Lamb, standing on Mount Zion! And with him were one hundred forty-four thousand who had his name and his Father's name written on their foreheads. (Revelation 14:1)

You have come to Mount Zion and to the city of the loving God, the heavenly Jerusalem, and to innumerable angels in festal gathering, and to the assembly of the firstborn who are enrolled in heaven, and to God the judge of all, and to the spirits of the righteous made perfect, and to Jesus, the mediator of a new covenant, and to the sprinkled blood that speaks a better word than the blood of Abel. (Hebrews 12:22–24)

That central mountain, a place of faith and promise and hope, gave focus to devotion. It was the navel of the world, the center of the universe.

> Great is the Lord,
> and highly to be praised;
>   in the city of our God is his holy hill.
> Beautiful and lofty,
> the joy of all the earth,
> is the hill of Zion,
>   the very center of the world
>   and the city of the great king.
>   (Psalm 48:1–2 BCP)

Everything radiated from Mount Zion, and everything converged toward it.

Still more important to Christians, and set beside the picture of the exalted Holy City, the daughter of Zion, is another hill outside old Jerusalem. It is in fact a low hill that bears the chilling name Golgotha, a place of death that thrusts its three crosses awkward against the sky. But religion teaches that nothing is simple; face value is deceiving. For this hill is the grandest mountain on earth. This mound of death is the place where death died, the hillock where hopelessness was destroyed, the exalted place where the gates of life eternal were opened to all who believe. We know Golgotha better by its less forbidding Latin name, Calvary. We boldly call churches by that name, and we adorn our altars with crucifixes to proclaim the central message of Christianity: light out of darkness, life out of death, life by means of death.

As the little shrine at the base of the Mesopotamian ziggurat was to the great shrine on its summit, so Mount Calvary is to the great mountain of the prophets' vision. It is a present and visible place, close to our life, set in our world to which our help has come from the surrounding hills. This hill points ahead and above and beyond to a larger sanctuary not made with hands, where pain and sorrow are done away and there is joy in God's presence forevermore. The transforming work of the cross on that hill outside Jerusalem leads at last to the enduring and eternal festival in the City of God.

That low hill called Mount Calvary becomes therefore the focus of all history and every human longing and need. It is the center of faith and source of hope, the place where the Messiah is enthroned. But the mountain we seek is found finally not in a geographical location but in the spiritual realm, and so we need not travel to find it. That place of conflict and victory is not only available and accessible to each individual; it is to be found in the otherwise unremarkable circumstances of any individual life. Ordinary activity becomes the locus of the cosmic battle, unobserved and unnoticed by many who look in from the outside, even as many did not notice any unusual happenings on Golgotha that Friday afternoon. Suddenly the ordinary erupts with significance, and the everyday breaks open to reveal undreamed of dimensions of divinity.

The word of the Lord has gone forth from Mount Calvary. Even now it is doing its work in the world, stinging consciences, prodding spirits, moving bodies, gathering peoples. There is a great stirring in all creation, and we begin to pulse with excitement. On the mountain a meal is being made ready, and the nations are being prepared to stream up the mountain to share the banquet in perpetual celebration and enjoyment of the God from whom and to whom are all things. That mountain, found in every human breast, is both source and summit of the faith.

Chapter Three

DAILY PRAYER
Hallowing Time

✛

The last third of the twentieth century saw a notable change in liturgical study and understanding. Older studies, such as Bouyer's,
concentrated on texts; the concern was primarily, and for many
almost exclusively, verbal. But beginning early in the twentieth century with the long-neglected French folklorist and ethnographer
Arnold van Gennep, there developed a renewed appreciation of
symbols that was picked up later in the century by anthropologists
such as Mary Douglas and Victor Turner, and by students of comparative religion, notably Mircea Eliade. This renewed attention
rather naturally encouraged liturgists to recover an understanding
of those large, deep, universal symbols employed in the Christian
liturgy but that have been part of many cultures of many times
and many places. Most symbols, in fact, were so deeply archetypal
that they struck a responsive chord in everyone who was able to
experience them. The woman in the gospel understood the power
of symbolic action, saying, "If I only touch his cloak, I will be
made well" (Matthew 9:20). The washing of Holy Baptism, the
cleansing and renewing bath, is such a universal symbol. Another
is the simple meal of bread and wine. But the most basic of all
images, experienced by all living creatures daily, is the alternation
of darkness and light. The basic diurnal pattern involves the regular rhythm of activity and rest. No organism can be always at rest
or always at work. The rhythm of the two is essential to life.

The idea of Daily Prayer may call to mind a pleasant countryside
with farmers and horses going to the fields at sunrise and returning
along unpaved roads to their hard-earned rest as the sun sinks low
in the sky and bells from the parish church announce Evensong.
Humans and animals and fields, we would like to think, all lived in
harmony then, working and resting, and the church accompanied

their simple rhythm with its own round of prayer. Such a picture is recalled in Oliver Goldsmith's *The Deserted Village* and in Thomas Gray's "Elegy Written in a Country Churchyard" (1751):

> The curfew tolls the knell of parting day,
> The lowing herd wind slowly o'er the lea,
> The ploughman homeward plods his weary way,
> And leaves the world to darkness and to me.

All of that dreamy picture is long gone (indeed, that was Gray's point), if it ever truly existed, the peaceful harmony shattered by the industrial revolution and two world wars. To talk about Daily Prayer in any traditional sense in the modern world seems perhaps hopelessly romantic. Electric power can turn night into day. Factories work around the clock. Night time is the best time for many — a time for parties, sports, theater, entertainment. For many, real life, meaningful life, begins when work is done, for then we have "time for ourselves."

We ignore the instinctive natural rhythms and powers, however, at our peril. Robert Frost, who has been both loved and dismissed as a simple nature poet, had a deep understanding of the mysterious forces at work in the world. In his poem "A Brook in the City," he describes a forlorn farmhouse now surrounded by houses and streets and, like a convict, forced to wear a number on the new city street on which it lingers awkwardly. Once the house that is now compelled to be a city house was embraced by a brook. Other evidence of the old farm is gone — the meadow has been cemented over, the apple trees cut and burned. The brook was "thrown/Deep in a sewer dungeon under stone," still alive, still running, but "in fetid darkness" no longer seen. Only ancient maps would show that a brook ran there. But, the poet wonders,

> If from its being kept forever under
> The thoughts may not have risen that so keep
> This new-built city from both work and sleep.

The brook, now controlled and underground, is no longer remembered. Civil engineers thought they could dispose of the unneeded stream, not realizing that it was "an immortal force." Their control was not absolute. Awesome powers remain, alive and active although now unseen and unrecognized, contributing to the discontent of those who live and work in "this new-built city," undermining its repose.[1]

Such are the lingering powers of night and day. Whether we live in the city or in the country, whether we work by day or by night or not at all, we are still subject to the deeply evocative symbols of night and day, darkness and light. Daily Prayer is rooted in those primal experiences of all creatures. There is a fundamental rhythm in the world, the rhythm of activity and rest, waking and sleeping. What makes unemployment so intolerable may be that having no work to do deprives us of what we dimly sense is our rightful share in the rhythm of work and rest. It cuts us off from the integral movement of the creation. Animals and birds and humanity too alternate activity and repose, each an extension of the other, resulting in a satisfying cycle. For those who have no work, their part in the fundamental rhythm is diminished, and that can be deeply distressing. In ancient times, the night was for sleep and the day was for work. That pattern is broken now; many work at night in factories that never rest in cities that never sleep. But it was ever so. When the sun sets and quiet descends on the world of nature, most creatures go to their rest, but not all. Nocturnal animals and insects then come to life. The night has never been quiet and the sky has never been entirely dark. As is so often the case when we observe the world and our experience of it, the picture is more complex and therefore more interesting than we at first suppose.

We begin in the darkness. It was so at creation, and it was so for each individual life. When darkness returns we experience a dissolution of perception and consciousness, and we slip back toward nonbeing. We sometimes used to teach children to pray,

> If I should die before I wake,
> I pray the Lord my soul to take.

It seems odd to suggest the fear of death to an innocent child, but the thought may be there already as it is in each adult.[2] The darkness reminds us of the nonbeing out of which we came and into which we will one day relapse. Each night is a descent along that slope. So we give children words with which to confront those fears, declaring that God is present even in the dark, even at the hour of death. The darkness suggests the womb at our beginning and at our ending, "whatever mystery of darkness lies beyond the portal of death."[3]

In the darkness we forcefully encounter our isolation and vulnerability. We are naturally afraid of what we do not know or understand. Darkness speaks of ignorance and fear. In the Old English epic *Beowulf*, the monster Grendel is characterized as a "rover of the borders" living in fen and fastness, a "walker in darkness." He is never described, and, because we cannot form a clear picture of him, we are the more terrified of his presence, as we are of all those unknown forces, which he represents, that come to us from the borders of life and understanding. Spenser in his *Epithalamion,* like many poets before and since, knows that darkness brings fears of creatures of the night, and he confronts such terrors even in the midst of a wedding celebration. Evil is out there, lurking unseen in the dark. Jesus says to those who have come to arrest him, "This is your hour, and the power of darkness!" (Luke 22:53), and at the crucifixion darkness descends (Luke 23:44).

The earliest rituals of which we have evidence were performed in the paleolithic caves in southern France and northern Spain about 30,000–10,000 B.C.

> A terrific sense of claustrophobia, and simultaneously of release from every context of the world above, assails the mind impounded in those more than absolutely dark abysses, where darkness is no longer an absence of light but an experienced force.[4]

That intense darkness plunges one into almost physical contact with the chaos of cosmic night and the other world. This is not the natural phenomenon of night. Natural night is never wholly dark, for there are stars, moon, fires, but cosmic night is an absolute and menacing darkness in which mysterious beings approach, divinities or monsters or both.[5]

Darkness, however, is not all negative. The darkness of the tomb can be a preparation for the darkness of the womb, and when we descend into the belly of the devouring monster, we may at the same time be entering into the womb of the mother for rebirth. Moreover, night is a time often associated with stillness and rest and peace, as it is in many prayers and hymns.[6] Holy Saturday, the Great Sabbath of Jesus' rest in the tomb between death and resurrection, is the primary symbol of the hope as well as the defeat associated with darkness. The darkness of that night is pregnant with promise as the disciples wait and watch for the first signs of dawn.

At last the rosy fingers of dawn begin to push back the cover of night, and sunrise comes with light and the fulfillment of the night of watching. Night fears are dispelled by the light that gives orientation and guidance. Darkness descends with the weight of gravity, pulling down the world and all that is in it toward the fearsome interior of the earth; but light is experienced as coming from above, in its luminous flight elevating the earth and all its inhabitants out of chaos and into order and purpose and life, drawing life toward its immeasurable heights.[7]

Dawn is the time to awake from the world of dreams into the knowledge and experience of reality. It dispels ignorance and fear, and replaces chaos with order, defeat with triumph, promise with fulfillment, death with life. In its ascendence and promise it looks to the future both of the day and of the life of the world.

The rising sun, for those with eyes to see, proclaims the rising Sun of Righteousness, the resurrection of Christ. Zechariah's canticle Benedictus makes that connection as it sings,

> In the tender compassion of our God
> the dawn from on high shall break upon us,
> to shine on those who dwell in darkness and the
> shadow of death,
> and to guide our feet into the way of peace.

St. Ambrose in his hymn to Christ *Splendor paternae gloriae* ("O Splendor of God's glory bright") prays,

> Morn in her rosy car is borne;
> Let him come forth, our perfect morn,
> The Word in God the Father one,
> The Father perfect in the Son.[8]

The masculine sun of world mythology conveniently becomes the image of Christ the Sun/Son. But this Sun surpasses the sun of the natural world, for he is "the sun that goes not down"[9] who fulfills the ancient prophecy, "The sun shall no longer be your light by day, nor for brightness shall the moon give light to you by night; but the Lord will be your everlasting light, and your God will be your glory" (Isaiah 60:19). In the heavenly city there will be no night "for the glory of God is its light, and its lamp is the Lamb" (Revelation 21:23, 25); as Zechariah had foretold, "There shall be continuous day" (Zechariah 14:7).[10] Already we, on whom the end of the ages has come (1 Corinthians 10:11), experience the unending day. Participation in Daily Prayer is a way of linking ourselves with continuity and with eternity.

Thus Evening Prayer and Morning Prayer, prayer as the sun sets and prayer as the sun rises, are the "two hinges" on which Daily Prayer turns.[11] They embrace the extremes of human experience: dark and light, below and above, loss of bearings and guidance, fear and confidence. Evening and Morning Prayer are the two principal "choir offices," sung in choir rather than at the altar and, unlike the Eucharist, not requiring an ordained leader. They are indeed not presided over, as is the Eucharist, but are a community act, the work of the whole assembly acting together in unison. When in Daily Prayer a single voice is heard, it need not come from a visible and identifiable person.

It is important that a consideration of these two principal hours of prayer begin with Evening Prayer, Vespers. The Eastern church, Isabel Hapgood explains, reckons its day after the pattern of Judaism, from sunset to sunset.

> Therefore the worship of God begins with the Evening Service, which typifies, in general, the Old Testament times, as foreshadowing our Lord Jesus Christ and his life on earth, and precedes the Divine Liturgy of the morning, wherein is typified the life of our Lord as set forth in the New Testament and his life in heaven.[12]

The Jewish pattern is essential: sunset to sunset. The alternative is to reckon the day from sunrise to sunset (or, more practically, from rising to retiring, from waking up to going to sleep.) In that reckoning, night drops out of the pattern, and the focus is unfortunately self-centered: the day is for me when I am awake. Life (and history) becomes a series of successive but distinctly separate days. A third possibility, reckoning time by the clock, from midnight to midnight is of even less help.[13] The relationship between the twenty-four-hour day and the alternation of darkness and light is lost altogether. The ancient pattern of Genesis, "There was evening and there was morning, the first day" (1:5), is worth preserving. In the account of creation given in the first chapter of Genesis, light, the first of the works of creation, broke in upon the uncreated darkness, establishing order and form and being. The evening-to-evening pattern was basic to the celebration of the Passover: "In the first month, from the evening of the fourteenth day until the evening of the twenty-first day, you shall eat unleavened bread" (Exodus 12:18). Indeed, if the only purpose of counting the days from evening to evening were to preserve a link of commonality with Judaism, that would of itself be eminently worthwhile.

Like Judaism, Christianity reckons time from sunset to sunset. At dusk, when anciently the lamps were lighted, Evening Prayer, Vespers, is sung. Its theme is recollection; its characteristics, inner peace and repose. In ancient times at Vespers, a nonbiblical hymn, *phos hilaron,* "Joyous light of glory," and Psalm 141 were sung. At dawn, when the rising sun dispels the last shadow of night,[14] Morning Prayer (Matins-Lauds) is sung. Its theme is resurrection; its characteristics are life, hope, vigor, duty. Anciently at Lauds a nonbiblical hymn, Gloria in Excelsis, and the *Laudate* psalms (148–150) were sung.

Thus, as the expression has it, time is sanctified. Human experience of time is deepened and transformed by regular prayer in the evening and in the morning. The passage of time is made to praise God and the works of God. In the words of the Easter hymn of Fortunatus, "Hours and passing moments praise thee in their flight."[15] We experience these times as proclamations of creation and of the death and resurrection of Christ. Time is no longer experienced as merely duration as the hours pass and the years slide by. Inevitably, certain days, hours, and times stand out with particular prominence in each individual life. To sanctify time is to heighten our awareness of the eternal significance of each moment lived in time. Not a moment is to be wasted, for each is an opportunity for some worthwhile deed — service of a needy neighbor, rest, pondering the work of God.

Time, it may be thought, needs no sanctification, for it came from the hand of the Holy One, who, having made darkness and light, sun and moon, signs for days and seasons and years, declared creation to be "very good" (Genesis 1:31). But time, like all creatures, was corrupted by the rebellious fall of humanity, and with the rest of creation "has been groaning in labor pains" (Romans 8:22) until the coming of Christ. At the incarnation, the creator entered creation, subject to time, the eternal limited by the temporal, and the redemption was begun.[16]

In Daily Prayer, the church, moved by the Holy Spirit, joins and extends the prayer of Christ, the body joining the head, in perpetual praise and prayer. The prayer is continuous, for it is an expression of the unceasing work of the Spirit of God and of the High Priest, and it is communal, joining heaven and earth, taking up the song that the morning stars began in order to accompany creation.[17] Those who pray Daily Prayer are members of an organic community. The celebrant is the whole church, in heaven and on earth, praying as a whole.[18] Such a view opens our hearts to the unlimited dimensions of God and the world. Its work is a duty and a joy. Its goal is none other than the praise of God, who, as the Te Deum sings, is "worthy of all worship"; but this praise enlightens one's entire life, all corners of daily life, opening abundant avenues of praise through discipline and service. John Keble understood well such urgent responsibility:

> If on our daily course our mind
> Be set to hallow all we find,
> New treasures still, of countless price,
> God will provide for sacrifice.
>
> Old friends, old scenes, will lovelier be,
> As more of heaven in each we see;
> Some softening gleam of love and prayer
> Shall dawn on every cross and care.
>
> The trivial round, the common task,
> Will furnish all we ought to ask;
> Room to deny ourselves, a road
> To bring us daily nearer God.[19]

The sanctification of time directs us toward that day when prayer and life will be one.

The Psalter

The Psalter, that great storehouse of prayer,[20] the prayer of mortals that is at the same time the word of God,[21] is the inspiration, principal means, and focus of Daily Prayer.

Praying the Psalter enables and encourages us to share in the perpetual praise of God. It is so for Judaism. Abraham Heschel observed,

> We never pray as individuals, set apart from the rest of the world. The liturgy is an order which we can enter only as a part of the Community of Israel. Every act of worship is an act of participating in an eternal service, in the service of all souls of all ages. Every act of adoration is done in union with all of history, and with all beings above and below.[22]

It is so in Christianity, as the church is bold to claim a share in Israel's history and practice and prayer. Dietrich Bonhöffer wrote,

> "Sing unto the Lord a new song," the Psalter enjoins us again and again. It is the Christ-hymn, new every morning, that the family fellowship strikes up at the beginning of the day, the hymn that is sung by the whole Church of God on earth

and in heaven, and in which we are summoned to join. God has prepared for Himself one great song of praise throughout eternity, and those who enter the community of God join in this song. It is the song that the "morning stars sang together and all the sons of God shouted for joy" at the creation of the world (Job 38:7). It is the victory song of the children of Israel after passing through the Red Sea, the Magnificat of Mary after the annunciation, the song of Paul and Silas in the night of prison, the song of the singers on the sea of glass after their rescue, the "song of Moses the servant of God, and the song of the Lamb" (Rev. 15:3). It is the new song of the heavenly fellowship.

In the morning of every day the Church on earth lifts up this song and in the evening it closes the day with this hymn. It is the triune God and His works that are extolled. This song has a different ring on earth from what it has in heaven. On earth it is the song of those who believe, in heaven the song of those who see.[23]

Night and day in their perpetual alternation until time will be no more show the ceaseless praise rendered by all creation and provide a glimpse and promise of the harmony of consummation.

Christian praise is specifically of the mystery of God's creating and redeeming love. It is the acknowledgement of what has already been done in the history of salvation as the seed that will blossom into fullness in the future. It is the expectation of its final and full achievement.

In praying the Psalter we participate in the sacred story, we appropriate it as our own. That which is dated we bring into our present. That which we see is unworthy we transpose to a higher key. Songs of war we can understand as songs of spiritual warfare.[24] The hateful words of the imprecatory psalms such as 109, in Alan Paton's description "the most terrible words that man has ever written,"[25] when taken into our own mouths become an honest recognition that as reprehensible as such words are, we nevertheless sometimes feel that way too.[26] As Bonhöffer observed,

A psalm that we cannot utter as a prayer, that makes us falter and horrifies us, is a hint to us that here Someone else is praying, not we; that the One who is here protesting his innocence, who is invoking God's judgment, who has come to such infinite depths of suffering, is none other than Jesus

Christ himself. He it is who is praying here, and not only here but in the whole Psalter.[27]

When the church prays the psalms, Christians hear not just ancient voices together with their own. Most of all the church hears the voice of Christ. A wise monk, following Bonhöffer, wrote,

> All these interruptions for prayer during the course of the day are not just to recite literary texts, however ancient or venerable, but to encounter the actual person of Christ and refresh our awareness of living in his presence.... What better way to have the mind of Christ among us than to make these prayers an important part of our life?[28]

In the Psalter are prayers known to Jesus and used by him as he walked among us. He helps us interpret those psalms that trouble us. The imprecatory psalms in his mouth are emptied of all of the imperfect motives, and Christ prays them with us "in solidarity with the desperate human cry for ultimate moral order and for justice."[29] Such, Bonhöffer found, as have thousands before and since, is the secret of praying the psalms in a Christian context. Bonhöffer wrote,

> The *man* Jesus Christ, to whom no affliction, no ill, no suffering is alien and who yet was the wholly innocent and righteous one, is praying in the Psalter through the mouth of his Church. The Psalter is the prayer book of Jesus Christ in the truest sense of the word. He prayed the Psalter and now it has become his prayer for all time.[30]

Therefore the Psalter can be our word, our prayer to God, and also at the same time God's word to us.

> Only in the whole Christ does the whole Psalter become a reality, a whole which the individual can never fully comprehend and call his own. That is why the prayer of the psalms belongs in a peculiar way to the fellowship. Even if a verse or a psalm is not one's own prayer, it is nevertheless the prayer of another member of the fellowship; so it is quite certainly the prayer of the true man Jesus Christ and his Body on earth.[31]

So Luther could call the Psalter "a little Bible" and declare that "there you look into the hearts of all the saints."[32] We find the whole range of human emotions, thoughts, responses, prayers, and cries. The psalms give us words to say that are better than our own words, sanctified by history and by the speech and life of Christ. The psalms teach us what prayer means: praying on the basis of the promises of God. The psalms also teach what we should pray. Although the scope of prayer in the psalms is far beyond the experience of the individual, nonetheless the individual prays in faith the whole prayer of Christ, "who alone possesses the full range of experiences expressed in this prayer."[33] So John Cassian in his travels to Egypt in the fourth century observed that the monks there did not seem so much to be reciting the psalms as to be re-creating them, for they said them from the heart as if they were extempore prayers.[34]

Reading the Bible

A significant feature of Daily Prayer as it is practiced in Protestant churches is the reading of Scripture. Historically, the principal office associated with reading from the Bible has been Matins, a predawn service. At other times, one brief lesson was read.

At the time of the Reformation in England, the Breviary offices were combined and simplified. A scheme was devised by which the entire Bible would be read through in a year in Morning and Evening Prayer. Thus one of the functions of the renewed office was instruction — teaching the people the Bible. It remains one of the attractive features of Daily Prayer. "Brief verses cannot and should not take the place of reading Scripture as a whole....Holy Scripture does not consist of individual passages; it is a unit and is intended to be used as such."[35]

But the reading of the Bible in Daily Prayer is not simply *lectio continua,* the continuous reading of portions of the Bible. The principle of Bible reading in Daily Prayer is *lectio divina,* spiritual reading.[36] One listens to a section of Scripture not as a lesson in biblical history, not as an exercise in critical scholarship (although for those trained in exegesis such questions and viewpoints inevitably run through the mind). One listens to hear the voice of God. That voice is heard by each in an individual way, according to the measure of understanding of each. One never finishes acquiring knowledge of the Bible's story.

The Scripture is a whole and every word, every sentence possesses such multiple relationships with the whole that it is impossible to keep the whole always in view when listening to details. It becomes apparent, therefore, that the whole of Scripture and hence every passage in it as well far surpasses our understanding. It is good for us to be daily reminded of this fact, which again points to Jesus Christ himself, "in whom are hid all the treasures of wisdom and knowledge" (Col. 2:3).[37]

Devotional use of the continuous reading of the biblical books requires all who want to hear to put themselves or to allow themselves to be found where God has acted once and for all for the sake of the world.[38]

> We become a part of what once took place for our salvation. Forgetting and losing ourselves, we, too, pass through the Red Sea, through the desert, across the Jordan into the promised land. With Israel we fall into doubt and unbelief and through punishment and repentance experience again God's help and forgiveness. All this is not mere reverie, but holy, godly reality. We are torn out of our own existence and set down in the midst of the holy history of God on earth.[39]

Such devotional reading turns our usual devotional practice and preaching upside down. It is not, Bonhöffer insists, that God is the spectator and sharer of our present life, however important that may be. It is rather that we must be reverent listeners to what may seem like an old story from the past. We must be participants in God's action in that sacred story. "Only in so far as we are *there*, is God with us today also."[40] That advice is against all that modern culture believes, against much that is taught in the churches. Indeed, Bonhöffer boldly and powerfully asserts, "It is in fact more important for us to know what God did to Israel, to His Son Jesus Christ, than to seek what God intends for us today."[41] Salvation is not to be found in one's own life history but only in the history of Jesus Christ. "Only in the Holy Scriptures do we learn to know our own history."[42]

Such devotional reading takes time and work. We should never begrudge such effort, for it is only by such strenuous effort that we can know our salvation and thus know ourselves. A good bit of that effort involves learning to listen. The collect composed for the 1549 *Book of Common Prayer* for the Second Sunday in Advent (now used for Proper 28) describes such careful and responsive listening in a succinct and memorable way:

> Blessed Lord, who hast caused all holy Scriptures to be writ-
> ten for our learning; Grant that we may in such wise hear
> them, read, mark, learn, and inwardly digest them, that by
> patience and comfort of thy holy Word, we may embrace,
> and ever hold fast, the blessed hope of everlasting life, which
> thou hast given us in our Saviour Jesus Christ.

The collect derives from Romans 15:4, the beginning of the epistle then appointed for that Sunday in Advent.[43] ("Written for our
learning" means "written for our instruction," as in the New
Revised Standard Version, not "written for us to memorize";
the archaic "patience and comfort" is perhaps better rendered
"steadfastness and encouragement," again as in the New Revised
Standard Version of the Bible. The conclusion may be related
to Colossians 1:27, "Christ in you, the hope of glory.") The
thought of this collect appears in diverse places within Christianity.
Guigo II the Carthusian wrote in *The Ladder of Monks,*

> Reading seeks for the sweetness of a blessed life,
> meditation perceives it,
> prayer asks for it,
> contemplation tastes it.
>
> Reading, as it were, puts food whole into the mouth,
> meditation chews it and breaks it up,
> prayer extracts its flavor,
> contemplation is the sweetness itself which gladdens
> and refreshes.[44]

John Wesley gave this advice on spiritual reading.

> Be sure to read, not cursorily or hastily, but leisurely, se-
> riously, and with great attention; with proper pauses and
> intervals, and that you may allow time for the enlighten-
> ings of divine grace. To this end, recollect, every now and
> then, what you have read, and consider how to reduce
> it to practice.... Read those passages over and over that
> more nearly concern yourself, and more closely affect your
> inclinations or practice....
>   Select also any remarkable sayings or advices, and trea-
> sure them up in your memory; and these you either may draw
> forth in time of need...or make use of.[45]

Lectio divina requires attentiveness to Scripture in relation to the
specifics of each individual life, leading to spiritual growth and

transformation. Such receptive, expectant reading is an encounter with the living Word, who demands our surrender and who slowly shapes us into the image of God.

Silence

The rhythm of Daily Prayer is that of night and day, darkness and light. It is also the rhythm of our words and God's word. It is further the rhythm of speech and silence, the two of equal importance. The silence of worship is not the awkward spaces when someone forgets what to do or the imposed silence of sometimes sullen respect while someone else is speaking or doing something. The silence of the liturgy is chosen and embraced as a time of receptive listening, allowing God, who is so often overwhelmed with our words, the opportunity to speak. Such a gift requires careful cultivation and cherishing.

In the winter there sometimes falls an immense and all-pervading silence. After a snowfall even the few subdued sounds of winter are muffled by the vast white blanket. Birds do not sing; the wind does not stir. The white silence becomes almost tangible. It is the deep, pervasive fullness that resonates before sounds are made or words are uttered, before the quiet is shattered by sound. Such silence returns us to the beginning, before time, to the instant before creation. As darkness both precedes light and succeeds it, so silence both precedes speech and succeeds it. That surrounding silence is a reminder of the limitations of human language and reason. Before the "most ancient of all mysteries," we fall silent, for in the presence of the Holy One human speech is inadequate to comprehend the vision of the divine majesty or to express our response to it. It is therefore small wonder that silence has been prized by the mystics to whom it seems right to communicate without words and to understand without knowledge that which is above words and knowledge.

> This I apprehend to be nothing but the mysterious silence and mystical quiet which destroys consciousness and dissolves forms. Seek, therefore, silently and mystically, that perfect and primitive union with the Arch-Good.[46]

So urged Hierotheus, who is purported to have been a convert of St. Paul's but who was perhaps a Syrian monk of the fifth century.

Perfect communion is beyond words. Love's favorite language is silence.[47] Thomas Carlyle wrote,

> Speech is too often not, as the Frenchman defined it, the art of concealing Thought; but of quite stifling and suspending Thought, so that there is none to conceal. Speech too is great, but not the greatest. As the Swiss Inscription says, *Sprechen ist silbern, Schweigen ist golden* (Speech is silvern, Silence is golden); or as I might rather express it: Speech is of Time, Silence is of Eternity.[48]

Silence is reverential quiet and wordless awe appropriate for an encounter with the divine. "The Lord is in his holy Temple; let all the earth keep silence before him" (Habakkuk 2:20). "Be silent before the Lord God! For the day of the Lord is at hand" (Zephaniah 1:7). "When the Lamb opened the seventh seal, there was silence in heaven for about half an hour" (Revelation 8:1). Silence is when God delights to work the most intimate and revolutionary deeds. Elijah learned it on Mount Horeb when the Lord was not in the wind or the earthquake or the fire but in "a sound of sheer silence" (1 Kings 19:11–12).[49] In the passage from the Wisdom of Solomon often recalled at Christmas, "While gentle silence enveloped all things, and the night in its swift course was now half gone, your all-powerful word leaped from heaven, from the royal throne...a stern warrior carrying the sharp sword of your authentic command" (Wisdom 18:14–16). Silence is a way of wonder.

As the quotations from the Bible imply, silence is also a way of waiting. Silence gathers and focuses our distractions and provides space for the mind and heart to wander freely. It is an expectant waiting, a letting go of what we so greedily and ignorantly clutch to our heart, an allowing ourselves to feel what D. H. Lawrence called the soft rocking of the living cosmos, a willingness to receive, leaving in communion with God space for God to speak.

Silence is, moreover, a way of surrender. It is ending our frantic activity and incessant chatter, yielding to God in "the surrender of silence."[50] It is letting go of all that we want and waiting upon God. The stern words of Psalm 46:10 command, "Be still and know that I am God."

While silence may be savored alone, in the liturgy it is a corporate experience that, perhaps surprisingly, binds those who share it more deeply than their common recitation of words can do. The Religious Society of Friends has demonstrated how meeting in silence is a gathering of power that builds and nourishes community. In corporate silence we help one another,[51] and spiritual cooperation is a necessary requirement of those who would worship.[52]

> In an ideal meeting for worship there should emerge from the concentrated spiritual exercise of those present a message which is in tune with this exercise. We are speaking of what may be something of a mystery to many, and which yet will be perfectly intelligible to those of certain experience — spiritual communion. After meeting, it is not unusual to hear someone say that his mind was engaged in meditation upon precisely the same subject or even the same verse of Scripture as the one to which utterance had been given by someone else.[53]

Such meeting in silence is a strenuous exercise. "The Quaker method of worship is the most exacting of all methods in the demands it makes upon the mind and spirit."[54] To those unused to it, silence may be irksome; it may be even terrifying to some who want to forget themselves in worship, for "silence seems to throw worshipers back upon themselves in a way they can hardly bear."[55] Members of the Society of Friends explain that they give rise to their best selves in silent meditation upon Perfection. They thus give a chance to "that of God" found in every human being to assert itself, to claim its rights, to assume guidance of the errant human spirit.[56] Liturgical Christians also know this Spirit in each believer calling, gathering, and enlightening the whole church. Silence is an important way of allowing that holy and life-giving Spirit to work. A Friend once asked the probing question, "Who would talk when God is at work?"[57] The silence of worship is "stillness which has the promise of the knowledge of God."[58] It is a stillness as alert and active as a sentry on guard, straining ear and eye through the darkness to catch the first and faintest sign of movement. Percy Dearmer observed that Quakers by their silent meetings have met, uncovered, and answered "the cultural weakness of Protestantism, which is still with us — the sacerdotalism that has led men to think that the rays of God's light can only reach the human heart through the distorted medium of a human preacher."[59]

In a Quaker meeting for worship after the last people arrive, the meeting "gathers" or "centers down," as the old phraseology had it,[60] and the concentrated and strenuous work of worship begins.

It is in such silence that liturgical worship, especially Daily Prayer, begins, from which it emerges, and to which it returns again and again. John Austin, a pious seventeenth-century Roman Catholic layman, in his edition of devotions in "the ancient way of offices," directs worshipers to stand a while in silence "to make the presence of God." He seems to mean more than simply "make [themselves aware of] the presence of God." Rather, Austin seems to understand that an assembly gathers in response to the Lord's promise, "Where two or three are gathered in my name, I am there among them" (Matthew 18:20), and their act of gathering claims that presence. It is a mystery claimed by others as well. "The prayer of two or three in fellowship is a greater thing than the prayer of the same persons in isolation, and as such has our Lord's express promise of power and reward."[61] Thomas Comber, the Dean of Durham, declared in 1684,

> These souls of ours are so clogged with Corruption, disturbed with Passions, and so constantly entertained with the Vanities which our Senses present us with that we find our Minds pressed down when we would lift them up to God.... So the Church directeth us first to prepare our hearts before we begin to pray. The Jews are taught when they enter their Synagogues to stand silently a while in the posture of Prayer before they begin their devotion.[62]

William Wistar Comfort reminds his readers that the fruitful use even of silence requires preparation. "One should not drop in casually to a Friends' meeting with the expectation of something mysterious happening. The mind and the spirit must be reasonably prepared in advance to receive and perchance to give the bread of life." The thoughts that arise in worship are often new creations, but novelty requires background. An expectant attitude, human love, reading and meditation all help prepare for worship.[63]

> The Quaker group silence, the cooperative brainwork of the entire assembly, the expectant hush, the sense of divine presence, the faith that God and man come into mutual and reciprocal correspondence, tend to heighten the spiritual quality of the person who rises in that kind of atmosphere to speak. But that group situation, important as it is, will not work the miracle of producing a message for the hour in a person who is sterile and has nothing to say.[64]

It is to such work of spiritual cooperation and cooperative spirituality that worshipers are summoned.

The principal act of breaking the preparatory silence occurs at the beginning of Morning Prayer, Matins, with the opening versicle, "O Lord, open my lips." The verse from Psalm 51:15 has point and effect if the Great Silence has been maintained through the night until that prolonged silence is ended by the mystery of God calling speech from silence as in the beginning of Genesis and a Lutheran eucharistic prayer begins, "You are indeed holy, O God, the fountain of all holiness; you bring light from darkness, life from death, speech from silence."[65] The miracle of creation, the miracle of language, the miracle of the ending of Zechariah's bondage to dumbness, the miracle of Jesus healing the one who was dumb are all renewed as a new day dawns and the vocal praise of God resumes in that assembly. But also before Evensong a time of silence is appropriate for the assembly to center down and make the presence of God. Before and during and after every service, there are times of profound silence to contemplate the mystery of God and the still greater mystery of the Holy One calling us into communion with God and therefore with each other.

Evensong

In silence and descending darkness the assembly gathers to mark the ending of one day and the beginning of the next. Daily, the condition of the chaos prior to creation is recalled and relived. But the assembly is a Christian congregation, and therefore the whole history of salvation cannot be set aside. A large lighted candle is carried into the assembly,[66] and the service of light begins. It is the time the ancients called the lighting of the lamps. Electricity has ended our dependence on fire for light. Indeed, light has become an ever-present force. City people move to the country and immediately install mercury vapor lights so that the stars are barely visible. The glow of cities at night interferes with astronomical observatories even in remote places. The light we have made burns between us and the primal darkness, driving the dark from our experience, rendering it remote and apparently irrelevant. Nonetheless, sometimes the power fails, and we are thrown back a century and more. Ancient fears arise anew, and we are surrounded by a hostile darkness that we can dispel only in the small circles of candles and torchlight. While we wait for "power" to be restored, we are suddenly and disturbingly in the grip of a force beyond our control. The darkness asserts its strength and reminds us of what we do all we can to forget: that one day, when the end comes, the darkness will be triumphant.

We bring a candle into a church at evening, and even though we can end the spell by simply switching on the electric lights, what we experience in that twilight is more than make-believe. The powerful symbol of darkness preserves its dread strength and is more enduring than the frail light we kindle. Striking a match and lighting a candle slows down what we accomplish in an instant with a light switch. The candle brought into the church is a way of dramatizing the mystery of light coming into the darkness and driving it back. It is a portrayal of creation and of re-creation, of Genesis and the gospel. Order conquers chaos, and life conquers death. We assert by our weak gesture with a candle, unnoticed by most of the world (and the church), that the power of triumphant darkness has been broken and one day will be gone forever. But still a gust of wind can push through a cracked window and disrupt our tentative little drama.

In contrast to the steadiness of electric light, candlelight may be described as a living light. Its fire throbs with life; it flares up, it dies down. It flickers as it consumes the candle. Like all living organisms, it must take in nourishment. The wax comes from bees, and so the candle is more clearly part of the living web of nature than is electric light.

During the lighting of the candles a venerable hymn is sung, perhaps the most ancient postbiblical hymn in the church's collection, *phos hilaron,* a gift of the Eastern church.

The Lutheran hymnal also provides a metrical translation by Henry Wadsworth Longfellow, "O gladsome light of the Father immortal"; *The Hymnal 1982, The United Methodist Hymnal* (1989), *The Presbyterian Hymnal* (1990), and the *Service Book and Hymnal* (1958) provide Robert Bridges's version, "O gladsome Light, O grace."

The hymn, in its original and in its metrical versions, is addressed to Christ the light of the world (John 8:12), and like many liturgical texts is an assemblage of many biblical passages and allusions. Central to them is Hebrews 1:3: "He is the reflection of God's glory and the exact imprint of God's very being, and he sustains all things by his powerful word."

Lutheran Book of Worship	*Book of Common Prayer*
Joyous light	O gracious Light,
of glory; of the	pure brightness of the
immortal Father;	everlasting Father in
heavenly,	heaven,
holy, blessed Jesus Christ.	O Jesus Christ, holy and blessed.
We have come to the	Now as we come to the
setting of the sun,	setting of the sun,
and we look to the	and our eyes behold the
evening light.	vesper light,
We sing to	We sing your praises,
God, the Father, Son,	O God: Father, Son,
and Holy Spirit:	and Holy Spirit.
You are worthy of being	You are worthy at all
praised with pure	times to be praised
voices forever.	by happy voices,
O Son of God, O Giver of life:	O Son of God, O Giver of life,
The universe proclaims	and to be glorified
your glory.	through all the world.
(p. 59)	(p. 112)

The opening lines of the hymn radiate Johannine themes but present difficulties because it is (deliberately, we may assume) ambiguous. Are the predicates spoken of the Father or of the Son? Both are grammatically possible, and the point is thus made that what is true of the Father must also be true of the Son. Jesus Christ is, as the Nicene Creed affirms, "Light from Light, true God from true God." "Whoever has seen me has seen the Father," Jesus said to Philip (John 14:9). Christ is the light radiating from the eternal, heavenly Father (John 1:9). Both the Father and the Son are appropriately praised as holy and blessed. As the sunlight lessens, we look to the vesper lights, which the church kindles to replace the fading light of day. We do more than notice that candles are being lighted or watch the servers as they perform their duties. We look to the light we kindle as our companion through the darkness. The gift of evening light, as we have seen, its flickering light alive, is a powerful symbol of Christ the Light, the Word through whom creation was accomplished, who drove back the darkness of chaos and error and sin and death, who is our guide through this shadowed world, our preserver from all threats and fears. Therefore the church, in its unending song, true to the favorite theme of the Eastern church from which this hymn came, sings to the Holy

Trinity. The content of the song is that the Triune God is worthy of praise by happy voices.

The hymn returns to its original theme, the praise of the Son of God, who as the word and breath of God is the Giver of life (John 10:28). He is appropriately lauded by all the world, that is, by all the created universe. Christ the Light is worthy (Revelation 4:11; 5:9).

Since this is an Eastern hymn, one would expect an emphasis on the work of the Holy Spirit, but, except in the name of the Trinity, the Spirit is not mentioned explicitly. One obvious possibility is that because the hymn is so ancient, already old in the third century,[67] it may not reflect or express a full trinitarian doctrine and theology. One of the titles of the Holy Spirit, however, is "the Giver of life," as in the Nicene Creed: "the Holy Spirit, the Lord, the Giver of life." And in many Eastern liturgies there are frequent references to "the holy and life-giving Spirit." If that is the intention here, the first stanza of the hymn refers to the Father and the Son; the third stanza to the Son and the Holy Spirit. The central stanza joins the first and the last with its praise of the Holy Trinity. The organization may be visualized thus:

> The Father and the Son
> The Father and the Son, and Holy Spirit
> the Son and the Holy Spirit.

It is a most subtle hymn.

Eleanor Irwin has suggested[68] that the second word in the Greek text, *hilaron* — variously translated as "gladsome" (Longfellow and Robert Bridges), "gracious" (*Book of Common Prayer*), or "joyous" (*Lutheran Book of Worship*) — is perhaps best translated as "cheerful"; the English word "hilarity" derives from it. Such a picture of a smiling, merry God is not contrary to the biblical pictures of God and Christ, but *hilaron* is never an epithet in the Bible for God or Christ. Deities in non-Christian religions were praised in this way: in the second-third-century *Corpus Hermeticum*, for example, Poimandres speaks of a revelation of the divine as *phos ... eudion te kai hilarion,* "a light clear and cheerful." The Christian hymn, Irwin suggests, may be declaring that only Christ is truly "cheerful." Christianity may again, as so often before and since, have appropriated the language of pagan worship for its own. In Christ, that is to say, is found the fulfillment of all the ancient hopes and dreams; what people dimly sensed is now present in clear light.

Phos hilaron may be understood as a gloss on the line from the psalmist, "In your light we see light" (Psalm 36:9). When the power fails we feel suddenly deprived, and we learn anew what it means to look for light or to wait for light. We learn again that, as it was for the psalmist, light is a wonderful mystery. We learn again that we, like a failing electric lamp, are often reluctant and unreliable receptors of light. So the ancient hymn identifies Christ as the Light that has its source in the eternal heavenly Father, and it suggests the necessary conditions for divine enlightenment. "You are worthy of being praised with pure voices forever." The purity of the voices of praise involves unity, as suggested by the purity of unison song as singers join together in one voice.[69] "May . . . God . . . grant you to live in harmony with one another, in accordance with Christ Jesus, so that together you may with one voice glorify the God and Father of our Lord Jesus Christ" (Romans 15:6).[70] The purity also involves charity, a love not only of God but of the neighbor through whom God's light may come to us. Such light cannot be generated by us or controlled by us or dispensed as we will. The most that the church, the most that the universe can do is provide a place that welcomes its appearing in all of its unpredictability and danger and comfort.

The hymn *phos hilaron* is a contribution of the Eastern church to Evening Prayer. The West had its own way of offering thanksgiving for light at Evening Prayer, comparable to *phos hilaron*. The Western thanksgiving was a solemn proclamation of praise, a continuation in a Roman context of "the old jewish notion that one blessed persons and things by giving thanks to God for them over them."[71] Hippolytus in the *Apostolic Tradition* (ca. 215) gives one ancient example; its relationship to the form of the eucharistic prayer is apparent.

> We praise and thank you, O God, through your Son, Jesus Christ our Lord, through whom you have enlightened us by revealing the light that never fades. Night *is falling/has fallen* and day's allotted span draws to a close. The daylight which you created for our pleasure has fully satisfied us, and yet, of your free gift, now the evening lights do not fail us. We praise you and glorify you through your Son, Jesus Christ our Lord; through him be glory, honor, and power to you in the Holy Spirit, now and always and forever and ever. Amen.[72]

The prayer has a trinitarian shape. It is addressed to the Father through the Son, who is mentioned by name and title twice in the course of the prayer; the Holy Spirit is named in the concluding doxology. The imagery is largely from the Fourth Gospel. God has "enlightened us" (John 1:9) with the unfading, incorruptible light (1:5), Jesus Christ. We reach the edge of night, having been filled and "fully satisfied" with the daylight, created for our pleasure. Behind these words may lie such passages as Psalm 104:13, "the earth is satisfied with the fruit of your work," and Sirach 42:25, "Who could ever tire of seeing his glory?" The language of daylight, created for our pleasure, that fills and satisfies us recalls, surely deliberately, the language of the Fourth Gospel with reference to Christ: Jesus Christ is the Light (1:4, 5; 8:12), who gives abundant joy (15:11; 16:24; 17:13), who fully satisfies our needs and desires (6:12).

The light of day is pleasant, encourages both mental and physical activity, is necessary for mental and physical health (by providing vitamin D). A lovely spring day makes us feel good, and when we come to its close, we have a sense of satisfaction. But in the liturgy nothing ever means only one thing. Every object, every activity points beyond itself. When the daylight fills the sky, as a seventh-century morning office hymn sings, "Now that the daylight fills the sky," it is a sign of God's grace and goodness to creation, providing for its needs. The daystar, the sun, is an image of Christ whose glory fills creation and enlightens every human heart. The light tells of resurrection and life, a sign of the abundant life intended for God's people: "I came that they may have life, and have it abundantly" (John 10:10). Only this light can fill us and fully satisfy us. It is that joy given by the risen Christ whose work was done so that our "joy may be complete" (John 15:11). We continue to enjoy God's blessing in the gift of the evening lights of lamps and candles, which, it is to be carefully noted, are not our own creations but partake of the mystery of light and reflect its source in God. People make candles; human skill crafted the oil lamps that illumined buildings of old; human ingenuity has made use of electricity as our primary source of light and power. And yet, candles can be blown out, oil lamps run out of fuel, electricity can be interrupted by power failures. Even modern technology that puts its massive machinery between us and fire is still ultimately dependent on the goodness of the Creator, whose creative kindness and generosity gives both daylight and light in the darkness, natural and artificial light.

There is a further lesson of the light: the light is never far from us. No day, no matter how stormy, is without a lessening of the darkness; no night is entirely deprived of light; no place in any life is beyond the reach of the glory of God; no situation is devoid of hope.

Another ancient thanksgiving for light is found in the *Apostolic Constitutions* (ca. 380). The form is like that of the thanksgiving in the *Apostolic Tradition.*

> We praise and thank you, O God, for you are without beginning and without end.
>
> Through Christ you are the creator and preserver of the whole world; but, above all, you are his God and Father, the giver of the Spirit and the ruler of all that is seen and unseen.
>
> You made the day for the works of light and the night for the refreshment of our weakness.
>
> O loving Lord and source of all that is good, mercifully accept our evening sacrifice of praise.
>
> As you have conducted us through the day and brought us to night's beginning, keep us now in Christ; grant us a peaceful evening and a night free from sin; and, at the end, bring us to everlasting life through Christ our Lord.
>
> Through him we offer glory, honor, and worship to you in the Holy Spirit, now and always and forever and ever.[73]

This thanksgiving is in the form of an elaborate collect.[74] It begins with an address to God. The thanksgiving opens with an extended invocation and ascription of praise to God the Father, who is eternal ("without beginning and without end"), the creator and preserver, Father of Christ, Giver of the Spirit, and ruler of all that exists, visible and invisible, echoing the affirmation of the Nicene Creed, "maker ... of all that is, seen and unseen."

The second element in the collect form is the antecedent reason. The thanksgiving recalls that God made the day for works of light (Romans 13:11–14; 1 John 1:5–7, 9–11) and the night for refreshment (Psalm 116:7).

The petition is the third element in the collect form, and this thanksgiving makes a fourfold request: accept our sacrifice of praise, keep us in Christ, grant us a peaceful evening, and bring us to everlasting light.

The fourth element in the collect form does not always appear; it is an expression of the desired result of the petition. The result desired is in the thanksgiving interwoven with the petition. The prayer is for peace, sinlessness, and life eternal.

The final element is the concluding trinitarian doxology. Notable in the conclusion is the phrase we offer praise to you "in the Holy Spirit." It derives from the insight of St. Augustine that the Holy Spirit is not simply the third person but the principle of unity in the Holy Trinity.

Modern thanksgivings are provided by the *Book of Common Worship*[75] and by *Lutheran Book of Worship,* the latter in the form of an abbreviated *exsultet,* with roots deep in Jewish devotion that thanks God with words of blessing.

> Blessed are you, O Lord our God, king of the universe, who led your people Israel by a pillar of cloud by day and a pillar of fire by night: Enlighten our darkness by the light of your Christ; may his Word be a lamp to our feet and a light to our path; for you are merciful, and you love your whole creation, and we, your creatures, glorify you, Father, Son, and Holy Spirit.[76]

This thanksgiving, opening with the Jewish *berekah* formula, recalls the exodus pilgrims led by the visible signs of God's presence — a pillar of cloud by day and a pillar of fire by night. For Christians, Christ is the pillar of fire, the light of the world, who illumines the darkness (John 1:4–5) with such clarity and brilliance that its light eclipses even the full light of day, making the pillar of cloud unnecessary. The candle points to a deeper reality, the word of God, that is, the preaching about Christ, which enlightens our path through the world (Psalm 119:105). The concluding doxology to the Holy Trinity praises the merciful love of the creator for all creation, to which all creatures respond in grateful praise. It is a humble assertion of our solidarity with all created things — the candle and fire and the assembly that sings to God's praise, as well as all creation, rocks and trees and air and animals and birds and fish. Humanity, we are reminded quietly, is but one kind of creature made by the diverse activity of God.

The second section of Evening Prayer is the psalmody. Psalm 141 has since ancient times been sung as a fixed part of Evening Prayer, where it accompanied the offering of incense. The antiphon, the second verse of the psalm, reflects the temple cult of ancient Judaism: "Let my prayer rise before you as incense, the lifting up of my hands as the evening sacrifice." Exodus 29:38–46 describes the daily morning and evening burnt sacrifice in the temple: a year-old lamb with flowers and oil and wine. Exodus

30:1–10 describes the daily incense offering. The psalmist understands incense as a symbol of prayer as its clouds rise into the heaven; in Revelation 5:8 and 8:3–5, incense is used to show the "prayers of the saints." The incense is a visible connection between the invisible prayers of the saints on earth and the prayers of the invisible hosts of heaven. The combined prayers praise the Lamb, whose work is the focus of the book of Revelation and which provides another meaning for the incense, widespread in the ancient world — that of purification. Indeed, the primary symbolism of the incense at Evening Prayer is repentance and purification, a visible sign of being surrounded and clothed with the righteousness of Christ. The text of Psalm 141, a psalm of repentance, and the prayer that follows it in the Lutheran order make this clear: "the incense of our repentant prayer ... that with purified minds we may sing your praises."[77] Only when we are so purified by the grace of God dare we take up the words of other psalms and canticles, appropriating for ourselves words of the ancient saints of God.

The order of the songs of praise in Evening Prayer as it is sung in the Roman Catholic and Lutheran forms is Old Testament psalms, a New Testament canticle (from the epistles or Revelation), and a postbiblical metrical hymn. The impulse to sing God's praise runs through the Hebrew Scriptures into the New Testament and on, beyond the world and time of the Bible down to our own, weaving one unbroken cord of praise, tying together all the centuries and all creatures in one endless garland of worship.

Traditionally, the hymn in the evening office deals with an aspect of creation, recalling again the pattern of Genesis 1, with each successive day of the week of creation beginning at sundown. The evening is the daily reminder and celebration of creation and the daily proclamation of the new creation, the mysteries of which were accomplished in the darkness of Christmas Eve and in the darkness of Easter Even. The light of life and hope is born unseen while the world sleeps.

The Bible is read and then pondered in silence. Such slow and meditative reading, balanced with periods of silent reflection, invites us to share the divine life, enlarges our heart, and leads to the union of God's will and ours.

After the reading, the assembly takes up the evening gospel canticle, the song of Mary, the Magnificat. With the blessed virgin we stand on the border of Old Testament and New and are witnesses to Law becoming Gospel, God becoming incarnate. The Magnificat is appropriately the gospel canticle for evening because in it the theme of creation prominent in the evening office is continued and expanded. The Magnificat presents from the point of view of Mary, in whom we see the church, the work that God is doing to rescue, remake, and renew the world. Mary is the model and paradigm of piety, patience, humility, and faith. Her response to the angelic announcement, *fiat mihi*, "Let it be with me according to your word" (reminding us of the words with which creation began, *fiat lux*, "Let there be light"), declares her acceptance of the will of God for her. It is the divinely empowered response that God elicits from those God calls to service.[78] When, therefore, the church sings her song, it joins her humble acceptance of what God intended for her and through her for the world.

Mary's spirit "rejoices" in God the Savior. So her song begins, "My soul proclaims the greatness of the Lord, and my spirit rejoices in God my Savior." That joy, as is especially clear in Luke's Gospel, is a principal characteristic of the age of the Messiah, the renewed community being called together by the gospel. "Joy," Baron von Hügel observed, "is the surest sign of the presence of God."

The evening canticle presents the mystery of the *Theotokos,* the God-bearer, the mortal woman who was the mother of God. She is called "blessed" by all generations through the regular repetition of her song and in her usual title in liturgical speech, the Blessed Virgin Mary. Her blessedness is no inherent holiness in her. It comes not from herself but from being the chosen instrument in the salvation of the world, the gate of heaven through which the Holy One of Israel chose to come to human life. It is not she but God's grace toward her that is praised.[79] Those who would do the holy virgin proper honor, wrote Luther, "must not regard her alone and by herself but set in the presence of God."[80] Apart from her Son, she is like the rest of us. In the Orthodox Church the virgin is never portrayed alone, by herself; she is always shown with her Son in whom her holiness consisted. As Luther observed, "She does not want you to come to her, but through her to God."[81]

Might, holiness, and mercy are the threefold attributes of the God who saves and in whom blessed Mary rejoices. She sings,

> The Almighty has done great things for me,
> and holy is his name.

The canticle praises and participates in God's revolutionary activity, turning the world and its expectations upside down. The arrogant mighty who feel no need of God are expelled from their seats of power on royal thrones and in corporate boardrooms; the humble and meek, the lowly and the downtrodden are exalted. Those at the top of worldly hierarchies are sent to the bottom, and those at the bottom are lifted to their places at the top. But it is not a matter of mere replacement or substitution, for the tyranny of those who have been deprived of power is often worse than the arrogance and oppression they replace. "New *presbyter* is but old *priest* writ large," John Milton lamented in an acute observation with perennial application.[82] The Virgin Mary recognizes and announces that a new social order of justice is at hand (see Luke 6:20–21). All our expectations are shaken; all logic is upset. The creator of the worlds is born into creation in a corner of the mighty empire of Rome; a virgin becomes a mother; a mortal becomes the bearer of God.

"He has mercy on those who fear him in every generation." The Magnificat is a song of the new creation appropriately sung as one day ends and the next begins. The old is passing with the dying day; the new is soon to dawn in its full radiance. The promise of mercy made long ago to the ancestors has been remembered; God has come to vindicate his people Israel; and God is preparing a greatly expanded family of Abraham's relatives. The family history begun long ago not only continues through all generations but increases, growing ever wider in its flow as the Gentiles are adopted into the family to share in the inheritance of Israel. The originating figure of the original covenant is Abraham the patriarch. The figure through whom the new creation begins is a woman, Mary, who stands as the New Testament analogue to father Abraham of the First Testament. Patriarchal traditions are being overturned to make a new, more inclusive family community. It is through Mary and her Son that the new people begins, a people who recognize no hierarchy, no ranking, no exercise of power one over another. It is a return at least in promise to the conditions of paradise before the fall, when the man and the woman were equal partners, before patriarchy (or matriarchy) existed. It is the beginning of a realm in which all human separations will be overcome, in which it will be said, "There is longer Jew or Greek, there is no longer slave or free, there is no longer male and female; for all of you are one in Christ Jesus" (Galatians 3:28).

The song of Mary has traditionally been accompanied by the offering of incense, honoring the altar with its fragrant cloud. This not only recalls and continues the incense offering in the evening and in the morning in the temple in Jerusalem that accompanied the daily sacrifices of a lamb. It also with its focus on a Christian altar shows the sacrifice of Christ the Lamb of God that the altar and its crucifix proclaim.

Each hour of Daily Prayer concludes with intercessions. The form varies from denomination to denomination, but the elements are comparable. In the Roman Catholic *Liturgy of the Hours* the prayer at morning and Evening Prayer consists of a brief litany, a different composition for each day, followed by the Our Father and the collect of the day. In *Lutheran Book of Worship*, Evening Prayer concludes with a version of the deacon's litany from the Liturgy of St. John Chrysostom (or another litany or a series of collects), the collect for peace, and the Our Father. In the *Book of Common Prayer* the office concludes with the Our Father, a set of suffrages, and a series of collects. It is the intention of each rite to make the prayers both particular and comprehensive. They are offered for specific people and specific situations, but they are also offered for "all sorts and conditions" of humanity, a great variety of particular occasions.

The intent of the prayer is summarized in the response in the litany, "Lord, have mercy." It is a universal petition, always appropriate in whatever situation. It echoes the thought of Magnificat and applies it to individual concerns. It pleads for God's gifts of grace, God's merciful favor, God's sustaining mercy to us and to all creation. To pray for God's mercy is to pray for God's kingdom. In the Eastern church there developed an intense devotion to the name and person and work of Jesus. It is concentrated in the Jesus prayer, "Lord Jesus Christ, Son of God, have mercy on me." The name Jesus contains all the gospel, the whole history of salvation, every need of the human heart. Its use in the Jesus prayer is a means of communion with God and with all who pray. That small but comprehensive prayer is like Mary the *Theotokos,* who contained, in the words of an English carol, "heven and earth in litle space."

A classic prayer in the Anglican and Lutheran forms of Evening Prayer is the collect for peace.

> Lord God, Heavenly Father, Thou Who createst holy desire, good counsel and right works: Give to Thy servants peace which the world cannot give, so that our hearts may cling to Thy commandments, and through Thy protection we may live our days quietly and secure from our enemies; through Jesus Christ Thy Son our Lord.[83]

The prayer dates from the Gelasian sacramentary in which it is the proper collect of the mass for peace. Luther Reed comments:

> This collect is rich in historic associations. We cannot but think of the troublous times in the latter half of the fifth century when it was composed — "when sieges and barbaric invasions made men's hearts fail for fear, when Rome but narrowly escaped the Huns and did not escape the Vandals; when the Western Empire itself passed away before Odoacer, and Odoacer was overthrown by Theodoric" (Canon Bright). Then, if ever, it seemed as if the church and Christianity itself might perish in the general ruin.
>
> Unhappily humanity has scarcely known a decade when, in some lands if not in many, wars and rumors of wars have not made this prayer appropriate.[84]

In its lovely cadences the prayer asks for that tranquillity of mind and heart, that inward calm that springs from the knowledge of God's mercy. It is an inner peace that is an island of calm amid the storm and waves of slander and injustice and scorn. It comes only from holy desires and good counsels that combine to issue in just works. Conversely, if all the world is quiet and none disturbs the wicked, they make themselves restless because there is an enemy within that upbraids them more loudly and wounds them more deeply than they can do to those who know the peace of God and the God of peace.[85] There are no holy thoughts in our minds, nor good purposes in our hearts, nor any righteous actions in our lives except through God's mercy. All of it is God's doing, for God alone can excite our feelings to desire what is good, engage our will to choose it, and strengthen our hands to do it.

God plants in us the seed of virtue and makes these holy desires to grow into prudent and holy purposeful resolves, and through divine providence and strength ripens them into just and righteous deeds, the fruit of which is peace. The prayer not only asks for God's gifts and aid but commits those who pray it to living that does not willfully deprive them of that peace nor hinder its growth and progress by stifling holy thoughts and breaking devout resolutions and neglecting good deeds.

Then, on the basis of this preamble and antecedent reason, one may ask for that distinctive gift of the risen Christ, a peace bestowed "not as the world gives" (John 14:27) or is able to give.

> For such peace is an inward calm, a "rest and quietness," the fruit of obedience to God's will and of trust in His pro-

tection. We do not ask to be removed from the assault and tribulations of the world, but from the fear of them, a gift that comes only to those who are resolved to do the will of God in devotion to His commandments.[86]

In the Lutheran and Presbyterian forms of the office (and in the *Liturgy of the Hours,* except for a concluding prayer), the Lord's Prayer, the words that Jesus himself taught his disciples and commanded them to pray, is the culmination and conclusion of the prayers. By the time of the *Didache* it had become the central and characteristic prayer of Christians, central to the formation of faith in every generation. We pray most of all because Jesus prayed and told us to do it too. It is Jesus Christ who prays, and we join in his intercession.[87]

The prayer is introduced in the Lutheran rite with the aspiration, "Lord, remember us in your kingdom, and teach us to pray." We are one with the penitent thief, and we ask to be taught how to pray in general and how to pray this prayer in particular with insight and understanding.

The opening words of the prayer, "Our Father," imply the communion of all humanity praying with Jesus Christ and also our communion with those who do not pray.[88] The very first word urges us to look at those people from whom we habitually feel separated and to understand that they and we have a common Father. Those above us, those beneath us, those of a different persuasion, those we denounce as utterly evil, those whom we have every reason to despise, those who have made themselves vile and are making the world like them — we must

> teach ourselves to think that in the very highest exercise of our lives they are associated with us. That when we pray, we are praying for them and with them; that we cannot speak for ourselves without speaking for them; that if we do not carry their sins to the throne of God's grace, we do not carry our own; that all the good we hope to obtain there belongs to them just as much as to us, and that our claim to it is sure of being rejected if it is not one which is valid for them also.[89]

Any prayer properly opens with adoration, the essential act of prayer, and the simple words "Our Father in heaven" express adoration mingled with thanksgiving that God is God.

Petition is not the first item in the Lord's Prayer, but it is right and proper nonetheless. The first three petitions of the Lord's

Prayer deal with the glory of God. We are commanded to take an interest in God's cause: God's name and kingdom and will.[90] As citizens of the city of God we must accept its constitution, its law, its order.[91] Prayer teaches us the virtue of abandonment as we pray "your will be done." The last four petitions concern us directly: give us, forgive us, save us, deliver us.

Each prayer concludes with "Amen." The prayer concludes as it began, with confidence. We conclude with the certainty that God has heard and declare our belief with the "Amen." What God will do with our requests for ourselves and for others is out of our hands. We may not get what we pray for. The refused prayer of Christ in Gethsemane the night before he died — "Take this cup from me" — is a clear example. C. S. Lewis quotes "an experienced Christian":

> I have seen many striking answers to prayer and more than one that I thought miraculous. But they usually come at the beginning: before conversion, or soon after it. As the Christian life proceeds, they tend to be rarer. The refusals, too, are not only more frequent; they become more unmistakable, more emphatic.[92]

Prayer, we come to learn, is simply giving God what we have.

Compline

Evensong accompanies and marks the setting of the sun and the gathering darkness out of which a new day will be born. During that darkness some members of the church sing Compline, night prayer. The simplicity and invariable text of this office have commended it to many who seek a richer prayer life, and it is included in the *Book of Common Prayer, Lutheran Book of Worship,* and the Presbyterian *Book of Common Worship.*

This going-to-bed prayer of the church (it is the way the church says goodnight) draws the obvious parallel between sleep and death, the darkness of repose and the nothingness of extinction. Three features of this simple hour are noteworthy: the confession, the brief lesson, and the antiphon to the Nunc Dimittis.

In the confession the leader confesses to God before the whole company of heaven (angels and saints) and to the assembly; then the assembly using the same words confesses to the leader. (It seems an easy thing to confess to God privately with no one to overhear or know. It is much more difficult and embarrassing to confess in the presence of others in increasingly visible proximity: God, the whole company of heaven, the brothers and sisters present in the congregation.) Each announces to the other God's pardon, which will bring them to everlasting life. The metaphors of guidance and direction in the pilgrimage journey underlie the confession.

The brief lesson or "chapter," which is really but a verse or two in length, is a use of the Bible that differs from the more extended readings in Evening and Morning Prayer and the scriptural proclamation in the Eucharist. Here, just before sleep, a long passage would be out of place. Instead, a verse is read as a maxim to ponder as sleep comes on, a watchword to give light in the darkness like the stars that preserve the sky from complete emptiness.

The gospel canticle for Compline is the third song from Luke's infancy narrative, the Nunc Dimittis, the song of Simeon, who, after long and expectant waiting, at last held in his arms "the treasure of all nations." An antiphon to the Magnificat at first vespers (Evening Prayer I) of the Feast of the Presentation of Our Lord in the temple (February 2) ponders the wonder of the scene: "the old man carried the child, but the child guided (*regebat*) the old man." It is, like Magnificat and Benedictus, a song of thanksgiving and fulfillment. Simeon waited in the darkness for the light of the nations, and when at last he held that light in his arms, he was prepared to depart from the temple and from this life. He had seen the future and had cradled the promised one in his arms. His song is appropriate for the church, whether an individual or an assembly, ready to depart, if need be, from the world. The Liturgy of St. John Chrysostom exclaims after the communion, "We have seen the true Light; we have received the heavenly Spirit; we have found the true faith. Let us bow down in worship to the Trinity Undivided, for he has saved us."[93] As the church enters the deepest darkness of waiting for the dawn, it is encouraged and given hope by the experience of aged (so we imagine him) Simeon. Even though the darkness seems complete, "the true light is already shining" (1 John 2:8).

That wonderfully evocative canticle is surrounded before and after with the antiphon-prayer, "Guide us waking, O Lord, and guard us sleeping; that awake we may watch with Christ and asleep we may rest in peace." Even sleep, we learn, is part of the life of obedient trust, an act of confident faith. Luther in the *Small Catechism,* after suggesting making the sign of the cross and saying the Apostles' Creed, Lord's Prayer, and an evening prayer of his own composition, directs, "Then quickly lie down and sleep in peace." Our peaceful sleep is an extension of our prayer, a declaration of our confidence in God's watchful protection. Such trusting sleep is our share in the Great Silence of the monasteries. St. Benedict declared in his *Rule* (42):

> And after compline no one shall be allowed to speak. If any be discovered to break this rule of silence, he shall be gravely punished: unless it be on account of guests and their needs; and even then it must be done with composure and moderation and gentleness.

Sleep following such prayers of commendation is a daily enactment of Jesus' rest in the tomb on Holy Saturday, resting in hope (Psalm 16:9–10) until the darkness ends in light and mortal life ends in the life immortal.

Morning Praise

As the sun rises, fulfilling the promise held in hope through the night, the church (or at least scattered individuals and communities of the church) joins again on behalf of all the endless song of creation and offers its morning praise.

The silence of sleep is ended with the psalmist's verse, "O Lord, open my lips," and its response, "And my mouth shall declare your praise." Again, as throughout the liturgy, the dependence upon God's initiative is clear. Without God, there can be no praise. The old monastic name for Daily Prayer that at first hearing sounds so impossibly self-righteous is exactly right: Daily Prayer is "the work of God" (*opus dei*). Human beings are instruments of praise that in the first and last analysis is not their own. This work of worship is not their own doing or achievement, and even the response to what God has done is inspired and filled and guided by the Holy Spirit. The opening versicle of Morning Prayer is also a recognition that our mouths are shut by our sin and only by the assurance of God's pardon are we able to speak again God's glory.

The lips having been opened by the Lord and the voice enlivened by God's Spirit, God's praise is declared in the little burst of praise to the triune God, the "lesser gloria," the Gloria Patri. Glory is ascribed to the Holy Trinity (in the original form of the song, "to the Father, through the Son, in the Holy Spirit") for everything God has done — affliction as well as enjoyment — in the past and in

the present and in the future, from the beginning of time forever.[94]
So the church pays tribute to each person of the blessed Trinity as
well as to the undivided Unity.

Such joyful song was begun by the angels in the morning of creation (Job 38:7), the beginning of time, and they and all creatures
continue it now in the present, and it will be prolonged throughout
all eternity. "As long as Goodness endures, Gratitude and Praise
cannot cease."[95]

The comprehensiveness of these few compact words embraces
all things as well as all times and all places and presents "at once
to our view all the Mercies of God, past, present, and to come."[96]
The song is an acknowledgement that all the good that ever was or
shall be done, with all that is now enjoyed in heaven and on earth,
proceeds from the everflowing Fountain "to whom this tribute of
Praise is, and was, and ever will be due."[97] Thus this little song is
both a declaration of the faith of the church and a rendering of our
homage. It is "orthodox" in the rich dual meaning of the Greek
for that word: right praise combined with right belief, making one
praise-filled confession of faith and faith-filled song of praise.

The ancient invitatory psalm is 95, the Venite, corresponding to
the fixed psalm of evening, 141. "Come let us sing to the Lord" is
more than one church member inviting another to join in Morning Praise. The invitation is not just the psalmist of old calling out
across the centuries for us to take up the old yet ever-new song.
The invitatory is heard as a divine invitation to add our voices to
the unending praise for which we and all creatures were created.

This invitatory psalm sounds the principal themes of the morning office: the entrance into God's presence with joy, thanksgiving,
and even noise ("shout"); the surpassing greatness of God, sovereign above all gods, who holds "the caverns of the earth" as well
as "the heights of the hills," who made the sea and molded the dry
land. The invitation goes out to participate in a progressive act of
adoration: from bowing to genuflecting to kneeling before the one
who made not only the natural world but human beings as well,
the one to whom we all belong. The interesting chiasmus (rhetor-
ical figures placed cross-wise) "people of his pasture" and "sheep
of his hand"(one would expect "people of his hand" and "sheep
of his pasture") reinforces the unity and equality of all creatures in
the eyes as well as the hand of God.

Anciently the morning office consisted principally of the *Laudate* psalms, psalms 148–150, with their repeated invitation and
ascription, "Praise the Lord." The practice is preserved in the *Lit-*

urgy of the Hours and in the Lutheran office. These psalms are in keeping with the principal theme of the office called Lauds, that is, Morning Praise, that rings out "when the rising sun has dispelled the last shadow of night."[98] It is a time of resurrection signified by awakening from sleep, of life and hope and vigor and duty; and the principal duty of God's people is God's praise.

Just as an extrabiblical hymn, *phos hilaron,* came to be associated with Vespers, so an extrabiblical hymn was associated with Lauds. It was the Gloria in Excelsis, called "the morning hymn" in the *Apostolic Constitutions,* deriving perhaps from the East and perhaps even written for Lauds. In the West the canticle has since been shifted to the entrance rite of the Eucharist.

The gospel canticle associated with Lauds is the Benedictus with its reference to "the dawn from on high" that will break upon us "to shine on those who dwell in darkness and the shadow of death, and to guide our feet into the way of peace." Like the Magnificat it too is a song celebrating the incarnation and the indescribable mercy of God who has "come to his people and set them free." It is a song soaked in Jewish pride and election. The God who is blessed is "the God of Israel" who has freed "his people" and raised up "for us," Zechariah sings with pride, a savior "born of the house of his servant David." He promised through the prophets that "he would save us from our enemies, from the hands of all who hate us," Zechariah continues. Zechariah moves backward through the layers of Israel's history, of which the present is the dawning fulfillment: the prophets who declared God's promise of rescue, the ancestors who received God's promises, the holy covenant concluded at Sinai, the solemn oath sworn to Abraham. "Each clause in this four-fold proclamation carries us one step farther back into antiquity"[99] to remind us that behind the continuity of Israel's history, now reaching its climax in the arrival of the Messiah, there lies the divine plan, to which God is everlastingly faithful. The morning canticle is a resounding affirmation of the messianic role of Jesus, bright with the promise of the opening day with its revealing and clarifying and cleansing light. In Jesus God has come to his people, fulfilling the promises of old.

Then, even more particularly, the song turns to focus on Zechariah's son, John the Baptist. "You, my child, shall be called the prophet of the Most High." The setting of this highly particular and exclusivist song, however, is the Gospel according to St. Luke, one of whose concerns is to show the universality of the gospel. So the canticle of Zechariah, for all of its pride in the promise and experience of Israel, is sung by the church as its own hymn, and the plural pronouns are understood to include Christians as well as Jews, for the church claims, we are together "his people." The great song not only will not let Christians forget their Jewish roots (spiritually we are all Semites, said Pope Pius XII). It reminds Christians that it is only by the grace of God that they dare breathe their claim on Israel's history and that they must receive that inclusion only with awe and gratitude that they have been grafted on to the Jewish family tree and given a share in being the people of God, children of Abraham. It is an insight appropriate to the morning and the dawn of a new day, bright with the promise of new and unexpected and undeserved mercies, a glimpse of the inclusiveness and peace of the kingdom of heaven. The verse in the Benedictus, "The dawn from on high will break upon us," is given in some ancient authorities "has broken upon us." This canticle, like the Magnificat, is on the boundary, rejoicing in the "now" and also in the "not yet." The daylight that dawns daily on the world is not yet the Day of the Lord. There have been decisive acts of liberation from slavery and sin, but the liberation is not yet completed.

The gospel canticles at Evening Prayer and at Morning Prayer, both revolutionary songs of victory and salvation, correct the assumption frequently made that religion is only personal and spiritual. These two songs, one of a mother and one of a father, are collective and concrete, rooted in Jewish society in ancient Palestine.[100] They are permeated with biblical, especially psalmic, language and spirit and follow the tradition of the Song of Miriam and Moses (Exodus 15), of Deborah (Judges 5), and of Judith (Judith 6). These are songs sung on the threshold of the new.

The Benedictus speaks first of the community, Israel, and then of the individual, John the Baptist. By extension, Christians find themselves included in the community, and each individual believer can be understood to be addressed when Zechariah speaks to "my child," the prophet of the Most High. The prayer of the day for the Third Sunday in Advent in *Lutheran Book of Worship* makes a similar broad application of the role and work of John the Baptist:

Almighty God, you once called John the Baptist to give witness to the coming of your Son and to prepare his way. Grant us, your people, the wisdom to see your purpose today and the openness to hear your will, that we may witness to Christ's coming and so prepare his way.

A notable passage is the concluding line of the canticle, "guide our feet into the way of peace." It recalls an insightful saying attributed to A. J. Muste,[101] the peace activist, "There is no way to peace; peace is the way."

Following the Benedictus, a classic morning prayer, the collect for grace, is said,

> Lord God, almighty and everlasting Father, you have brought us in safety to this new day: Preserve us with your mighty power, that we may not fall into sin, nor be overcome by adversity; and in all we do, direct us to the fulfilling of your purpose; through Jesus Christ our Lord.[102]

The prayer complements the text of the Benedictus impressively. "The dawn from on high shall break upon us," Zechariah sings confidently; as Christians daily greet the dawn the church prays to God who has "brought us in safety to this new day," the unfolding day on the calendar and the new day of Christ and the new covenant.

The prayer asks a twofold petition: to be preserved from the occasions leading to sin and to be brought safely through adversity.[103] The petition echoes the Lord's Prayer: "save us from the time of trial, and deliver us from evil." The prayer also recognizes that avoiding sin is not enough; we must do things as well to accomplish God's will. "In all we do, direct us to the fulfilling of your purpose." This petition also echoes the Lord's Prayer, "your will be done," and Luther's explanation, "To be sure, the good and gracious will of God is done without our prayer, but we pray in this petition that it may also be done by us."[104] That is the "way of peace" of which Zechariah sang. The focus is entirely on God, who has brought us to this new day, whose mighty power alone can preserve us from falling into sin and being overcome in adversity, the fulfilling of whose purpose is to be the purpose not just of some but of all we do.

The Lutheran office appends to Morning Prayer a paschal blessing, a little office of the resurrection, sung at the font to conclude Morning Prayer on Sundays. Its principal focus is the great canticle that has found a place in the *Liturgy of the Hours,* in the *Book of Common Prayer,* and in Lutheran books — Te Deum. It is a magnificent and powerful reminder of the magnitude of what we do when we presume to worship God, the Lord, the eternal Father. Our praise and acclamation join the worship of all creation: all the mystical ranks of myriad angels sing in endless praise to the thrice-holy God of power and might, whose glory cannot be confined to one dwelling place but floods out and fills heaven and earth. The praise of the thrice-holy is taken up also by the triple praise of the bright company of apostles, the noble fellowship of prophets, the white-clad host of martyrs. On earth their praise is joined by that of all the church militant praising the Father of boundless majesty, the Son worthy of all worship, and the Holy Spirit, our defender and guide. The cause of this universal acclamation is what has been done for us in Christ, the King of glory, the eternal Son, who became confined in flesh to set us free, who bought us with the price of his life-blood, overcame the deadly stinger of the evil one, opened the kingdom of heaven to all believers, and reigns at God's right hand in glory, who will come to be our judge. On the ground of that sacred history of self-sacrificing love, the church presumes to pray that "the eternal Son of the Father" would not remain aloof from us but continue the work of helping each of us, bought with the price of his life, and bring us with all who believe and all the apostles, prophets, and martyrs whom we have joined in praise, to everlasting glory. The largest and most exalted choir combines to praise the largest and most exalted view of God, the thrice-holy Trinity. Such is the purpose of Daily Prayer.

Chapter Four

THE EASTER VIGIL
Hallowing Memory

✠

In his "Autumn Journal," Louis MacNeice, referring to the ancient
Greeks, wrote:

> And how one can imagine oneself among them
> I do not know;
> It was all so unimaginably different
> And all so long ago.[1]

So the past often seems to us: distant, different, and beyond recovery. Christianity in its most characteristic and central liturgical
service, the Easter Vigil, rehearses significant events from Israel's
distant history and connects them with events in the life of Christ
as interpreted through the eyes of the young Christian movement.
The roots of this service lie deep in the very different world of the
Bible, when miracles seemed not at all extraordinary. It was a very
different world then.

The Great Vigil of Easter attempts to build bridges to that far-
off time and world. With the roar of traffic outside, the church
turns off its electric lights and in the darkness kindles a fire. Suddenly, as the flames leap up, the remote ages leap to life and we
can at least half-believe that we are contemporary with our distant
ancestors in the faith and, more surprisingly, that they are contemporary with us. We are not just playacting, pretending to be ancient
people without modern utilities. In the Easter Vigil we remember
the past in such a way that we find ourselves among those events.
The past, we learn in the firelight, is not dead after all; those ancestors move to our own time, emerge from the darkness of centuries
and millennia as the flickering light illumines their faces, and the
past lives again. Rather, the past never died. It had simply been

71

obscured by changing civilizations and by the increasing rush of events, by wars and industry and conveniences. The "past" has been there around us, beside us, even in front of us all along, all the time. We just did not see it.

History, we must learn, does not lie behind us, growing ever more distant as if we were looking out from the back of the last car of a speeding train watching the tracks swiftly recede into invisibility. History is what advances, not what lies behind. It is a reminder that what we may think was left behind was not laid to rest and that it still awaits our reckoning with it. The religions that derive from the Bible lay great emphasis on memory, keeping the past in mind and so keeping it alive, recognizing its continuing power and influence.

The mind of peoples shaped by biblical religion is a vast storehouse of memory reaching even into the mists of the beginning of the race, back beyond record, back even beyond our understanding, into a time separated from us by millennia of diverse and divergent human life and experience. Aspects of the past, apparently long obsolete, are kept in the memory because in them Jews and Christians still find lingering clues of transcendence, the precise meaning of which may no longer be entirely understood but that nevertheless preserve important insights that may yet open again with new and unexpected meaning.

The Moon

Daily Prayer makes symbolic use of the regular, dependable cycle of night and day, the most obvious rhythm of the earth and its creatures. Passover and Easter, however, derive from another basic rhythm of the earth and its satellite, only somewhat less apparent: the cycles of the moon.

Human beings, we may imagine on the basis of the experience of each individual life, reckoned early with the daily loss and recovery of light and came to know that after the night would come the dawn. This regular and dependable cycle can be seen as a daily proclamation of resurrection, and it has been so understood in Daily Prayer and by poets such as John Milton, who consoled himself in *Lycidas,* the great elegy lamenting Edward King, "a learned friend, unfortunately drowned in his passage from Chester on the Irish Seas, 1637,"

> Weep no more, woeful shepherds, weep no more,
> For Lycidas, your sorrow, is not dead,
> Sunk though he be beneath the watery floor;
> So sinks the day-star in the ocean bed,
> And yet anon repairs his drooping head,
> And tricks his beams, and with new-spangled ore
> Flames in the forehead of the morning sky:
> So Lycidas sunk low, but mounted high,
> Through the dear might of him that walked the waves.
>
> (lines 165–173)

The image of sunset and sunrise was effective for Milton in this instance because Edward King, like the sun, went under the sea to the west of England and like the sun will, it is asserted, again mount high into the sky. Henry Francis Lyte's familiar evening hymn, "Abide With Me, Fast Falls the Eventide," (1847) makes effective use of the parallel between the end of the day (sunset) and the end of individual lives ("Swift to its close ebbs out life's little day"), and in its final stanza looks forward to the breaking of a new day in the new world of heaven. But the daily cycle was not the only symbol of resurrection.

A more ancient measure of time was by lunations, as ancients watched the moon wax and wane and disappear for three days and wax again. The moon extends over a longer period the message that the daylight returns daily, and it does so in ways that awoke the wonder of the ancients. The pale light of the moon encourages awe and reverence more than does the intense light of the sun. The face of the moon combines both light and shadow. The moon regularly and noticeably progresses through its cycle of appearance, increase, wane, disappearance, and reappearance. Moreover, the reappearance is not immediate but occurs only after three days of darkness. Thus the moon seemed closer to human experience of growth and decline and death than did the daily movement of the sun, for the sun does not change so noticeably in appearance from day to day. Each new day appeared as a fresh opportunity as, for example, it was sometimes thought in ancient China that each day brought forth a new sun. The moon was more clearly the same moon throughout the month, and its disappearance and return served as the pattern that promised that the disappearance of individual people and communities was never total and final. The perceived pattern was more than wishful thinking, for the duration of the cycle of the moon, twenty-nine days, closely approximates the menstrual cycle in women. Women bear in their bodies the wonderful power to conceive life and to give birth and to nourish children. The moon influences not only human life but the seas and the soil as well. Its gravitational pull causes tides in the oceans of the earth. The moon governs agriculture, especially planting, in many societies, even in America at the beginning of the twenty-first century.

It is therefore not surprising to find that anciently, almost universally, every important ceremony took place at certain phases of the moon.[2] So significant were the lunations that even solstices and equinoxes were not exactly determined by the movement of the sun but were approximated to the nearest new or full moon. Lunar rhythms mark monthly intervals, but they also serve as the archetype of more extended periods.

Passover, and therefore Easter, are related to the moon, specifically to the first full moon after the spring equinox, the nomadic new year. The precise relationship between the moon and Passover is probably beyond recovery. The explanation that Passover was held at the full moon so that pilgrims journeying to Jerusalem could travel by moonlight is clearly a later pragmatic rationalization. We can understand why the moon was a widespread object of wonder and even of worship throughout most of the ancient world, but we do not know precisely why the moon and Passover maintained their intimate identification. Festivals of new moons persisted throughout the Bible.[3] For centuries they were part of a triad of celebrations: yearly festivals, monthly new moons, and weekly sabbaths. As the centuries passed, increasing emphasis was placed on the sabbath rather than the celebration of the new moon with which it was usually joined, but nonetheless the identification of the Passover with the first spring full moon remained unchanged and unchallenged. In Christianity, which inherited and consistently maintained the lunar connection, the calculation of the date of Easter involved other astrological observations, including the nineteen years of a complete sidereal cycle, the time it takes for the stars to return to their places in the turning of the heavens.

The celebration of Passover and its near relative Easter preserves a deeply symbolic relationship with a natural cycle that, like night and day, goes beyond the confines of one religious tradition to embrace the experience of all humanity through the ages from the most distant and unrecoverable past. Even though it is lost to our complete understanding, Jews and Christians have assiduously maintained the relationship with the spring full moon, answering

voices that call faintly across the millennia to the depth of our being, voices beyond our hearing but surely not beyond influencing
us. Such is Jewish and Christian profound regard for the past. Such
is the healthful power of tradition, which is another name for history that advances with us into the future and still requires, even
demands, our attention.

The moon is, in Mircea Eliade's words, "the first of the creatures
to die, but also the first to live again."[4] The lesson of the moon is
the proclamation of the central event and message of Christianity:
the death and resurrection of Christ. It is the *Pascha,* the Passover,
renewed and extended to all the human race.

The Spring

Passover-Easter is not tied to every moon throughout the year, but
only to one: the first full moon of the spring. It is the time of
the annual celebration of rebirth and renewal as life in its abundance emerges from the temporary death of winter. There is the
general human awareness of rebirth in the spring and, in the temperate zone of the Northern Hemisphere, life emerges from its
hiding places: leaves return, flowers bloom again, birds migrate
north. One of the pleasures of Middle English literature is its interest in the beauty and delight of the spring celebrated in lyrics
and in longer works such as the Prologue to Chaucer's *Canterbury
Tales* and in *Sir Gawain and the Green Knight.* For more than
thirty-five years Hal Borland (1900–1978) wrote a nature editorial each Sunday for the *New York Times* and a quarterly article
for *The Progressive.* They were wonderfully wrought statements
about what was happening in the natural world, while the rest
of the news dealt with the usual diet of political struggles, economic crises, warfare, and scandal. The editorial for Easter Day,
April 2, 1972, spoke of the human need when winter passes and
spring comes "to participate in the triumph of life so obvious all
around."[5] In 1975 he wrote that

> spring is life arisen from the dead of winter, and truth Tri-
> umphant over the dark forces of denial. It is the green of the
> most persistent life we know, the green of the leaf, of the ba-
> sic, life-giving leaf. It is the instinctive reaching for the sun,
> the innate belief in the power beyond.[6]

"I know that if a crocus can happen again, anything can happen."[7]

In the Northern Hemisphere, where Judaism and Christianity began, the annual rebirth and renewal and renovation of the world provides the setting for the celebration of the deliverance accomplished by God at the Red Sea and on the cross. The themes of Passover are manifold. Theodor Gaster has suggested that of the complex of ideas that today make up the Passover festival, the central theme is release: on the seasonal plane, the release of the earth from the grip of winter; on the historical plane, the release of Israel from slavery in Egypt; on "the broad human plane," the release from bondage and idolatry.[8] This release is not to be understood as simply escape, for it is a positive achievement as well: reaping the new grain, the birth of Israel as a nation, the attainment of freedom and the vision of God. The three planes of the festival, moreover, are parallel to each other. "The dark and dreary winter" corresponds to the era of slavery and to the night of ignorance, and the "burst of new life in the spring corresponds in turn to the flowering of Israel and the burgeoning of freedom."[9] In its basic form, then, Passover is one of the innumerable seasonal festivals known to the history of religion as a celebration of the beginning of the agricultural cycle. Anciently, such festivals involved a shared meal of pure and uncontaminated food that would impart new life and vigor, and the sprinkling of the blood of a sacrificial animal as a mark upon those who participated in the ritual and as a sign of God's favor.

Judaism and Christianity, however, are not simply nature religions, as if their message is merely the rebirth of nature, as if their teaching could be reduced to flowers. The focus of Judaism is emphatically on the rebirth of a people from slavery, and the focus of Christianity is emphatically on Christ's resurrection. Yet it should not be overlooked that the *setting* of the celebration of the exodus and the cross is incorporated into the Jewish and the Christian proclamation. Nature, as it were, joins in the praise of the life given and restored by God. Nature is heard proclaiming the resurrection. Fortunatus's great Easter hymn *Salve, festa dies* welcomes the happy morning of the resurrection:

> Earth her joy confesses, clothing her for spring,
> All fresh gifts return with her returning King:
> Bloom in every meadow, leaves on every bough,
> Speak his sorrow ended, hail his triumph now.
> "Hell today is vanquished, heaven is won today!"

> Months in due succession, days of lengthening light,
> Hours and passing moments praise thee in their flight.
> Brightness of the morning, sky and fields and sea,
> Vanquisher of darkness, bring their praise to thee.
> "Welcome, happy morning!" age to age shall say.[10]

It is clearly not that the story of Christ's resurrection is one of the illustrations of the new life that spring brings to the earth. Rather, the reverse is true: the new life of springtime is a celebration of Christ's resurrection. The spring, nature's resurrection, is both a symbol of Christ's resurrection and nature's way of greeting the risen Lord. It is as if nature cannot help but join in the praise and the greeting of that morning that transformed the world and all that is in it. The natural renovation is itself transformed from the cycle of yearly renewal to a sign that because of the victory of Christ, "trampling down death by death, and on those in the tomb bestowing life,"[11] nothing can be the same again. Nature's rebirth becomes another voice of praise made particular and specific in its new context. It is now applied to the work of the Son of God. In Christianity (and in Judaism, one might add), G. Van der Leeuw has pointed out, "nature is not our mother but our sister."[12] And nature as our sister must be redeemed along with us.

Sacred Time and Space

In the celebration of the new year in ancient societies, certain characteristic features appear with great frequency. New fires are lighted,[13] evil is expelled,[14] the royal rule is renewed and the ruler triumphs over death,[15] the dead return,[16] water is sprinkled on people and objects,[17] sexual license is allowed,[18] there is feasting, seeds are sown.[19] The world was thought yearly to regress into chaos, and "everything that time had soiled and worn, was annihilated,"[20] the world and everything in it was created anew and reborn to begin a new life. "The sacred calendar periodically regenerates time."[21] Renewal is the key to the celebration of the new year.[22] And the ancient celebration of the new year has shaped the Easter Vigil.

The daily cycle, "while earth rolls onward into light,"[23] is, as the previous chapter has suggested, a repetition and a renewal of creation. This daily cycle, moving from darkness to light more perceptibly than does the slowly turning year, is intensified and particularized in the Easter Vigil. The ancient vigil, a watching prayer, was a preparation preceding great feasts and consisted of readings and silence and prayer. But most ancient of all, most dramatic, most intense is what Augustine called "the mother of all vigils," the passage of the night from Holy Saturday to Easter Day. It takes its participants from death to life, from defeat to hope.

The central experience and teaching of Christianity is the complex of events surrounding the death and resurrection of Jesus Christ, so intimately connected with each other that they form one event, one proclamation. The completed sacrifice of Christ on Calvary, together with its validation in the resurrection, breaking out of the world of space and time into a new dimension and a new time, the eighth day, is finished and unrepeatable. In the wonderful redundancies of the old *Book of Common Prayer,* Jesus Christ "made there (by his one oblation of himself once offered) a full, perfect, and sufficient sacrifice, oblation, and satisfaction, for the sins of the whole world."[24] Nonetheless that completed and unrepeatable sacrifice is contemplated anew daily in the symbolism of Daily Prayer, weekly in the celebration of the Lord's Supper on the Lord's Day, yearly at Easter, and once personally in each individual's death.

In secular life we are accustomed to experiencing time as a straight line along which we move. (Einstein's purported question to the ticket collector, "When does Madrid reach this train?"[25] provocatively changes the perspective, but the image is the same.) We move through time or time moves past us, and what has passed seems gone beyond recovery. "But O for the touch of a vanish'd hand, / And the sound of a voice that is still," Tennyson yearned.[26] It is the appalling shock of the death of a loved one that we struggle to acknowledge and accept. "Will I never again feel his touch?" I cried to myself when my father died. Are those gentle eyes permanently closed, and is the familiar voice forever stilled? Will I never again be able to share with pride my accomplishments with him or tell him my disappointments? The experience of yesterday, we believe, whether joyful or painful, is past, and we cannot recall it or re-live it. And as "time passes," we are increasingly distanced from that experience.

Students of liturgy have a deep and abiding interest in the past not because they are antiquarians (although, to be sure, some are indeed students of that useful field of study) but because they know that the past is not dead. It is not even past. "... Yesterday, today, and tomorrow are IS: Indivisible: One.... It's all *now* you see.

Yesterday won't be over until tomorrow and tomorrow began ten thousand years ago."[27] Ritual gives us a means by which we can overcome the distance that time wedges between *now* and *then*. It provides a means by which we can enjoy sustained, renewing recourse to the past. We have already seen how Daily Prayer consecrates and clarifies and interprets the meaning of the daily cycle of sunset and sunrise. Each morning the sun rises, defeating the darkness and ordering the chaos as it did on new year's day and as it did at the original creation.[28] The three moments of today and new year and creation are experienced together. Each day and each new year's day repeat the first sunrise of creation, and each repetition coalesces with and is practically identical with the original event. For the duration of the ritual, there is no separation. The events of the past are experienced as present realities. The past comes alive, moves into the present, and is experienced anew as a present contemporary event. We become eyewitnesses to what we ordinarily recognize as long past and far behind us, and those distant events become contemporary with us, filled with meaning for our time and our lives.

In a religious celebration, participants emerge from ordinary temporal duration and recover sacred time in which a sacred event is reactualized. In such sacred time the formative and archetypal events are, as Eliade never tired of explaining, indefinitely recoverable and infinitely repeatable. "It is an ontological, Parmenidean time; it always remains equal to itself, it neither changes nor is exhausted."[29] At each celebration, the participants find the same sacred time...the same as was recovered the previous year or a thousand years earlier. Thus the one sacred time is infinitely recoverable at every celebration, no matter how often the celebrations take place. Sacred time "appears under the paradoxical aspect of a circular time, reversible and recoverable, a sort of eternal mythical present that is periodically reintegrated by means of rites."[30] In ritual, *then* and *now* become one, joined in a representation of that eternal present, which is an experience now of the time of heaven when all will exist in an eternal present, when time will be no more.

The clearest example in all the Christian liturgy of the reintegration of time occurs in the Exsultet, the Easter proclamation sung by the deacon by the light of the paschal candle. "This is the night," the deacon sings again and again. The proclamation says not, "This is the anniversary of the night"; not, "Tonight we remember what happened long ago"; but, "This is the night"

when God delivers the children of Israel, when Christ rises from
the tomb, when heaven and earth are joined. All the events of sacred history become contemporary with us and we with them as
separation in chronological time is overcome.

Ritual is also a means by which geographical separation can
be overcome. As ritual makes available sacred time by which the
past is made contemporary with us and we with it, it also makes
separation in geographical space dissolve. In everyday secular experience "the place of each locality is unambiguously fixed."[31] We
assume that there is a difference between *here* and *there*. Jerusalem is on one side of the earth, and New York is on the other;
we would never confuse the two. We can measure in exact miles
the actual space that separates the two cities. But what ritual as-
sumes is that a place can be present in several locations and all at
the same time. As with time, space...here and there...coalesces
and becomes one, without separation. The United States is ancient Palestine, this parish church is Jerusalem. In ritual, space is
made one.

Another way of putting this is to say that ritual actions are
symbolic actions, and, to use Paul Tillich's language, symbols,
understood on the profoundest level, participate in the reality to
which they point.[32] The rituals of religious worship are more than
"merely" symbolic. They participate in the reality of the cosmic
events they celebrate.[33] They are our share in those events.

Mircea Eliade described the characteristic feature of archaic religion as the "eternal return." Rituals can reverse the progress of
time and bend the line of temporal progression into a circle and
return to the archetypal, formative event. In the Easter Vigil one
sees clearly such an eternal return. As the White Queen remarks to
Alice, "It is a poor sort of memory that only works backwards."[34]

The Easter Vigil, by its use of the Jewish and Christian celebrations of Passover, nourishes memory and with it, hope. In the Bible,
"to remember" is a most powerful and vigorous action. Throughout the ancient world, to "remember" was to keep alive. In Old
English society the bard was a highly honored and essential member of a king's court because the fame a hero achieved by courage
was made to endure by the composition and songs of the bard, the
scop. A name is kept alive by remembering it. In later times Shelley
wrote confidently of more tender memories,

> Music, when soft voices die,
> Vibrates in the memory.[35]

But always there is the haunting awareness that such remembrance cannot keep one's fame alive indefinitely.

> Memory fades, must the remembered
> Perishing be?

worried Walter de la Mare.[36] So the hatred of enemies expressed itself in the desire that their name be blotted out (Psalm 109:13; Exodus 17:17). Their name will be forgotten when the family or tribe ceases to exist. An enemy that has been killed is not exterminated until the name of that enemy is entirely obliterated.

In everyday use, memory is a frail and fading recollection of a past event that saddens because what is gone cannot be recovered. William Cowper wrote wistfully in his *Olney Hymns,*

> What peaceful hours I once enjoyed!
> sweet their memory still!
> But they have left an aching void
> The world can never fill.[37]

In a secular song Thomas Moore (1779–1852) lamented what had been lost with the passing years.

> Oft, in the stilly night,
> Ere Slumber's chain has bound me,
> Fond Memory brings the light
> Of other days around me;
> The smiles, the tears,
> Of boyhood's years,
> The words of love then spoken;
> The eyes that shone,
> Now dimm'd and gone,
> The cheerful hearts now broken![38]

To remember in its most profound sense is more than just to keep in mind. It means also to keep in action. God spoke through the prophet Malachi, "Remember the teaching of my servant Moses" (4:4) and means of course that the people are not simply to keep the law of Moses in mind but to obey it.

This suggests a second characteristic of memory in its biblical use. It is usually not the action of an individual only but of the community. The memory and commitment to action is enhanced and strengthened when it is a communal activity, done in concert with others. Its most powerful and dramatic use is that in 1 Corinthians 11:24f, "Do this for the remembrance of me." The Eucharist is a bringing back out of the past into the present the sacrifice of Christ, indeed Christ himself, crucified and risen.

Third, the verb "to remember" is used in a majority of instances in the Bible with God as the subject. God remembers individuals, mercy, promises, and in so doing acts to protect and deliver.

Memory is seldom simple. It acts like a magnet that attracts to itself an odd assortment of associations that enrich it with many layers of meaning.

> It is a funny thing what the brain will do with memories and how it will treasure them and finally bring them into odd juxtaposition with other things, as though it wanted to make a design, or get some meaning out of them, whether you want it or not, or even see it.[39]

The Great Vigil of Easter, Christianity's central celebration, has taken into itself the deepest and most evocative symbols known to humanity: silence, darkness, fire, water, bread and wine. The vigil is nothing less than a representation of the creation and the remaking of the world. Here is the entire history of salvation in dramatic form from creation to the resurrection.

Emptiness

The candles and the lamps in the church have been extinguished since Good Friday, the day light died, to show the death of nature in sympathy with the death of the Son of God. As the overwhelming Passion hymn by Friedrich von Spee and Johann Rist, *O Traurigkeit,* puts it, "O sorrow deep...God's self lies dead" (*Gott selbst liegt todt.*) Struck dumb by the enormity of the deed, the world is plunged into an awesome silence. Following the celebration of the passion and death of Christ, churches in Spain were locked until the beginning of the celebration of Easter. In a time when churches were open always day and night and were the resort of people for a variety of reasons, their being shut spoke of the dread deed of crucifixion. The voice of the church was stilled, Christians were dumb to tell[40] what had been done. There was no place to flee for comfort; there was no place to hide. The church was closed. Such was the cost of the annulment of the sins of individuals and the community.[41]

A congregation gathers in a darkened church to keep vigil as they await the first signs of the dawn of the day of resurrection. But as they gather in silence and darkness they are retreating further back into the past, behind the time of Christ, behind the Passover, behind the patriarchs, to a time before time, to the original empti- ness out of which creation came. The congregation is drawn back into the primordial night. To recall that time and to recreate (or to de-create) that nothingness deprived of all sound and light out of which the cosmos came, the congregation gathers in silence and darkness. We leave the familiar world of perpetual illumination and withdraw into at least a semidarkness. Vestiges of light may re- main, coming in through the windows perhaps, for in such a world as we know, it is almost impossible to shut out all light. But in fact a vestige of light in the darkened church can enhance the meaning. The light seems as it were on the point of being extinguished,[42] engulfed by the surrounding shadows.

Silence too is necessary. It too marks a detachment from the world of sound and distraction. It is the silence of waiting, of ex- pectation, not without a certain fear, of some movement in the darkness, some sound to break the stillness. Submerged in silence and darkness, the congregation is being prepared by undergoing a regression into chaos, which is at the same time a unifying, wor- shipful, and expectant waiting for an action that is beyond our summoning.[43] Distance is abolished. We are waiting for God to do something.

Fire

Into this empty but expectant darkness and silence comes a spark, and a fire leaps up. The original command of the Creator has its intended effect again: *fiat lux,* "Let there be light," and there was light. Creation has begun; re-creation, renovation is under way.

Anciently, fire was "the most precious of possessions, to be re- newed only with difficulty probably not merely because the process itself was arduous, but certainly and primarily because the fire's living power must never be allowed to perish, and could only be restored in a traditional, sacramental manner."[44] Christianity therefore retains in many places the practice of striking the new fire from flint and steel. Ritual is always conservative; Joshua was com- manded to circumcise the Israelites with flint knives, as in Stone Age times (Joshua 5:2–3). Striking flint and steel is an inefficient method of obtaining fire, but it reminds us how precious fire was anciently, how difficult to strike.

The new fire that is struck (or "begotten." as some ancient stories would have it) is the first living creature to have a role in the
Easter Vigil, the first to be seen by the participants. It is at first not
entirely comforting. Faulkner noted

> the struck match which doesn't dispel the dark but only ex-
> poses its terror — one weak flash and glare revealing for a
> second the empty road's the dark empty land's irrevocable
> immitigable negation.[45]

One may remember also the beacon of fire spoken of in the opening lines of Aeschylus's *Agamemnon* (early fifth century B.C.) that
in the course of the terrible events of the drama brings not light but
deeper darkness. No living symbol is entirely under our control.
Moreover, the Easter fire entering the darkness, unlike the sudden
brightness of electric light, preserves shadows that slide along the
walls and spring from obstacles as the light moves into the church,
giving shape and a wonderful subtlety to the building and to the
congregation. The flicker of living flame provides a delicate play of
light on any nearby surface; carvings and moldings enfold darkness
and offer forward surfaces to our sight.[46]

The lighting of a new fire is an important feature of the new
year celebration of many ancient peoples. On new year's eve the
fire is put out and is ritually re-lighted on new year's day: "The
new fire signifies the appearance of a new World."[47] Ritual combat
between two opposing groups is another feature of many ancient
new year celebrations, and fire is part of such a contest between
darkness and light, "a reactualization of the cosmogonic act."[48]
The darkness is identified with chaos, and "the rekindling of fire
symbolizes creation, the reestablishing of forms and of limits."[49]

Fire originates in the heavens — in the sun and in lightning (in
Greek mythology Prometheus stole fire from the gods and brought
it to humanity), and that can be an overwhelming, even a terrifying power. Such fire can destroy. The ancient people of northern
Europe lived under the multiple threat of destruction by the forces
of nature, flood and ice and fire. In the Old English epic *Beowulf,* Hrothgar built the hall Heorot (that is, hart), and the bard
describes it with foreboding. "The hall stood tall, high and wide-
gabled: it would wait for the fierce flames of vengeful fire."[50] It was
as if human habitations, like the world itself, waited fearfully for
the destruction that doomed all things. Fire could thus serve as a
valuable symbol of the terrifying face of divinity, as in the story of
Moses and the burning bush (Exodus 3:1–6).

But fire has another face, that of a power spreading warmth and light, kindled by human beings to be the flame of the hearth. The various fire cults of the ancient world focused on terrestrial fire, kindled to flame by humanity and living together with us.[51] We are fascinated by certain qualities of fire in a fireplace. It is alive, changing continually, in constant motion, "and yet there is constancy in it. It remains the same without being the same." It dances as if it had an inexhaustible source of energy and suggests power, grace, and lightness.[52] In ancient Rome there was a highly developed domestic cult in which the father of the family was the priest of the flame and his sons (flamines) the kindlers, but the care of the hearth was entrusted to the women.[53] On the first of March, at the beginning of the old Roman year, the fire was extinguished and immediately rekindled, assuring prosperity for another year. This devotional focus on fire was extended to the state in which the hearth fire (Vesta) became the deepest mystery, on which the community's security depended: "the temple of the Vesta, the eternal fire, and the fatal pledge for the continuance of the Roman empire deposited in the shrine."[54] Thus human life and the life of the fire existed in a reciprocal relationship: they participated in each other.

Moreover, fire was understood to be a cleansing power. Together with water it is the great means of purification; indeed, fire was regarded as much the more potent, for it had the power to destroy. So John the Baptist speaks of baptism with fire (Matthew 3:11; Luke 3:16). Those who see the new fire at Easter cannot help but remember the cross marked in ashes on their foreheads forty days before, on Ash Wednesday, at the beginning of Lent. Those ashen crosses tell of the destruction of the old, of purification and cleansing.

The new fire is kindled, and by its frail flame a great candle is prepared, a pillar of fire as in the days of the exodus, to lead us, like our forebears in Israel "through the night of doubt and sorrow"[55] of our pilgrimage toward the promised land. The candle is marked with the sign (a cross) and the letters of a title of Christ (Alpha and Omega) and penetrated with five grains of incense for the five wounds of Jesus in hands, feet, and side. In the liturgy of this night and, with lesser emphasis, throughout the fifty days of Easter the candle is treated ritually as if it were Christ.

As the paschal candle is lighted from the new fire the minister says, "May the light of Christ, rising in glory, dispel the darkness of our hearts and minds." The statement instructs us in the meaning of the resurrection and of the candle. Christ, like the rising

sun, drives out from hearts and minds the darkness and all that
the darkness suggests: fear, ignorance, confusion, hopelessness, despair, grief. Christ is like the new fire, a living flame, rising up in the
darkness, giving light, pushing back the curtain of shadow, loosen-
ing the grip of gloom. The splendid candle represents to us the light
of Christ as its flame rises upward from the wick bringing light and
joy. In its irresistible leaping upward fire suggests also the carrying
of sacrifices and with them the hearts and spirits of those who offer
them heavenward.

In Evening Prayer the candle is a sign, a dramatic portrayal that
"Jesus Christ is the light of the world."[56] In the Easter Vigil, however, the paschal candle is treated as a still more potent symbol,
almost indistinguishable from what it represents, Jesus Christ. It is
not that Christians have in their regression become fire worshipers
but that the candle and its flame show to those with eyes to see
how all things point to Christ and proclaim his glory. The candle
remains wax, and Jesus Christ remains the Son of God, but the
symbol so participates in the reality to which it points that it is
nearly — but never entirely — identical with Christ. In the Hebrew
Bible the ark of God was such a potent object. Made by Moses and
Aaron from acacia wood and gilded inside and out, it was received
by them (and by their enemies) as a symbol of the presence of God
among the people of Israel and was regarded with such awe and
devotion that it was *as if* it were God among them. Uzzah, who
rashly presumed to reach out his hand to steady it as it was being
drawn by oxen, was struck dead for his presumption (2 Samuel
6:6–7). A mortal had dared to touch [the symbol of the presence
of] God. This may seem a primitive conception of the sacred, but
it shows an acute sense of God's terrible majesty.

Yet more clearly, the deacon who carries the candle into the
church sings of the candle, "The light of Christ" (*lumen Christi*).
The deacon does not sing, "This candle represents the light of
Christ," "This candle reminds us that Jesus Christ is the light of the
world," nor "This candle you see is a way of dramatizing vividly
Jesus' claim in the Fourth Gospel, 'I am the light of the world.' "
The words accompanying the procession with the candle are simply, "The light of Christ." We begin to see and understand the
latent power of symbols. The Easter candle is not "merely a symbol"; rather, it is nothing less than a symbol. The congregation,
remembering the long night of silence and desolation following the
death of Christ, can only reply with full hearts to this proclamation
of the light of Christ, "Thanks be to God."

By the light of the paschal candle, now set in a prominent place by the altar and adorned with flowers, the deacon begins the "most extraordinary passage in all the liturgy," the Exsultet. Some, even those who love the liturgy, sometimes ask, Can any Christian congregation be expected at the dawn of the twenty-first century to understand and appreciate the highly concentrated and exalted poetry of the Exsultet, packed as it is with arcane biblical and theological references?[57] The only correct answer to such questions must surely be, No, but so what? Probably no congregation in Christian history has been adequately prepared to appreciate all the references and allusions of this grand and soaring song of praise. Indeed, many parts and passages of the liturgy are beyond the full comprehension of individuals and congregations — the Nicene Creed, for instance, to say nothing of the nature of Christ's presence in the Holy Communion. To eliminate the Exsultet because it is beyond us is to take the route of those denominations and congregations that abbreviate the Apostles' Creed because they cannot comprehend what it means to confess that Christ "descended to the dead" or, in the older translation, "descended into hell." It is a concession to ignorance and an unwillingness to be taught.

The Exsultet may be understood as an expansion of the thanksgiving for light employed at the beginning of some forms of Evening Prayer. The first part of the great song with its traditional melody, compatible with the ancient tone for the preface verses, is a large invitation to Easter joy and praise. The hymn moves in eversharpening focus from great to small, from innumerable invisible choirs to the individual deacon who takes up the song this night. It is a poetic expansion of the traditional preface of the Eucharist, the purpose of which is to link earthly praise with that of the choirs of heaven. The Exsultet attempts even more, presuming to arouse first the choirs of angels in heaven; then second, the earth itself, the natural world; third, our mother, the Christian church; fourth, the congregation gathered in this place; and finally, the singer whose voice speaks for all Christians of all times and all places, inviting the grand chorus of people and nature and angels to "join with me in praising the lovingkindness of almighty God." It is an impulse similar to that which motivated the epic poets of classical times such as Homer and Virgil and their later imitators such as Spenser and Milton, following a brief statement of their theme, to begin with an invocation of the muse, for no unaided mortal is worthy or able adequately to sing the grand theme. As a human singer requires divine help to sing the story of Odysseus, so a deacon, "in my unworthiness" numbered among God's ministers, requires angelic and earthly and human assistance to attempt an adequate song in praise of the resurrection.

Then, following the preface verses, which establish a context of mutual regard and concern and give expression to the spirit of unity that is to characterize the church, the actual Easter proclamation, the *praeconium*, begins. It is right, salutary, proper, and healthful that we should praise God the Father together with God the Son (it is clear that this is a Western text; the Holy Spirit is not mentioned until the concluding doxology) "with full devotion." What is appropriate is not always possible in human affairs, of course, and what the Exsultet declares to be appropriate is beyond the reach of any congregation, for who can claim to have offered "full devotion"? Our attention is always incomplete, our fervor always too cool, our intensity limited. That is why the deacon begins by asking for help from the angels and earth and church, better to approach adequacy in praise of the central event of history. The devotion is as full as human imagination can manage in the sense that this enormously rich and suggestive Great Vigil makes use of insights and ideas and actions from across the breadth of human experience on this planet, and archetypal symbols that evoke in us the deepest echoes. It is perhaps not too much of an exaggeration to claim that no fuller ritual than this has been devised by mortal mind.

The occasion of this praise is first described in terms of one pictorial understanding of the atonement. Jesus Christ, the second Adam, paid the debt (that is, death) of the first Adam, the representative of the entire human race, and released us from bondage to original sin. In the words of an eighth-century office hymn, *Jesu, nostra redemptio*, as translated by John Chandler,

> But now the bonds of death are burst,
>   The ransom has been paid;
> And thou art on thy Father's throne
>   In glorious robes arrayed.[58]

Passover and Easter merge into one festival, the former preparing for the latter, the latter fulfilling the promise of the former, each illuminating the other. "This is the Paschal Feast," the deacon sings. At the first Passover a lamb was slain, and its blood marked the doorposts of the people of Israel held in bondage in Egypt, to protect them from the angel of death. At the new Passover, a greater lamb was slain, whose blood sanctifies the homes of the faithful. The doorposts of the homes in Egypt were transformed by the blood into doors of deliverance, doors that would close on the old life of slavery and open into the promised land. The doors of the believers marked with the blood of the Lamb of God become the gate of everlasting life, the image central to the collect of Easter Day. Old and new coalesce, time is made one. Judaism and Christianity (from a Christian perspective at least) merge into one celebration.

The first of five declarations that "this is the night" begins, merging the centuries into one. Mythical time is an eternal time. "From the point of view of the mythical consciousness, the past has never passed away; it is always here and now."[59]

1. This is the night when Israel, delivered from slavery, was led through the Red Sea dry shod, or as John Mason Neale's translation of St. John of Damascus's hymn, "Come, Ye Faithful, Raise the Strain," quaintly puts it,

> Led them with unmoistened foot
> Through the Red Sea water.[60]

The biblical text (Exodus 14:22) says that "the Israelites went into the sea on dry ground, the waters forming a wall for them on their right and on their left," but what was dry ground for them was clogging mud for the pursuing Egyptian chariots.

2. This is the night in which the fire of the candle and the fire of the resurrection purges away by destroying the "darkness of sin." The cleansing of Ash Wednesday and of the Lenten fast is brought to completion.

3. This is the night in which paradise is regained. Believers are rescued from the gloom of slavery in Egypt and symbolically from the depression caused by sin, are renewed by being brought out of the house of bondage as a new people, a nation, and restored to their former state of holiness. The celebration of this most holy night joins not only Passover and Easter but with them also the Garden of Eden and the hope of heavenly paradise. The promised land and heaven make room for the possible as opposed to passive acceptance of the present state of affairs. It overcomes the natural inertia of humanity and bestows a new ability to grow into the full stature of the image of God.[61]

4. This is the night when, in another vigorous description, Christ the strong hero breaks the chains of slavery and death and comes forth from the gloomy dungeon a triumphant victor. The

image has inspired hymns and poetry. Fortunatus's hymn, "Welcome, Happy Morning! Age to Age Shall Say" (*Salve, festa dies*), prays to Christ the victor, "Loose the souls long prisoned, bound with Satan's chain."[62] An early Latin hymn translated by Olavus Petri into Swedish and from Swedish into English by George Henry Trabert declares,

> We thank thee, Jesus, that thy hand
> · Hath freed us from sin's galling band;
> No more its bondage need we fear,
> The year of liberty is here.[63]

St. John of Damascus's eighth-century hymn puts it:

> Neither might the gates of death,
> Nor the tomb's dark portal,
> Nor the watchers, nor the seal,
> Hold thee as a mortal.[64]

The Old Saxon epic *Heliand,* written in the first half of the ninth century, describes the resurrection, mixing biblical and pagan motifs. "There was the spirit coming, by God's power, the holy breath, going under the hard stone to the corpse! Light was at that moment opened up . . . ; the many bolts of the doors of Hel were unlocked; the road from this world up to heaven was built!"[65]

The monetary image returns in the Exsultet, recalling the "debt of Adam to the eternal Father," discharged by the redemptive death of Christ. We would have no profit, the deacon's song declares, in being born (under such an enormous debt) "had we not also been redeemed." The debt was ours, but we had no way of paying it. The profit we now enjoy is entirely due to another. This thought leads to a series of exclamations of gratitude. How wonder-filled is God's descending to us in love. How beyond price and telling is God's goodness, that to buy freedom for a slave God paid the price of a Son.

The transaction is indeed so wonderful that it can only be described by paradoxes: Adam's sin was necessary to show the depth of God's love that washed it away by the death of Christ. Adam's sin was a happy fault (*felix culpa*), for it required such a great Redeemer as the Son of God.

The song returns to its praise of this night, "which alone was worthy to know the time and the hour wherein Christ arose again from hell." Nature — in this case, night — has the faculty to know and understand what is kept from mortal minds, the exact time when the tomb cracked open and Christ returned from the place of the dead with freed captives in his train.

5. Once more the cry is raised, "This is the night." It is the night foretold in Psalm 139:12. It is a night so holy, so powerful, so central to Christianity that its accomplishment is sevenfold. It (a) sends wickedness fleeing, like the pursuing Egyptian army; (b) washes away sin; (c) restores innocence to a race that had lost it; (d) restores joy to those who mourn; (e) casts out hate, for all are reconciled by the work of this night; (f) brings peace, which is more than the absence of strife and is a deep and abiding harmony; and (g) humbles earthly pride, for none of this is a human achievement. It all had to be accomplished by Another.

Our response to such overwhelming and selfless generosity can only be an offering of praise. The candle takes on yet another dimension and is understood as an offering of thanksgiving that is able to teach us our duty and obligation. The mystery of fire, like the mystery of the godhead itself, is not diminished no matter how often it is divided and borrowed. Candle after candle can be lit from its flame, and the flame is not made less; it burns as steadily and as brightly as before. The lesson of the candle is that the natural world has a role in this unity and praise. The bees who produced the wax for the candle are servants of God, too, and teach us the essence of generosity: giving without expectation of any return. The candle duplicates and extends the lesson: its wax feeds the flame, fulfilling its purpose by giving freely of itself, expending its own life for the good of another. The bees teach the candle, and the candle teaches us: sacrificial service is the lesson. Together the bees and the candle proclaim the sacrifice of Christ and summon us to follow their example. This is truly a blessed night in which a wonderful unity and a divinely ordered harmony are declared. Heaven and earth, divine and human are made one.

The proclamation portion of the Exsultet concludes, and the final sections are a prayer for the candle, for the church, and for the congregation. The extraordinary prayer for the candle on the literal level is simply a request that the candle may continue to burn in God's honor throughout the night until sunrise. But even that simple prayer says more than meets the eye. The candle is to burn in God's honor. Again we are reminded that we cannot honor God without divine assistance. For the candle to honor God on our behalf requires cleansing and purification, and again we are in the realm of symbol. We ask that we may see not just the flame of a large candle but in that flame the light of Christ, cleansing and purging all that is impure in our intention and desire. We ask that even when we are no longer watching, when the ritual is finished, that the candle that shows the resurrection will continue to drive out all that night represents and indeed be received as one of the lights of heaven, joining the sun, moon, stars, and planets. We ask that the candle, which human hands have made, be taken up to a place with the lights of heaven installed by the Creator. There is in this curious idea a hint, so delicate that we hardly notice it, of the next stage of the Easter mystery, the Ascension in which Christ the light is taken up into heaven.

The prayer for the candle continues, asking not only that the sun, the morning star, may find the candle still burning at dawn, but that Christ, who is "the morning star that never sets," will find the ardent faith and devotion that set up this paschal candle still strong at his coming in the day of his power. The prayer concludes with a request for God to rule, govern, and preserve the whole church (entire and of one piece, universal and catholic) and to grant the crowning gift, peace.

The Readings

The next section is the heart of the vigil. A series of significant lessons from the Bible is read, reviewing the revolutionary essentials of the biblical way of life. The Easter Vigil compresses the whole of the ancient baptismal preparation into one night. As the lessons are read, the congregation again becomes catechumens listening, learning, being shaped in mind and heart, encouraged to probe motives, to test commitment, to increase understanding, to change their lives. The several stages of the ancient catechumenate are compressed into one night: we are hearers (auditors) and competents (*competentes*); we undergo scrutiny in the light of the readings; we expel Satan and evil from our life as individuals and as a community; we receive anew the words of the Apostles' Creed and the Lord's Prayer. Two worlds intersect in this great service, and we are involved in the combat between the church and the world.

Each reading is followed by silence for meditation on its meaning, after certain readings a canticle is sung, and after each reading a prayer is said to draw out an interpretation of the reading. This portion of the vigil in the ancient church was extended for a very long time, through the night as the church waited for signs of the rising sun/Son. The mood is now more meditative and the pace more relaxed than during the singing of the intensely packed phrases of the Exsultet. After that challenging, daunting, over-whelming poem, the more familiar words of the Bible come almost as a relief.

Nonetheless, modern congregations may find it difficult to shift into a slower meditative mode. We are used to speed and continuous excitement and agitation. If a television show begins to drag, we change the channel. We are not used to silence; we are not used to meditation. We do not know what to do when nothing seems to be happening. In his tightly packed, multileveled epic *The Faerie Queene*, Edmund Spenser (1552–1599) works to create a certain quiet in our minds, for great ideas cannot be hurried. He adds an extra syllable to the concluding line of each stanza. The resulting six-stress Alexandrine, as it is called, has the effect of putting a brake on the speed of the narrative so that each stanza rolls gently to a stop, encouraging the reader to pause and savor the pleasures and insights of the completed stanza before going on to the next. Spenser demands of his readers "a still brooding attention, not a perpetual excitement."[66] It is not a modern method of storytelling, and we may grow impatient with it. But, as C. S. Lewis observes, although the *Faerie Queene* may fail to gain some readers, it seldom loses those it has once gained: "I never meet a man who says that he *used* to like the *Faerie Queene*."[67]

In the Easter Vigil in the silence that follows each reading we have time to think, to ponder and consider the significance of the passage, and we have the prayers to guide our understanding. The readings are instruction as well as proclamation and celebration. They review the past, highlighting certain events and themes for our devotion. In their diversity they serve as a reminder of the wealth of events and insights that are brought together in the Great Vigil. They present an assembling of events and responsibilities: creation of heaven and earth (Genesis 1:1–2:2), the destroying and renewing flood (Genesis 7:1–5, 11–18; 8:6–18; 9:8–13), the obedience of Abraham in being willing to sacrifice his only son (Genesis 22:1–18), the death and deliverance at the Red Sea (Exodus 14:10–15:1), the invitation to the thirsty poor to "come to the waters" (Isaiah 55:1–11), the holy wisdom vouchsafed to Israel (Baruch 3:9–37), the spiritual renewal promised by the vision of the valley of dry bones (Ezekiel 37:1–14), the restoration of Jerusalem (Isaiah 4:2–6), the institution of the Passover (Exodus 12:1–14), the resurrection of Jonah from the belly of the great fish

(Jonah 3:1–10), the obligation of those with whom God makes a covenant (Deuteronomy 31:19–30), the deliverance of the three young men from the fiery furnace (Daniel 3:1–23, [Song of the Three 1–2, 23–27], 24–29). Themes of creation and recreation, death and deliverance, obedience and sacrifice, punishment and renewal, hope for the future and corresponding ethical obligations arise and merge in the richness of the biblical record, and no one reading teaches only one lesson. Each individual who listens is able to hear in the readings a message that is personally applicable that night. Each member of the congregation is thus encouraged to compose a personal sermon on the basis of the texts that are read.

We do not simply review what God has done in the past. As the ritual erases the separation of time and space, what is described in the readings becomes contemporary and a personal experience. Bondage is broken, slavery is ended. We hear this in our own experience as a declaration that our intolerable self-enclosure is breached, the walls of self-centeredness are shattered, our prison is torn down. We are redirected to live no longer for ourselves but "in Christ." The self in Christ does not, however, become thereby diffused or dispersed. The self that emerges from the re-creation (the "I") is the self that finds its center elsewhere, no longer in itself but in life together with and for others.

So when we hear the creation account(s) from Genesis, it is not just a poetic vision of how all this wonderful world began. It is heard by us as a statement of God's intention for the world. The story of the flood of Noah's time tells us of death and destruction and the renewal of the original creation. Abraham's aborted sacrifice of Isaac teaches us the virtue of radical obedience to God. What is required of us is a total cleansing and remaking, redirecting us outward toward others, from isolation to community, from individuals to a people, the church. From the Red Sea a nation, Israel, emerged. From the waters of baptism a community, the church, is born.

Water

The readings that prepare for the service of baptism have already introduced the next great archetypal symbol, water. Fire is a great mystery, an emblem of divinity, a dangerous friend, a destroyer and a cleanser, necessary to human life. But water is a yet greater mystery, a greater necessity for creation. Life is possible without fire, but life is not possible without water. G. Van der Leeuw reports a conversation held in 1938 between an interviewer and a native of Surinam (Suriname).

Man cannot live without water.

Q. But what about fire?

Oh, no, sir. We cannot compare fire with water. Man can make fire, but water, only God alone can do this. Water is everything that lives, it is essential for man, animals, and plants. It is only man who cannot live without fire.[68]

Water is more important than fire. It symbolizes and incorporates into itself the whole of potentiality.[69] Like fire, water has a double face: it is both friend and foe. It gives life, and it can take life. It is both preserver and destroyer. Water is thus a still more profound if a less obvious representation of divinity.[70] It suggests generative, reproductive forces. Rain falls on a field and the crops grow. In both the Genesis 1 account and in the understanding of modern evolutionary biology life comes from the water. Water, like fire, blends change and permanence. It seems alive, continuous, energetic; but whereas "fire is adventurous, quick, and exciting, water is quiet, slow and steady. Fire has an element of surprise; water an element of predictability."[71]

In Greek mythology Aphrodite, the goddess of desire, was associated with water. She rose from its foam; her priestesses washed in the sea to honor her and to renew their virginity.[72] Fire always keeps us at a distance and so reveals one aspect of divinity, the *mysterium tremendum* that is removed from us. Water reveals another, more approachable and intimate aspect of divinity. Water invites us not just to come near and touch but to wash in it, plunge ourselves into it, and be totally surrounded by its cleansing, soothing, and invigorating qualities.

"In any analysis, there is always a danger of breaking apart or reducing to separate elements what was a single unity, a cosmos, in the minds that produced it."[73] In the mythology of many peoples the moon is associated with water as the source of the waters of life.[74] Both moon and water "govern the periodic appearance and disappearance of all forms"[75] and give a cyclic development to things everywhere. Moreover, fire and water are found in association.[76]

"All over the world the source of living water is accounted a joyous miracle."[77] A well is a source of wonder.[78] There is preserved in the book of Numbers (21:17–18) the little, perhaps fragmentary, song of the well:

> Spring up, O well! — Sing to it! —
> the well that the leaders sank,
> that the nobles of the people dug,
> with the scepter, with the staff.

The living water or the water of life brings fruitfulness and prosperity. Its power extends into the next life and its water bestows eternal life. The sacred river appears in Ugaritic (Canaanite) and Mesopotamian mythology as well as in the Bible, where it flows from the temple (Ezekiel 47:1–2; Joel 3:18; Zechariah 14:8; Revelation 22:1–2). Psalm 46 describes the return to chaos during the cosmic upheaval of the latter days, but in the middle of the tumult (as in the middle of the psalm verses) there is firmly established a renewed Eden, now no longer a garden but the city where God dwells, refreshed and gladdened by a river.

Water is, as Tertullian noted, an emblem of the formless state into which God spoke the creative word. It is "one of those things which, before all the furnishing of the world, were quiescent with God in a yet unshapen (*impolita*) state." The fluidity of water suggests that it contains in itself all possibilities and so is the source of all things. Water, Tertullian observes, venerable because of its antiquity and because of its dignity, is doubtless more pleasing to God "than all the other existing elements. For the darkness was total thus far, shapeless, without the ornament of stars; and the abyss gloomy; and the earth unfurnished; and the heaven unwrought: water alone — always a perfect, gladsome, simple material substance, pure in itself — supplied a worthy vehicle to God."[79] (The "gladsome" character of water suggests a parallel with the "gladsome" light of the evening candle in the hymn *phos hilaron* of Evening Prayer.) Water precedes all forms as the primeval waters, and it upholds all creation.[80] Immersion in water symbolizes a dissolution of forms, a return to the time before creation and order, a total regeneration, and emerging from the water is a repetition of creation, a new birth. "Every contact with water implies regeneration"[81] because dissolution into the formlessness of preexistence is followed by a new birth and because immersion fertilizes and increases the potential of life and of creation.

"Life, strength, and eternity are contained in water."[82] Such living water, the water of life, is not available to everyone in the same way in mythology, for it is found in places difficult to get to and belongs to demons or divinities. But in the Bible and in Christianity, specifically in Christ, the living water that gives eternal life is available to all who will come to it. That is the point of the reading from Isaiah 55, "Ho, everyone who thirsts, come to the waters."

When an object or person is immersed in water, form is dissolved, the thing or person ceases to exist.[83] Immersion is therefore the equivalent of death, death of the individual and destruction of the cosmos in a flood in which all forms cease to exist. Water nullifies the past and restores the purity and integrity of the dawn of the world. Thus, in the account of Noah's flood, read at the Vigil, the world was destroyed by the water out of which it had come, and after the devastation in which all drowned except the eight people in the ark, a renewed creation was brought forth from the water that both destroyed and gave life. If forms are not regenerated by being periodically dissolved in water, Eliade observes, they will crumble, exhaust their powers of creativity, and finally die away. Humanity would eventually be completely deformed by sin and, emptied of its seeds of life and creative powers; it would waste away, weakened and sterile. Such is the situation portrayed in T. S. Eliot's *Waste Land*. Instead of permitting this slow regression into subhuman forms, the flood effects an instantaneous dissolution in water, in which sins are washed away and from which anew, regenerate humanity will be born.[84] The reading from Genesis 7 and 8 is more than just a review of what took place long ago under the original covenant and that Christians, guided by 1 Peter 3:18–22, see as a prefiguring of baptism, which annihilates the old nature and gives birth to the new in each individual. There is also the continuing relevance of regular and repeated renewal. Not that baptism can be repeated, but by our making regular recourse to it, using it daily, our powers are restored.

Water, Eliade observes acutely, can never get beyond its own mode of existence, can never express itself in forms. Water can never pass beyond the condition of the potential, of seeds and hidden powers. Thus Easter and baptism are never ends in themselves; they give the human race the power to develop according to its renewed potential. So the lesson from Deuteronomy (31:19–30) read in older versions of the Vigil lays out the ethical obligations of those who bind themselves to the ancient covenant.

> As soon as it has separated itself from water, every "form"
> loses its potentiality, falls under the law of time and of life;
> it is limited, enters history, shares in the universal law of

change, decays, and would cease to be itself altogether were it not regenerated by being periodically immersed in the waters again, did it not again go through the "flood" followed by the "creation of the universe."[85]

Ritual purifications with water are performed to bring into the present for a fleeting instant that time when the creation took place and are a symbolic reenactment of the birth of the universe and of the new person.

All of this rich mythological background to Holy Baptism is not to say that the Christian sacrament is simply a borrowing of pre-Christian ideas. Such symbols as fire and water are archetypal and universal. They are the products of an intuition that the cosmos is a unity and that humanity is a specific mode of being in the cosmos.[86]

Baptism

The readings completed, the focus of the vigil turns to the font, which is prepared for the administration of Holy Baptism.[87] Water in mythological thinking has feminine characteristics, and the font has been likened to the womb of mother church. As the Spirit once moved over the water to begin creation and as the Spirit once moved upon the Virgin Mary so that she might conceive and bear the Son of God, so now the church asks that the same Spirit will move over the font so that it might become fecund and bear new children of God, for by baptism we are born of water and the Spirit.

The thanksgiving is said over the water, a thanksgiving primarily for the gift of the sacrament of baptism, but it ranges wide across the biblical record to gather significant images of baptism in references to water as an agent of cleansing and renewal.

In the course of the thanksgiving, the *Book of Common Prayer* directs the celebrant to touch the water. Earlier rites had directed the celebrant to divide the water with the hand, making the sign of the cross in the water. It was a rich symbol. The cross is a sign of blessing, obviously, putting the sign of Christ in, not just on, the water to consecrate it. As the paschal candle is treated as if it were Christ, bearing his sign, so now the water, a creature and gift of God, is, as it were, baptized so that those who emerge from its water are not just reborn but reborn into the baptized people of God. Also, dividing the water leaves no trace of the cross drawn in it.

The fire is infinitely divisible without loss; water makes a complementary assertion. It is indivisible: whatever is drawn in it quickly disappears and its wholeness returns. (The young poet John Keats, knowing that his life would be short, suggested that his epitaph be "Here lies one whose name was writ in water.") That character of persistent wholeness and indivisibility of water teaches and shows the unity of all who have been baptized. And further, the cross drawn across the water of the font divides it into four quadrants — north, south, east, and west. The suggested compass points indicate the worldwide mission and spread of the church. After Pentecost, when the Easter mystery had been completed, the apostles spread throughout the world to extend the ministry of the risen Christ whose Spirit they bore and who impelled them in their missionary enterprise.

A second, more dramatic and more obvious action during the thanksgiving may complement the celebrant's touching the water. At the conclusion of the prayer, the Easter candle is lowered into the water/font/womb. The significance is clear to those who know how to read symbols. The symbol of Christ is inserted into the water, the phallic candle into the womb. This is not a fanciful interpretation by post-Freudian students of mythology who can find sexual symbolism everywhere. Apparently in some places in the medieval church, the candle, having been lowered upright into the font, was then tilted so that some of the molten wax would fall like semen into the water. The medieval clergy, and probably many of the laity too, knew quite well what they were doing! Here is further evidence that the Easter Vigil is a species of new year celebration, for the presence of erotic activity — whether sexual excess to mark the return to chaos, or sexual activity to participate in the renewal of the new creation — was a conspicuous feature of the new year festival in many cultures.[88] It needs to be made clear, however, that the sexual symbolism is present in the Easter Vigil not to shock or for itself alone but as a sign of the intimate union of Christ and his bride the church, as well as the intimate union of God with each baptized person and of each of the baptized with one another. Sex in the liturgy shows the transcendence of the duality of self and other, of male and female, of God and humanity.

There follows the renunciation of Satan and the affirmation of the baptismal (Apostles') creed. In ancient rites this was the dramatic highlight of the baptismal action. The candidates would face the darkness to the west, where the sun had set, and thrice renounce the devil and all his works and all his ways. Some would

spit in the direction of the setting sun. Later in the continuing celebration of Easter, the collect for the third Sunday after Easter
would remind new Christians of their obligation to have nothing
to do with evil.

> Give strength to all who are joined in the family of the
> Church, so that they will resolutely reject what erodes their
> faith and firmly follow what faith requires.[89]

The older translation, used in the English *Book of Common Prayer*
and borrowed from there for Lutheran use, was

> Grant unto all them that are admitted into the fellowship of
> Christ's religion that they may eschew those things that are
> contrary to their profession, and follow all such things as are
> agreeable to the same.[90]

The verb translated "resolutely reject" or "eschew" is still more
vigorous in the original Latin of the Leonine sacramentary; it is
respuere, "to despise," "to spit upon." The reference to "their profession" is clearly a reminder of what the candidates had professed
at their baptism, the Apostles' Creed. They have been admitted into
Christ's religion, joined to the family, through Holy Baptism.

Having dramatically renounced Satan and all his empty pomp,
the candidates would turn toward the east, toward the rising sun
and the Son "who goes not down,"[91] to affirm the threefold profession of faith in God the Father, God the Son, and God the Holy
Spirit. The struggle of Lent and, for many, the struggle that had
continued for years, was at last at an end. Satan, defeated, slunk
away into the darkness of death, and the candidate embraced and
was embraced by Christ and his church giving light and life. Such
ritual combat between two opposing forces or groups was another
characteristic of new year celebrations. It was an annual expulsion of demons, diseases, and sins.[92] The expulsion culminated in
sending away from the community a person or animal regarded as
the vehicle through which faults of the entire community are carried away beyond the reach of the inhabitants. In the practice of
the ancient Hebrews, the scapegoat was driven into the wilderness
(Leviticus 16:7–28). So too in Christianity: conversion was a matter of martial combat with a range of unseen forces. The divine and
the diabolic were locked in mortal battle over and within each of
the candidates.

The candidates then disrobed and went down into the water
naked for baptism in the name of the triune God. Going into

the water was a return to the womb for rebirth. "Naked I came from my mother's womb, and naked I shall return there," said Job (1:21). The nakedness of the candidates was perhaps also a confession of their defenseless condition. Without protection, they were immersed in the water to be clothed with the righteousness of Christ, and then as they emerged from the water they were clothed with the white baptismal garment. Those familiar with Jewish traditions might recall passages in the Mishnah such as, "The Egyptians...were punished naked"[93] and "God punishes the wicked naked."[94]

Feasting

The procession returns from the font to the altar where the final act of the Easter Vigil, the Holy Communion, is celebrated. In the past, the Litany of the Saints was sung during this procession, invoking the prayers of a host of holy people and reminding the newly baptized of the great company of saints of whom they are now a part.

> Before us and beside us,
>   Still holden by thy hand,
> A cloud unseen of witness,
>   Our elder comrades stand:
> One family unbroken,
>   We join, with one acclaim,
> One heart, one voice uplifting,
>   To glorify thy Name.[95]

"We are surrounded by so great a cloud of witnesses" (Hebrews 12:1).

The transition from darkness to light, from death to life is now reaching its completion. At the singing of the Gloria in Excelsis at the beginning of the mass, bells are rung — tower bells and hand bells — the statues, images, icons, and crosses that had been veiled during Holy Week are uncovered and those that had been removed are returned to their places; flowers and plants abound, giving fragrance and perfume like the aromas of good deeds; musical instruments of many kinds support and supplement the song of the congregation.

Throughout this vigil mass, Christ's gigantic, irresistible force of life[96] dominates as on no other day of the year. The collect for the Vigil asks God

who made this most holy night to shine with the glory of the Lord's resurrection: Stir up in your Church that Spirit of adoption which is given to us in Baptism, that we, being renewed both in body and mind, may worship you in sincerity and truth.[97]

The ancient prayer joins Christ's resurrection and our resurrection in baptism. It gathers into one those newly baptized at the Vigil and those who, baptized long before, renew their baptism at this service. It joins Passover, the festival of unleavened bread, and Easter, asking for the Holy Spirit, given in baptism, to guide our celebration of the festival "with the unleavened bread of sincerity and truth," as 1 Corinthians 5:8 (the former epistle for the mass of Easter Day) commands. Before the Gospel, "alleluia," the joyous and perpetual song of heaven, not heard in the Western church since Lent began, can be contained no longer and breaks out in pent-up abundance, being sung again and again to welcome the Gospel, Matthew 28:1–10. The proper preface for Easter joins Passover and Easter, identifying Christ as the Passover lamb, sacrificed for us to take away the sin of the world (as the communion hymn Agnus Dei declares: "Lamb of God, you take away the sin of the world, have mercy on us"). By his death he has destroyed death (when he died, death died), and by his rising he has restored our life.

The meal of Holy Communion is the culmination of the Great Vigil. The feast is yet another characteristic of new year celebrations,[98] concluding the preparatory fasting as the mood moves from grief to joy, from despair to hope, from death to life. It is a celebration of a new age, a time of perfect peace and reconciliation and unity. Tacitus described the worship of Nerthus or Mother Earth "with days of rejoicing and merrymaking in every place she honors with her advent and stay. No one goes to war, no one takes up arms; every object of iron is locked away; then, and then only, are peace and quiet known and prized...."[99]

In the Eucharist, a human necessity, taking nourishment, is broadened and deepened and transformed until it incorporates the essential proclamation of Christianity. It becomes in St. Augustine's phrase, a visible word, a word that is not only spoken and heard but a word that is seen and touched and tasted. (See 1 John 1:1–3.)

The word that proceeds from the mouth of God takes on substance so that it can enter not only our ears but our mouths and bodies as well.

For the critic George Steiner, Holy Saturday has profound secular meaning. There is, he observes, one particular day in Western history about which neither historical record nor myth nor Scripture make report. It is a Saturday, and it has become the longest of days. Good Friday has meaning for Christians as the day of the cross, the day of crucifixion. Non-Christians too, Steiner observes, also know of the message of Good Friday in injustice, suffering, waste of lives and dreams. Sunday for Christians is the day of resurrection, and for non-Christians too Sunday can be a day of hope, an intimation of a justice and a love that have conquered death.

> But ours is the long day's journey of the Saturday. Between suffering, aloneness, unutterable waste on the one hand and the dream of liberation, of rebirth on the other. In the face of the torture of a child, of the death of love which is Friday, even the greatest art and poetry are almost helpless. In the Utopia of the Sunday, the aesthetic will, presumably, no longer have logic or necessity. The apprehensions and figurations with the play of metaphysical imagining, in the poem and the music, which tell of pain and of hope, of the flesh which is said to taste of ash the spirit which is said to have the savor of fire, are always Sabbatarian. They have risen out of an immensity of waiting which is that of man. Without them, how could we be patient?[100]

T. S. Eliot said that the essential vision for a poet is a vision of the boredom and the horror and the glory.[101] In our everyday life we know well the boredom that plods along without distinctiveness or interest, without flashes of illumination. There is the horror we see often in world events and occasionally even in our own lives, and the ultimate horror of Good Friday when humans rejected the most powerful demonstration of love, when mortals put God to death. And there is the glory that, by the deathless grace of God, we can still glimpse from afar and occasionally see close by us.

The Pascha, that rich complex of events that is Passover and Easter, is the eye through which everything and everyone must one day pass, to which everything tends, and from which everything emerges, transformed, into worlds beyond what we can know here, worlds as yet unknown, worlds even undreamed of.

In the grand and powerful celebration of the Easter Vigil, we have the essence of Christianity set before us, as on that most holy night we pass with Israel and with Christ from death to life. The ancient celebration joins Good Friday and Holy Saturday into one action. The passion, death, and resurrection of Christ are all here. So is our dying and rising in Holy Baptism and its yearly and daily renewal. The Great Vigil of Easter is the model for everything else we do in worship. It is, to put it quite simply, *the* service. It is a concentration in one service of what Christian worship does throughout the year. Every Sunday is a celebration of Easter, a proclamation of the resurrection of Christ on the first day of the week. Every day, from sundown to sunrise, is a renewal of that movement from darkness to light, as even the cycle of night and day tells of death and resurrection in all their richness and mani- fold meaning. The resurrection makes us see in a new way and in a new light our entire experience. This night has indeed enlightened the world and everything in it.

Chapter Five

THE CHRISTIAN YEAR
Hallowing the Seasons

✠

There is a comforting certainty in the dependable round of nature. When all else goes wrong, days and seasons remain. Every living creature responds to such certainties. Religious people respond still more deeply to the cycles of the natural world. The cycle of night and day is hallowed by Daily Prayer and is intensified in the Easter Vigil, which moves in its profound way from darkness to light. The turning of the seasons also has been of religious significance to the human race since we emerged on this planet, and so naturally Judaism and Christianity have hallowed the progression of the seasons with a calendar that differs significantly from the secular calendar.

One with the World

In English literature as early as *The Wanderer* (preserved in one manuscript transcribed ca. 975), nature conspires to reflect a person's mood. In that Old English poem the lonely searcher for a new lord and a new hall tries to console himself,

> He who is alone often lives to find favor, mildness of the Lord, even though he has long had to stir with his arms the frost-cold sea, troubled in heart over the water-way had to tread the tracks of exile.[1]

In the medieval *Second Shepherds' Play* the solitary shepherds appear on the wagon-stage at the opening of the play, each complaining about the cold weather and the ruthlessness of society. In *King Lear,* a violent storm shakes the stage as Lear is shaken in anguish. We have a deep correspondence to the natural world in which we live.

Human beings have, we suppose, been freed from our bondage to the soil, but we may still be bound to our origins more deeply than we know. In the spring there is an awakening of life around us, and we cannot escape a stirring in our blood as well. We luxuriate in the abundance of the summer. In the fall a melancholy settles over the land and us. In the winter the silence simplifies the world. We are not strangers on the earth, nor are we its lords. We are not independent. We come from nature; we exist by the processes of nature; we live every moment in absolute dependance on nature. We can live some five weeks without food, five days without water, five minutes without air. We cannot be against nature; we can only be one with it. If out of ignorance or apathy or aggressiveness we tear the fabric of which our own life is a part, we destroy ourselves as well as the mighty structure from whose womb we were born, in whose web we have had our unfolding history, and whose support and companionship in life is the primal place and ground of our existence.[2] We are one with the air, the water, the land, the leaf.

> Whence comes the boast that man possesses the earth? Summer gives it the lie every hour of the day. Life is the possessor, an infinity of life that will outlast all winters, even outlast the follies of mankind. Summer proves it, summer, the achievement beyond all human dreams and capacities.[3]

We are sustained by the certainty "that no matter how cold or bitter the winter, there will be violets again...that spring will follow winter."[4] If we listen carefully we may hear the rhythm that beats through the life and substance of everything we know. It is there in the atom, in the sunlight itself, in the color of the sunset, in the throbbing of the human heart, the crying of the winter wind, the progression of the seasons, the wheeling of the years. "We live by it, beings of that rhythm in our very breath, in our speech, in our songs, in our birthing and loving and in our growing old."[5]

> Maybe we need to learn these things anew each year. Perhaps we need to face the snowstorm and feel the frost underfoot to know that there is both ice and fire in earth, even as in the stars; to know that the big assurances endure.[6]

The continuity is as old as life, and the great rhythms beat through the least of us as through the universe.[7]

Like sunset and sunrise, the turning of the seasons is not a sudden, datable occurrence. We may mark the equinoxes and the solstices exactly by assigning a precise time to sunset and sunrise, but they are nonetheless aspects of a gradual process, movement that blends themes and modulates our perceptions. The large pattern is sure and dependable, but within the overarching certainty there are variations.

> The sun was warm but the wind was chill.
> You know how it is on a April day
> When the sun is out and the wind is still,
> You're one month on in the middle of May.
> But if you so much as dare to speak,
> A cloud comes over the sunlit arch,
> A wind comes off a frozen peak,
> And you're two months back in the middle of March.[8]

There is a perverse playfulness in the world that will not allow us to take it for granted. It is a living and lively force with which we have to do.

In the biblical world, time is a matter of ripening, fullness. St. Paul wrote to the Galatians, "When the fullness of time had come, God sent his Son, born of a woman, born under the law, in order to redeem those who were under the law, so that we might receive adoption as children" (Galatians 4:4–5). In Acts 2:1, "When the day of Pentecost had come," the verb *sumplerousthai*, translated "had come" in most modern versions, is related to the word "fullness" (*pleroma*) and has the sense of filling up (as in Luke 8:23, "the boat was filling with water") or completing the interval of days before an event. The Authorized Version translated appropriately, "When the day of Pentecost was fully come." Biblical time is such a ripening to completion, fullness, the time for an event to happen, the time for an emotion to be felt, the time for a harvest to be gathered, the time to celebrate the completion of a harvest. Time is thus an emblem of our communion with God. The cycle of the seasons of the year, rooted in the natural world, has been a significant inspiration for Christian prayer. The turning of the hours of each day, the first day and the eighth day, the passage of the seasons, all are manifestations of the death and resurrection of him who is First and Last, Alpha and Omega.

The purpose of the church year is a liturgical appropriation of the life of Christ. It is, however, not a simple reliving of the life of a man from Nazareth from birth to death and afterward. Christ is belittled if we commemorate only his thirty-three-year life on earth until the Ascension and Pentecost. Such an approach would confine his life to ancient Palestine, reduce Christ to a human level, and invite a separation between our life and his. Such a view, deprived of a clear and intimate connection between our life and his, is spiritually barren and devotionally debilitating. In keeping the church year we do not live vicariously the life of another, nor do we make believe that we are living in another time and place. Rather, the purpose and function of the church year is to provide a kind of template by which our lives are given a common shape and order to encourage the living of *our* life in the light of past events that are not past (memory) and in expectation of the future that is already our possession (hope).

> Standing in the living present,
> Memory and hope between,
> Lord, we would with deep thanksgiving
> Praise thee most for things unseen.[9]

The goal is a life that participates in Christ's life. It is a real life — his and ours — that ultimately is, or should be, one. The purpose is not chronology but identification.[10] The church year fosters a living historical sense, by investing the present moment of our life in Christ with heroic significance.

This understanding frees us from a chronological review of the historical life of Christ from beginning to end, from birth to ascension, as obvious as that may seem to be. Our preoccupation with time and our misunderstanding because we think only in linear terms leads us to assume that a historical review of the life of Christ is what the annual year of the church is all about. Our loss of a sense of the timeless world of liturgical celebration has led to a loss of a sense of participation in the proclamation and praise of the liturgy and of the liturgical year. A renewed sense of the timelessness of liturgical celebration points to that condition when time itself will be done, yet even now participates in that timeless state (heaven) suggested by "angels and archangels and all the company of heaven," the sabbath rest, and that state of repose St. Augustine spoke of at the beginning of his *Confessions,* "You have made us for yourself and our hearts are restless until they find their rest in you."[11]

The continual rush of time that so torments us deprives our lives of dignity and meaning. The year, however, is capable of being experienced in such a way as to give it coherence. The church year is a way of ordering time to make it coherent and manageable, and to invest it with a sense of purpose, direction, and meaning. The year has a theological dimension (time is eschatological; it is not mad but going somewhere), and the year has a moral dimension (time is ethical; it has significance and dare not be wasted). The church year is a way of recalling and reliving the experience of Christian people, that is, the church, in disciplined obedience, celebrating the joy of the resurrection-ascension-pentecost, the spread of the faith throughout the world, and the eager expectation of the consummation.

As it evolved over the centuries, the church year is a dense, close-packed work. As with any work of art, several levels are experienced simultaneously: Passover and Easter and our present life; Bethlehem, today, and the end. Here, under the vision of the church year, everything holds together, every image reinforces and is absorbed into the ultimate meaning, leaving us with as much a sense of mystery as of clarity. Coleridge observed that some of the best poetry remained only "generally and not perfectly understood."[12] Yet, for all its complexity, the church's year is not impossibly complicated. It makes use of a limited number of profound, deeply evocative symbols — darkness and light, fire, water, food. But these are each so rich that they provide an inexhaustible source of insight and ideas and inspiration. The Irish poet and mystic William Butler Yeats observed,

> Anyone who has any experience of any mystical state of the soul knows how there float up into the mind profound symbols whose meaning ... one does not perhaps understand for years.[13]

So it too with the church's life. Symbols rise to consciousness that may not be understood for centuries. But the wholeness of the liturgy preserves them for us so that they are available when we need them.

The Christian Pilgrimage

One enormously rich and suggestive archetype that shapes the year of the church is that of the pilgrimage. Christianity identifies itself with ancient Israel, having Egypt behind and the promised land ahead. The chains of slavery have been broken and the land of bondage sealed off by a wall of water. We cannot return to the past, as much as in our perversity we may sometimes long for it. We can only fare forward through peril and danger until we are safely across Jordan's water and settled in the promised land, and our journey is done.

The Puritans who came to America in the early seventeenth century reexperienced the life of the ancient Israelites, for they too had to cross an ocean that lay between them and their old life of persecution and peril in England, and they faced an uncertain life in a "howling wilderness"[14] in the new world.

There is a rhythm in the universe, the rhythm of night and day, of the regular progression of the seasons, of the turning of the years. Everything that lives shares in that rhythm.

> Each has his or her place in the procession.
> (All is a procession,
> The universe is a procession with measured and perfect
>   motion.)[15]

The form of the world is never static. "The fundamental form of process is cyclical movement, the alternation of success and decline, effort and repose, life and death which is the rhythm of process."[16]

The cycles of the natural world remind those who see and listen to them that humans are but transients on the land. Woods and wilderness usually get along better without us, and the natural world is not there simply for our convenience and use. The abundant proliferation of spring reminds us that we can cut grass and chop brush and prune trees and try to prevent erosion from eating away the land. But when we stop controlling the growth, pastures and fields are overrun by birch and sumac, fences rust and rot, the dooryard is a seedy weed-patch,[17] and a tumbledown house, crowded by a thicket, becomes at last

> no more a house,
> But only a belilaced cellar hole,
> Now slowly closing like a dent in dough.[18]

We human beings are but transients. Gabriel Marcel called humanity *Homo Viator*[19] and so each of us is. We are passing visitors to a scene that will endure without us.[20]

We have lost sight of our transitory place on the earth, and we have forgotten the ancient practice of walking. It was once a life shared by mendicant friars, beggars, pilgrims, bards, travelling artisans; but we have not practiced this way of life for some time. As long ago as the eighteenth century Samuel Johnson noted, "A French author has advanced this seeming paradox, that *very few men know how to take a walk.* "[21] In the twentieth century John Hillaby, a naturalist and historian, demonstrated that such knowledge was not yet entirely forgotten.[22] Throughout human history religious people have believed that life is about taking a walk, making some kind of journey.[23] It may take the form of an outward pilgrimage to a religious site or shrine or it may be (or may at the same time be) an inward journey into the depths of being toward spiritual growth and exploration. Throughout the world pilgrimage seems a natural religious activity.[24] Mecca attracts two million visitors each year; a tide of men and women flow to the Ganges at Allahabad (Prayaga) for the great festival held there every fifteen years. The sense of exile, of not being entirely at home in this world, of being aware of a separation from the source of meaning pervades the biblical understanding of the human condition. Religious people are therefore people on the way. A religious society is not a perfect society, and the defining characteristics of the church — unity, holiness, catholicity, apostolicity — are best understood as vocations to which the church is called, not static possessions. In biblical terms we are between Sinai and Sion.

Thus, within the cycles of the day, the month, and the year, the Christian life is given a direction and a goal. This life is not a cycle of endless repetition, but it is a life that is going somewhere, under the large and controlling metaphor of the pilgrimage.

Cain in his self-pity lamented that he was "a wanderer on the earth" (Genesis 4:14), and he "went away from the presence of the Lord, and settled in the land of Nod," that is, the land of wandering. He was a wanderer, however, because he was a fugitive. He was on the run because he had murdered his brother. Cain, who had been a settled farmer, a "tiller of the ground," was required as his punishment to live the nomadic life of his brother Abel, "a keeper of sheep." In larger terms, humanity, created to live in God's presence in paradise, was now to live outside the garden as a wandering nomad in the land of Nod, east of Eden. Human desire wanted to keep God at a distance; God's desire, however, continued to be for community and companionship.

Abraham is the archetypal figure of pilgrimage. In answer to the summons of God, he and his family left their own country and went in search of the promised land, opening the way to a new way of life and belief. It was echoed in the experience of

Saul on the road to Damascus. Abraham travelled with his family and Saul travelled alone, but both were set on "the nomad's way" (Judges 8:11 JB). It is a powerful and recurring image. The exodus experience of nomadic life in the wilderness was a preparation for the eventual return to the promised land. Homelessness and the hope of return was a central theme of Judaism after A.D. 70, and in each of the exodus experiences, God too seemed in exile in the wilderness. In the New Testament also, the writer to the Hebrews employs the motif of wandering or journeying. The image of pilgrimage shaped medieval European religious life and literature as well. Chaucer's *Canterbury Tales* are not only the report of an imagined pilgrimage from Southwark to the shrine of the popular martyr Thomas a Beckett at Canterbury; they are also a representation of the pilgrimage of all sorts and conditions of humanity, joined in a common enterprise for a variety of reasons and motives, through this world to the next. The parson says in the prologue to his tale,

> I wol yew telle a myrie tale in prose
> To knitte up al this feeste, and make an ende.
> And Jhesu, for his grace, wit me sende
> To shewe you the wey, in this viage,
> Of thilke parfit glorious pilgrimage
> That highte Jerusalem celestial.[25]

Indeed, the metaphor of life as a journey can be traced from Homer to Joyce and Beckett and beyond.

The polarity between stabilization and evolution, stagnation and growth,[26] preservation of old forms and the production of new ones is preserved in its tension by the image of the pilgrim and so of the church year that maps out a pilgrimage route for wayfarers.

By returning to an old figure of God's people as pilgrims — begun in the Old Testament with the epic journey of Abraham and Sarah, revived in the Middle Ages and by John Bunyan, and rediscovered by the American Puritans and by the Second Vatican Council — we may find an answer to the psalmist's question, "How shall we sing the Lord's song in a strange land?" (Psalm 137:4 KJV). The suggestive image of the pilgrim making a way through the world to a particular destination can serve as an ordering motif in understanding what the church is about in keeping its own peculiar calendar and year.

A pilgrimage journey involves a threefold process: separation, transition, and incorporation.[27] (1) The separation required by a pilgrimage makes necessary sacrificing what is familiar and comfortable. Abraham had to leave his native country and relatives. The pilgrimage also requires a certain loss of innocence, as Adam and Eve, representing the human race, began in paradise but had to leave it, having tasted of what was forbidden them. The separation, it must be noted, involves loss. (2) The resulting transition, moreover, is a time of hardship and suffering. The difficulty and pain are given meaning by the constant focus on the goal of the journey, the sacred place, understood as the center of the universe, the place of the fullest presence and permanent abode of God. A pilgrimage is an exposure to trial and hardship, the perilous passage from a confining but comfortable world into a world the vastness of which we can hardly surmise. We are told little about Abraham's journey. The exodus is described in more detail. It was a time of deprivation and homelessness and longing during which not only Israel was in exile; God was in exile with them in the wilderness. (3) The concluding state of incorporation includes the experience of grace sought by the journey but experienced not as earned but as an undeserved and even unexpected gift, for no preparation, no matter how diligent, can provide foreknowledge of just what to expect. Like Abraham, one can only trust the goodness of God, which is a complex goodness involving, among other things, the command to sacrifice his only and beloved son Isaac.

In its metaphorical use, beginning with Abraham, the pilgrimage journey is not a mere visit and return. It is a one-way trip. Abraham did not return to what had been his home, nor did he desire to return there having reached the promised land. Even when a pilgrim journeys to a pilgrimage site, Jerusalem for example, there is often little report of the return trip. The focus is on the destination, which does more than renew, restore, rejuvenate. It so transforms those who reach it that they cannot be the same again, and, as T. S. Eliot suggests in his poem *The Journey of the Magi*, should they return home, they do so deeply changed and no longer able to enjoy or even feel at home in their original country. Their true homeland, they have come to learn, is elsewhere.

For all of the disconcerting discovery afforded by the pilgrimage, the metaphor of the pilgrimage journey also involves an impulse toward making sense out of a chaotic world and toward a new social order. The culmination of such an epic journey is the foundation of a city: Rome for Aeneas, Jerusalem and the new Jerusalem for the biblical writers,[28] the City of God for Augustine. The end of the labor is not individual salvation but the establishment of a new and purified society of order and harmony in which everything clearly works for the common good and above all the glory of God.

The Beginning of the Year

The journey of pilgrims over "the nomad's way" therefore requires its travellers to be out of step with the world, for they are following a different calendar; they are responding to another rhythm. To make the pilgrims' path correspond to the highways of the world is to deprive it of its power to transform. To make the pilgrims' calendar reflect the secular calendar is to undermine the pilgrims' purpose. There is no reason to expect Christian pilgrims through the year to be in harmony with the world, for they, like Thoreau, march to a different drummer.[29] While the world celebrates its Christmas with an orgy of merchandising before the year's end, the church keeps its somber yet hopeful Advent. When the world has finished with its Christmas, the church begins its twelve-day Christmastide. The world has its New Year, but the day is largely ignored by the church in its focus on the beginning and the conclusion of the Christmas celebration — the Nativity of Our Lord and the Feast of the Epiphany.

The church's new year occurs at a different time from that of the world. Indeed, like Judaism with an echo of an ancient new year at Passover[30] ("This month [Nisan] shall mark for you the beginning of months," Exodus 12:2) and Rosh Hashanah in the autumn on the first and second of Tishri (late September–early October),[31] the church has a dual new year also.[32] The First Sunday in Advent, "the Sunday nearest to St. Andrew's Day (November 30), whether before or after," is generally explained as the beginning of the Christian year. Liturgical books begin with Advent because Advent seems to be a preparation for the celebration of the birth of Christ, leading, as the church's year rolls on, to the commemoration of his death and resurrection and ascension and return as king. Thus Christianity has its new year begin in the late fall, a couple of months later than Rosh Hashanah. (The autumnal new year in Judaism was surely developed on the pattern of the day as understood in the first chapter of Genesis. As the day begins with sundown and continues through the night of waiting for the dawn and the fullness of daylight and concludes with sunset, so the year correspondingly may be understood to begin in the autumn, continue through the dry season, the winter of emptiness and waiting for the renewal of life in the spring and its flourishing through the summer, and conclude in the ripeness of autumn with which the year begins again.) But there is an important sense in which Christianity, like Judaism, has a new year in the spring as well. Indeed, the most profound understanding of the Christian year identifies the clear break in the cycle of the year as occurring not with the beginning of Advent, for the concluding time after Pentecost turns toward a contemplation of the last things — death and the judgment — which are also a theme of Advent. Rather, the clear break in the turning of the year happens with Ash Wednesday. The beginning of the penitential season of Lent comes as a sober interruption of our enjoyment of life. The joy of Christmas and the Epiphany gives way to "the cold cheer of Lent"[33] announced by Ash Wednesday with its chilling but healthful reminder of death.

In liturgical books such as *The Taizé Office*[34] one finds a clear presentation of a common outline of the Christian year. There are two cycles, Incarnation and Redemption, each centered around a great feast, Christmas and Easter; each including preparation (Advent and Lent), celebration (Christmas Day and Easter Day), and fulfillment (the Christmas season and the Easter season); and each celebration concluded with a related festival (the Epiphany and Trinity Sunday). The church year in such a view is thus a kind of ellipse with two foci. Intellectually and didactically, it is a clear, balanced, and satisfying scheme. Devotionally, however, it is not easy to shift from one cycle to the other. There is no truly transitional time; there are just the Sundays after the Epiphany and after Pentecost until the next cycle begins. Moreover, the scheme is theologically misleading, for there are not two separate actions but one saving act of God which must be taken together as one whole work bringing us to the heavenly Jerusalem where myriads of angels together with the righteous made perfect worship God (Hebrews 12:22–23).

The church year is a creedal statement, but it does not follow the logical order of the Apostles'[35] and the Nicene creeds. The church year is a work of symbolic memory,[36] the process by which we not only repeat past experience but reconstruct it. Such deconstruction and refashioning is the way of art in all its forms. A novelist's arrangement of events within the linear flow of words often departs in varying degrees from strict chronological order. Moreover, portions of a narrative may be connected without regard to chronology through such devices as image patterns, leitmotifs, analogy, and contrast. Much modern poetry — that of

Eliot and Pound, for example — undermines the inherent connect-
edness of language, forcing the reader to perceive the elements
of the poem not as unrolling in time but as juxtaposed in space.
"Spacial form" is a general label for these different narrative tech-
niques.[37] Art never simply reflects or reproduces nature or reality.
"When art intervenes it unmakes nature in order to make it otherwise."[38] It is not that art gives a false message, contrary to reality,
but that the artist has in mind and spirit another order of beauty
and attempts to interpret the most profound yearning inscribed in
the human heart: "to discover the world which lies beyond this
visible world."[39] Imagination is a necessary element of true recollection. We *imagine* the past. Goethe gave his autobiography the
tile *Dichtung und Wahrheit* (*Poetry and Truth*).

> He did not mean that he had inserted into the narrative of
> his life any imaginary or fictitious elements. He wanted to
> discover and describe the truth about his life; but this truth
> could only be found by giving to the isolated and dispersed
> facts of his life a poetical, that is a symbolic shape.[40]

St. Augustine in his autobiographical *Confessions* does not relate
the events of his life. He tells the story of his conversion, which is
"the repetition and reflection of the universal religious process," of
humanity's fall and redemption.[41] Augustine could not understand
his own life except in the symbolic language of the Christian faith.
So in the church year the life of Christ is presented to be relived and
reexperienced by his followers. This is not done, however, in a flat-
footed, unimaginative, strictly chronological review from birth to
death and resurrection and ascension. That approach could never
touch our lives. It would remain simply historical and commem-
orative. We would simply observe the life of another. What the
church does in its yearly presentation of the work of Christ is show
it in such a way that it can be experienced by its celebrants two
thousand years and more afterward. Christians have had the experience of the death and resurrection of Christ, have handed on that
tradition into the present, and carry the experience into the future
as their hope and confidence.

The central event, the beginning and the end, is the *Pascha,* the
unitary celebration of the death-resurrection-ascension, the dying
and rising that give meaning and focus to all other events of that
life and ours. The Easter Vigil therefore properly has the characteristics of a new year festival, for that is indeed what it, like Passover,
is: the beginning of a new year and a new life of God-given grace.[42]

Ash Wednesday and Lent prepare for the celebration of Easter, and the celebration of the queen of feasts extends through Ascension and Pentecost and the work of the church until the parousia, of which Christmas is the promise and the Epiphany the culminating foretaste. Then Ash Wednesday breaks into the round of the year once again with its preparatory anticipatory message of death and resurrection.

The spring of the year is the time when (in portions of the Northern Hemisphere) life in all its variety begins anew. The natural world is reborn and comes to exuberant life. In the ancient Near East and elsewhere, as in ancient Rome,[43] the spring was the time for warfare. "In the spring of the year, the time when kings go out to battle" (2 Samuel 11:1) is translated "the turn of the year" in the Jerusalem Bible and the Revised English Bible, and "the return of the year" in the Anchor Bible.[44] The turn of the year in the spring occurred after the onset of the dry season, but in addition to practical concerns, there may also be more obscure ritual and religious reasons for setting out to battle at the time of the vernal equinox. The ritual sword dances popular in England as a celebration of spring seem associated with the practice of a nature cult.[45]

In *Lutheran Book of Worship* the exhortation to the congregation at the beginning of the Ash Wednesday liturgy combines effectively the idea of turning and of springtime warfare.

> ... by our sin we grieve our Father, who does not desire us to come under his judgment, but to turn to him and live.
>
> As disciples of the Lord Jesus we are called to struggle against everything that leads us away from love of God and neighbor. Repentance, fasting, prayer, and works of love — the discipline of Lent — help us to wage our spiritual warfare. I invite you, therefore, to commit yourselves to this struggle and confess your sins.... [46]

The spiritual warfare is a process of turning. The opening lines of T. S. Eliot's *Ash Wednesday* are a translation from Guido Cavalcanti and also echo a sermon by Lancelot Andrewes:

> Now at this time is the turning of the year.... Everything now turning that we also would make it our time to turn to God.... Repentance itself is nothing but a kind of circling ... which circle consists of two turnings.... First a turn wherein we look forward to God and with our whole heart

resolve to turn to Him. Then a turn again wherein we look
backward to our sins wherein we have turned from God. . . .
The wheel turns apace, and if we turn not the rather these
turnings may overtake us.[47]

Christians who keep the church year are called to follow Christ
into death and beyond. His struggle is to be theirs, and their struggle becomes his. The memorable action that gives the name to the
day — the imposition of ashes — is a reminder of our mortality
and of the urgency of the Lenten discipline. The full understanding
of Easter begins with the solemn proclamation of Ash Wednesday,
"You are dust, and to dust you shall return." Lent is a time to sort
out the transitory from the permanent, what is passing from what
abides. The ashes, moreover, tell of cleansing (anciently, ashes were
used as a cleansing agent) and of renewal, for they are also a sign
of the washing in baptism, the ashes being a penitential substitute
for water.

Throughout the world, myths of a hero's quest have four aspects: *agon* or conflict, *pathos* or death (often the mutual death
of hero and monster), disappearance of the hero, and the hero's
reappearance and recognition.[48] These four archetypal aspects can
be identified in the struggle of Christ also: *Agon* of the temptation and the garden of Gethsemane (Lent), death (Passion Sunday
and Good Friday), disappearance (Holy Saturday), and reappearance and recognition (Easter and the resurrection appearances).
Christians share these experiences in the church's year by going
through the wilderness to Jerusalem (the *agon* of Lent), eating
the new Passover in which the Lamb is put to death destroying death, waiting in the emptiness of Holy Saturday for the first
signs of life and light of Easter morning, and recognizing and welcoming the risen Christ in Word and Sacrament and in others
in need.

Einar Billing, the Swedish bishop and theologian, taught during
the early decades of the twentieth century that the exodus provides
the central category for interpreting the Bible (both Old and New
Testaments) and the mission of the church as well. The exodus
was an event in which a people experienced unexpected deliverance from bondage, and the deliverance came about through the
breaking of the power of the oppressor and the opening of an until then impossible future for those who had been oppressed. The
exodus thus provides a basic principle of interpretation of God's
action. Judgment opens the way for the creation of something new

and unexpected: such is the work of the God "who gives life to the dead and calls into existence the things that do not exist" (Romans 4:17).

In the days of Lent we embark on an exodus journey toward the veiled future that lies on the other side of change. The Gospel for the First Sunday in Lent, to set the theme and the length of the season, is the story of Jesus' temptation by Satan. It is the analogue to the story of the fall of humanity. In Eden the first Adam succumbed to the tempter; in the wilderness the second Adam resisted the wiles of the tempter. Paradise lost is becoming paradise regained. The forty years Israel spent in the wilderness of Sinai, tested and humbled, are recapitulated in the forty days Christ spent in the wilderness of Judea, enduring humiliation for his people, and are not just reenacted but reexperienced by the church during the forty days of Lenten testing and preparation.[49] We, like the ancient Hebrews before us, go through a desolate wilderness that is of our own making. Once placed in paradise, we have made of it a wilderness. Our goal is Canaan, the new land that is our old and permanent land from which we have been exiled. There, "all idol forms shall perish / And error shall decay"[50] in a land prepared and purified by God, who will at last be recognized and worshiped as Lord alone. Eden, ruined by our sin, will be restored by God's power (Isaiah 51:3). Meanwhile, as we make our yearly way through the barren wasteland, baptismal images abound in the Lenten liturgy and readings — when we learn to see them.

The key to Christian life is a reliving of the Easter mystery. The church year therefore has its organizing focus on Easter, which is primary and central, at once past and present, communal and personal.[51] Easter is no more behind us in the past than is our sinfulness.[52] The church year finds its culmination in the feast of promise (Christmas), which arrives as the world grows dark. When the world ends, the promise is fulfilled. The gloomy chill of winter is broken, and death is denied its last word.

Traces of such an understanding of Easter, rather than Advent, as the central and renewing event of the year lingered in the medieval calendar. The beginning came with Pre-Lent, the three Sundays before Ash Wednesday — called Septuagesima, Sexagesima, and Quinquagesima — which led into Lent, which prepared for Easter, which was celebrated in stages to Ascension and then to Pentecost.[53] The annual reading of the Bible in Daily Prayer began with the first chapter of Genesis on Septuagesima in the early spring, the beginning (in the Northern Hemisphere) of the natural year.

Just as Christ's resurrection from the dead is the central fact of the Christian life, so the celebration of Easter is the center of Christian worship. "We are Easter people, and Alleluia is our song," Augustine declared. Because of the centrality of Easter, a period of preparation developed to ready participants for it, and this preparatory period was eventually extended to forty days, suggested by the forty years Israel spent in the wilderness preparing for the promised land and the forty days of fasting and prayer given to Moses (Exodus 24:18), Elijah (1 Kings 19:8), and Jesus himself in preparation for their work.

Thus Lent and Easter, Ash Wednesday through the Day of Pentecost, is to be understood as one whole season, consisting of forty days of preparation and fifty days of fulfillment. Both parts of the season are themselves divided. The time of preparation consists of the days of Lent (an initial day followed by five weeks, Ash Wednesday through the fifth week of Lent) and Holy Week. The time of celebration consists of an initial day, Easter Day, followed by six weeks of celebration until the Ascension, and then the nine-day novena of prayer for the fulfillment of the promise of Easter in the gift of the Holy Spirit.

It is important to keep separate Lent and the Passion. The long-standing identification of the two, deeply ingrained in Lutheran devotion particularly, may be psychologically damaging and is theologically misleading. Lent is a time of self-examination, discipline, purification — growth, as the derivation of the English name for the season suggests: Lent is from *lencten,* the lengthening days of springtime. It is a time of renewal focused on baptism. The ashes of Ash Wednesday with which and in which Lent begins are signs of purification and cleansing. The English custom of using unbleached linen paraments and covering statues and adornments is a portrayal of the inward focus of the season.

The veils should be of white linen, brown holland, or of silk (*not* of crepe). But nothing whiter than the toned white of homespun linen should be used; the white linen of which surplices are made...does not have a good effect. The beauty and significance of the Lenten white will be at once appreciated if this is remembered; for the walls of the church being distempered in a toned white (as they should be) the veiling of pictures, reredos, &c., causes them to be lost in the general back ground till Easter comes again.[54]

Such visual austerity emphasizes the understanding of Lent as a time of inward purification and growth. The propers for Lent — the collects, verses before the Gospel, offertories — emphasize life, not death and gloom.

Holy Week is the time for concentration on the passion and death of Christ, particularly on the Sunday of the Passion ("Palm" Sunday) and Good Friday. The collect for the Sunday of the Passion focuses on the passion and death of Christ, but, it is to be noted, not to the exclusion of his resurrection:

> Almighty and everliving God, in your tender love for the human race you sent your Son our Savior Jesus Christ to take upon him our nature, and to suffer death upon the cross, giving us the example of his great humility: Mercifully grant that we may walk in the way of his suffering, and also share in his resurrection; through Jesus Christ our Lord.... [55]

The verse before the Gospel, "The hour has come for the Son of Man to be glorified" (John 12:23), and the Offertory — "Truly, truly, I say to you, unless a grain of wheat falls into the earth and dies, it remains alone; but if it dies, it bears much fruit. If anyone serves me, he must follow me; and where I am, there shall my servant be also; if anyone serves me, the Father will honor him" (John 12:24,26)[56] — also counter any morbid emphasis on the death itself, for the death of Christ was in the Fourth Gospel, paradoxically, also his glorification.

The paschal mystery we seek to explore defies limitation, and it is constantly urging us to see more than what appears on the surface. Most importantly, the old unity of cross and resurrection as one event must be preserved. The church has with its liturgical year bought the Lucan chronology of Good Friday, the holy sabbath of rest, Easter Day, followed forty days later by the Ascension, followed ten days after that by Pentecost. It is of course helpful to devotion to separate the events this way and spread them over fifty days, for we cannot meditate and reflect upon everything at once. But we must be aware that such is only one way of seeing the paschal mystery, one scheme of ordering it for contemplation. By reading St. John's Passion on Good Friday every year and by making readings from the Fourth Gospel prominent during the Sundays of Easter, the church has suggested — perhaps too subtly — that there is another way of ordering the events that also has validity. In John's understanding, Jesus' resurrection, ascension, and sending of the Spirit all occurred on the same day and are clearly one event. The division of the one unitive event into separate actions is schematic only and needs the counterbalance of the unified view.

For several centuries the Great Vigil of Easter was the total and unitive celebration of the redeeming work of Christ. Until the third century, Good Friday was observed only by a solemn fast; there seem to have been no special liturgical observances. Maundy Thursday became a separate celebration only when the movement toward historicizing the year was well under way in the fifth century. The point that needs to be remembered, then, is that the cross and the resurrection belong together. Each without the other is not only incomplete but seriously misleading. Without the resurrection the cross is defeat and the triumph of death; without the cross, the resurrection is unreal and irrelevant to the human condition. In the cross we see triumph; in the resurrection we still see Jesus' wounds. This is clear in the oldest approaches to Good Friday. When it became a separate observance, it was not, as the ancient Good Friday hymns make clear, a day of death, defeat, and desolation. Rather, in the death was victory, in the defeat was triumph. Christ died, but with that death, death died, and its lasting grip was broken. A dramatic encounter was enacted between God and the ancient enemy, between the forces of life and the forces of death, and death by winning lost the war. St. Ephrem, a deacon (d. 373), wrote of Christ,

> Death slew him by means of the body which he had assumed, but that same body proved to be the weapon with which he conquered death. Concealed beneath the cloak of his humanity, his godhead engaged death in combat; but in slaying our Lord, death itself was slain. It was able to kill natural human life, but was itself killed by the life that is above the nature of mortals.[57]

Death and life are paradoxically and mystically mingled.

> At length death came upon Eve....Thus the mother of all living became the source of death for every living creature. But in her stead Mary grew up, a new vine in place of the old. Christ, the new life, dwelt within her. When death, with its customary impudence, came foraging for her mortal fruit, it encountered its own destruction in the hidden life that fruit

contained. All unsuspecting, it swallowed him up, and in so doing released life and set free a multitude of humanity.[58]

More familiar perhaps is the hymn *Pange lingua gloriosi* by Venantius Fortunatus (530–609):

> Sing, my tongue, the glorious battle;
>   Of the mighty conflict sing;
> Tell the triumph of the victim,
>   To his cross thy tribute bring.
> Jesus Christ, the world's Redeemer,
>   From that cross now reigns as King.[59]

Fortunatus in another hymn, *Vexilla regis prodeunt,* wrote of the cross as sign of triumph.

> The royal banners forward go,
> The cross shines forth in mystic glow
> Where he through whom our flesh was made,
> In that same flesh our ransom paid.
>
> Fulfilled is all that David told
> In true prophetic song of old;
> How God the nations' King should be,
> For God is reigning from the tree.
>
> O tree of beauty, tree most fair,
> Ordained those holy limbs to bear,
> Gone is thy shame, each crimsoned bough
> Proclaims the King of glory now.
>
> Blest tree, whose chosen branches bore
> The wealth that did the world restore,
> The price which none but he could pay
> To spoil the spoiler of his prey.[60]

Similar ideas are expressed in the proper preface of the cross for passiontide:

> ...we...offer thanks and praise to you, O Lord, holy Father, through Christ our Lord; who set the salvation of the human race upon the tree of the cross, so that, whence death arose, thence life also might rise again, and that he, who by a tree once overcame, might likewise by a tree be overcome; through Christ our Lord.[61]

Satan, the tempter, who by a tree in Eden once overcame humanity, is overcome by the cross of Christ. The cross on Calvary replaces the tree in the garden: the tree that was for humanity the tree of death is replaced by a new and more potent tree of life. So the cross was seen devotionally as giving off a "mystic glow" and was seen in visions as exalted and bejeweled and shining with heavenly splendor.

The *Pange lingua* sings to the cross,

> Faithful cross! above all other,
>   One and only noble tree!
> None in foliage, none in blossom,
>   None in fruit thy peer may be:
> Sweetest wood and sweetest iron!
>   Sweetest weight is hung on thee,
>
> Bend thy boughs, O tree of glory!
>   Thy relaxing sinews bend;
> For awhile the ancient rigor
>   That thy birth bestowed, suspend;
> And the King of heavenly beauty
>   Gently on thine arms extend.[62]

The wood of the cross becomes pliant, its hardness softens; the instrument of death becomes a life-giving mother nursing at her breast her new child. (John Mason Neale's translation emphasizes the maternal character of the cross: "And the King of heavenly beauty / On thy bosom gently tend.") On the cross, the instrument of death, life is born.

The same paradoxical unity of death and resurrection is found in the sermons of the early teachers of the church. Ephrem says with marvelous vigor and bold imagery,

> Death trampled our Lord underfoot, but he in his turn treated death as a highroad for his own feet. He submitted to it, enduring it willingly, because by this means he would be able to destroy death in spite of itself. Death had its own way when our Lord went out from Jerusalem carrying his cross; but when with a loud cry from that cross he summoned the dead from the underworld, death was powerless to prevent it.

> We give glory to you, Lord, who raised up your cross to span the jaws of death like a bridge by which souls might pass from the region of the dead to the land of the living.[63]

St. Theodore the Studite (d. 826 in Asia Minor) praises the cross yet more extravagantly:

> How precious the gift of the Cross, how splendid to contemplate! In the Cross there is no mingling of good and evil, as in the tree of paradise. It is wholly beautiful to behold and good to taste. The fruit of this tree is not death but life, not darkness but light. This tree does not cast us out of paradise, but opens the way for our return.
>
> This was the tree on which Christ, like a king on a chariot, destroyed the devil, the lord of death, and freed the human race from his tyranny. This was the tree upon which the Lord, like a brave warrior wounded in hands, feet, and side, healed the wound of sin that the evil serpent had inflicted upon our nature. A tree once caused our death, but now a Tree brings life. Once deceived by a tree, we have now repelled the cunning serpent by a Tree. What an astonishing transformation! That death should become life, that decay should become immortality, that shame should become glory! Well might the holy Apostle exclaim: *Far be it from me to glory except in the cross of our Lord Jesus Christ, by which the world has been crucified to me and I to the world!* The supreme wisdom that flowered on the Cross has shown the folly of worldly wisdom's pride. The knowledge of all good, which is the fruit of the cross, has cut away the shoots of wickedness.[64]

To be faithful to the original tradition, we must understand and preserve the unity of the cross and the resurrection as one event. The traditional rites for Holy Week and Easter preserve in a dramatic and powerful way this unified view of the work of Christ.

The Sunday of the Passion, "Palm" Sunday, introduces the yearly experience of the death and resurrection of Christ. The service begins with a commemoration of Jesus' entrance into Jerusalem. The people gather, preferably in a place other than the church building to help them understand that they are the crowd that met Jesus outside the city. Palms are distributed. The processional Gospel for the year is read. A solemn thanksgiving, which parallels the thanksgiving in Holy Baptism and in the Eucharist, is said, blessing the palms and those who carry them; and the procession goes forth singing the traditional hymn, "All glory, laud, and honor." Then, the procession completed, the day's liturgy begins, and its emphasis is on the Passion. The memorable procession with palms with its Gospel telling of the triumphal entry, it must be remembered, is but a dramatic prelude to the service of the day, and the real name of the day is the Sunday of the Passion; "Palm Sunday" is but a nickname.[65] Through the Middle Ages into the second third of the twentieth century, the Gospel for the mass on this Sunday was the Matthew Passion (Matthew 26–27); in the present lectionary the Gospel is a reading of one of the three Synoptic passion accounts. That long review of the whole Passion, from the supper to the burial, is the theme of the day and the week. We are reminded that we are not simply walking through the week with Jesus, with Sunday as the remembrance of the triumphal entrance into Jerusalem, but rather we are meditating devotionally, liturgically, dramatically upon the whole saving event. So the whole passion narrative is read on Sunday and again on Friday. We are thus warned against a compartmentalized understanding of this great story.

Monday, Tuesday, and Wednesday of Holy Week have traditionally been treated as ordinary days of Passiontide and do not traditionally have a separate, distinct character. But the rites of Maundy Thursday, Good Friday, and Easter Eve are the most important of the entire year, for in them is commemorated the event by which the world and all that is in it have been transformed. Those three days, the sacred triduum (the holy "three days"), are the central celebration of Christianity, the high holy days of the new covenant. All that comes before, Christmas and Epiphany, and all that comes after, the season after Pentecost looking toward the final appearing of Christ, comes to a focus here and has its concentrated expression in these three days.

On Thursday, anciently, penitents were reconciled in preparation for the celebration of Easter. The Lutheran rites have a form of this practice in the extended absolution that begins the Maundy Thursday liturgy, answering the extended confession of the Ash Wednesday liturgy. The Gospel for the day gives the new commandment to love one another, enacted in the washing of feet that follows, as the participants in the service are about to witness once more the boldest expression of love the world has ever known, the cross. The service concludes with stripping the altar of its linens, paraments, ornaments, while Psalm 22 is sung. It is a dramatically powerful action, and the people leave the darkened church in silence. The commemoration of the institution of the Holy Communion becomes almost secondary to the great and compelling theme of love as it is known in the new covenant, sealed by the blood of Christ.

On Friday, an austere service has been traditional. It begins with the entrance of the ministers in silence and the praying of the collect for the day. The Gospel is the Passion according to St. John (18–19). The broad and inclusive intercessions are in the form of an ancient bidding prayer. A large, rough-hewn cross is then brought into the church, and before it, in some churches still, the shattering experience of hearing the reproaches takes place, in which God is heard condemning the church for its faithlessness in the face of such overwhelming love. An adaptation of this experience is given in Johann Heermann's powerful hymn "Ah, Holy Jesus":

> Who was the guilty, who brought this upon thee?
> Alas, my treason, Jesus, hath undone thee.
> 'Twas I, Lord Jesus, I it was denied thee;
> I crucified thee.[66]

Saturday, the Great Sabbath, is the supreme day of rest. As on the seventh day God rested from the work of creation, so on the seventh day God rested from the work of redemption. But after the setting of the sun, the church gathers to begin the great watch for the signs of the dawn of Easter, the day of resurrection.

The Great Vigil of Easter is the culmination of the entire liturgical proclamation of the church. The grand service gathers its imagery from the archetypal symbolism of the religious impulse of all peoples of the earth as it moves from darkness to light, from chaos to order, from death to life. The most ancient symbols in the history of religion are here: fire and water and food. In the Exsultet and throughout the service we are reminded that the entire universe is involved in this saving action. As the fall corrupted all creation, destroying the relationship between people and God, people and each other, people and animals, people and the soil (see Genesis 3:14–19),[67] so the restoration cleansed all the world. The seventeenth-century mystical poet Henry Vaughan (1622–1695) wrote of Adam, "He drew the curse upon the world, and cracked / The whole frame with his fall";[68] and Fortunatus's *Pange lingua* sings of Christ the second Adam,

> He endures the nails, the spitting,
> Vinegar, and spear, and reed;
> From that holy body broken

Blood and water forth proceed:
Earth, and stars, and sky, and ocean
By that flood from stain are freed.[69]

There is in that hymn a profound understanding of sin and a correspondingly profound understanding of redemption.

The first part of the vigil centers around light, the second part explores the mystery of water in all its richness, and in the third part the essential elements of a meal, bread and wine, become vehicles for renewal and life. One of the psalms associated with Easter is Psalm 114, *In exitu Israel de Egypto,* "When Israel went out from Egypt." The Latin combines paradoxically the ideas of deliverance and of the exile in the wilderness that followed. Moreover, the word "exile" derives from *ex* ("out of") and the Latin root *salire* ("to leap"), the same etymological root that produces the word "exult."[70] Thus etymologically the exile of Lent and the Exsultet of Easter are two faces of one event.

With that grand and powerful and indeed overwhelming service of the Easter Vigil, the celebration of Easter begins and continues not just the following day nor even for a week but for a "week of weeks," the great Fifty Days (the original meaning of "the Pentecost"). Thus the forty days of Lenten discipline are balanced by the fifty days of rejoicing; preparation is more than matched by fulfillment. In this expanded view of Easter, from a day to a week to fifty days, there is a subtle echo of ancient Judaism. The Jubilee year occurred every "sabbath of years." The Book of Leviticus records the law:

> You shall count off seven weeks of years, seven times seven years, so that the period of seven weeks of years gives forty-nine years. Then you shall have the trumpet sounded loud; on the tenth day of the seventh month — on the day of atonement — you shall have the trumpet sounded throughout all your land. And you shall hallow the fiftieth year and you shall proclaim liberty throughout the land to all its inhabitants. (Leviticus 25:8–10)

(The last phrase is inscribed on the Liberty Bell in Philadelphia.) The jubilee year was a sign of the peace of paradise. Thus, together with the sabbatical year, the "sabbath of the land" every seven years ensures that the land rests from cultivation and so participates in honoring the Creator. The whole land — all the inhabitants of the land and the soil itself — share in the peace of the sabbath, a sign of perfection and the absolute sovereignty of God. All slavery is abolished and freedom is proclaimed throughout the land. The parallel with Easter is clear.

Such an understanding of Easter extending fifty days is essential. All eight Sundays of Easter, including the Day of Pentecost, are of a character notably different from the other Sundays of the year, for they are an extended celebration of the paschal mystery. The Sundays of Easter set the tone and character of all the Sundays of the year, bringing gladness and life and hope to every week of the year, for Sunday is more than a weekly remembrance of the resurrection; it is also the eighth day, the sign of the new creation, already begun among us. These Sundays of Easter help to show why it is important for Christians to gather on the first day of the week to celebrate the paschal mystery week by week on the day of resurrection.

The weeks of Easter explore the Alleluia, the Easter song par excellence, the song the angels sing in heaven (Tobit 13:22; Revelation 19:6). The early teachers of the church found it full of mystic significance. In the Middle Ages the word was treated almost as if it were a person, put away and buried before Lent and resurrected with great rejoicing when Easter began. Easter hymns and texts abound with repetitions of "alleluia."

> It is a cry of heavenly joy. In this sense the first Christians received the word and used it as a song of joy, of heaven, and of resurrection. It is embedded in the oldest structure of the liturgy; centuries pass by as it rises from the lips of Christians, and it will continue to be sung until the end of time, and then forever in the heavenly Jerusalem.[71]

Weekly through the year and daily throughout Easter the Alleluia preaches a deep and lasting joy. During the Easter season the church is too joyful to kneel. Flowers and plants abound to show the new life. The paschal candle burns by the altar throughout the fifty days to show the presence of the risen Christ in his church.

With Easter lasting seven weeks, one need not pack the entire resurrection Gospel into the sermon on Easter Day. Indeed, in past lectionaries, the Gospels appointed for that day (in medieval lectionaries, Mark 16:1–18, and in the twentieth-century revisions, John 20:1–10) each tell only of the fearful and unnerving encounter with the empty tomb. The Gospel for the Easter Vigil, Matthew 28:1–10 (originally 28:1–7), does present an appearance of the risen Jesus, but it is a startling one. As the women run from the tomb, "Suddenly Jesus was there in their path" (Matthew 28:9 NEB), and he says, "See you in Galilee." We begin the first week of Easter by looking into the empty tomb. It is sufficient for this day to ponder the fact that Jesus was not where they had left the body, a fact that upsets all our expectations and securities.

The Second Sunday of Easter is the Sunday of St. Thomas, and the Gospel is the same for all three years. The theme is the struggle to believe the impossible message of resurrection. We are invited to join Thomas's cry of recognition and faith, "My Lord and my God."

The Third Sunday of Easter sets before us an appearance of the risen Jesus: in Year A it is the appearance of Jesus to two disciples at Emmaus (Luke 24:13–35); in Year B it is his appearance to the Eleven in Jerusalem (Luke 24:36b–48); in Year C it is Jesus' "third appearance" in St. John's account, to the disciples by the Sea of Tiberias (John 21:1–19).

The Fourth Sunday of Easter presents the image of the Good Shepherd. The Gospels for each year are drawn from John 10. In this lovely image is distilled the essence of the cross-resurrection event: the selfless concern of the Shepherd; the death of the Shepherd who lays down his life for his sheep in the ultimate expression of his love; the divine claim ("I am the Good Shepherd," as opposed to the wicked shepherds who are only out for themselves) shown in the resurrection, for death could not hold the Son of God; and a view of the end and of the consummation when there will be "one fold and one Shepherd." Old Testament and New are bound together, David and the Son of David, God the Shepherd and Jesus the Shepherd, this life and the next.

The Fifth Sunday of Easter presents general pictures of life and growth. In Year A, the many rooms in the Father's house (John 14:1–14) suggest the richness of the new life that is offered to us. In Year B, we learn the importance of remaining attached to Christ the vine who is the source of life (John 15:1–8). Cyril of Alexandria wrote,

> The Lord calls himself the vine and those united to him branches in order to teach us how much we shall benefit from our union with him, and how important it is for us to remain in his love. By receiving the Holy Spirit, who is the bond of union between us and Christ our Savior, those who are joined to him, as branches are to a vine, share in his own nature.

From Christ and in Christ, we have been reborn through the Spirit in order to bear the fruit of life; not the fruit of our old, sinful life but the fruit of a new life founded upon our faith in him and our love for him. Like branches growing from a vine, we now draw our life from Christ, and we cling to his holy commandment in order to preserve this life.[72]

In Year C we learn the new commandment of love (John 13:31–35). St. Augustine explains:

Love does indeed renew the one who hears, or rather obeys its command; but only that love which Jesus distinguished from a natural love by the qualification, "As I have loved you." This is the kind of love that renews us. When we love as he loved us, we become new, heirs of the covenant and singers of the new song.[73]

The new song is, of course, "Alleluia."

The Sixth Sunday of Easter turns our attention toward the expectation of the gift of the Spirit, for the Easter proclamation is not yet complete. Year A combines the praise of the Spirit of truth with the command to love (John 14:15–21); Year B (John 15:9–17) emphasizes love with the subtle hint of the Spirit: the Father will give you "whatever you ask in my name" (v. 16); Year C tells of the promise of the Spirit and of the gift of peace (John 14:23–29).

Ascension day, forty days after Easter, marks a further stage in the proclamation of the Pascha. It is the last of the resurrection appearances, but Easter still continues. The season thus begins and ends with the absence of Jesus. On Easter Day we see only the empty tomb; from Ascension Day on we see him no more. It is, however, not that he is gone; it is that he is beyond us.

The Seventh Sunday of Easter each year draws its Gospel from Jesus' high priestly prayer of John 17. Thus we are reminded of the function of the ascended Jesus as intercessor, praying for his church, for us, even now and to the end of time. We can no longer see him, yet his work continues more urgently, more universally than during his earthly ministry when he was confined to space and time.

The feast of Pentecost, the fiftieth day of Easter, concludes the paschal celebration and is the culmination of the week of weeks. Like Christmas and Easter Day, this third great festival of the year has its appointed vigil. Vespers is appropriately sung Saturday evening to mark the beginning of this last of the fifty days and as an

echo of the Great Vigil of Easter. Pentecost is thus to be understood
not as a separate event but rather as part of the whole proclamation of Easter. The Spirit gives the church life; it is, as Pius XII
described the Spirit, the "soul of the church." As Easter began with
the water of baptism, so it ends with the living water of the Spirit,
all part of one act of initiation and incorporation into the life of the
body of Christ. St. Cyril of Jerusalem taught the newly baptized
under his instruction:

> This is a new kind of water, a living, leaping water, welling
> up for those who are worthy. But why did Christ call the
> grace of the Spirit water? Because all things are dependent
> upon water.... [74]

In the Fourth Gospel, water is symbolic of the Spirit. We recall that
on Ash Wednesday the ashes are symbolic of water, too, but the
ashes are a dry and penitential symbol. So that distant beginning
of our preparation for Easter and its culmination at Pentecost are
subtly bound together.

The emphasis of the Gospels for the Fifth and Sixth Sundays of
Easter is on love rather than life, and at first this may seem odd.
The traditional collect for Easter Day, from the Gregorian sacramentary, used in the earlier Roman, Episcopal, and Lutheran rites,
also seems to be less clearly focused on the resurrection than one
might expect:

> Almighty God, who through thine only-begotten Son Jesus
> Christ hast overcome death, and opened unto us the gate of
> everlasting life: We humbly beseech thee, that as thou dost
> put into our minds good desires, so by thy continual help we
> may bring the same to good effect; through the same, Jesus
> Christ our Lord.... [75]

The Lutheran liturgical scholar Luther D. Reed quoted approv-
ingly the opinion of the authors of the *Tutorial Prayer Book* that
"the petition of this collect 'has the merit of associating a consis-
tent Christian life with the Resurrection, but seems inadequate to
the greatest festival of the Christian year.' "[76] This collect may not
make its point as clearly as we might like, but it is a typical understatement in the quiet but profound manner of the classic prayers
of the church. Ethical renewal is a prominent point of the Easter
proclamation in the preaching and teaching of the formative years
of the church, and so it is no wonder that this theme became embedded in the principal collect of the church year. *Lutheran Book*

of Worship preserves the traditional collect; the Roman and Episcopal rites have replaced this Gregorian collect with one from the earlier Gelasian sacramentary and the Missale Gallicanum vetus that has a different petition:

> Almighty God, who through your only-begotten Son Jesus Christ overcame death and opened to us the gate of everlasting life: Grant that we, who celebrate with joy the day of the Lord's resurrection, may be raised from the death of sin by your life-giving Spirit.[77]

The new life means exactly that: a renewed way of living in which desire and action are one. It is in our midst a sign of the perfection of heaven, as Peter Abelard's hymn declares:

> Wish and fulfillment are not severed there,
> Nor do things prayed for come short of the prayer.[78]

Theodor Gaster said of Passover and Pentecost:

> In the Jewish tradition, the deliverance from Egypt is important only because it paved the way to Sinai — that is, to Israel's voluntary acceptance of its special and distinctive mission; and what the Seder narrative relates is the whole story of how Israel moved progressively from darkness to light, from the ignorance and shame of idolatry to the consciousness and glory of its high adventure.[79]

That movement, from Passover to Pentecost, from deliverance to acceptance of the Law, is also basic to the Christian Passover. In itself Easter is not complete until the paschal mystery is shown in all that Christians say and do. Resurrection has meaning for the world to come, of course; it also has meaning for this life now and requires a renovation of life *here* to prepare for and reflect life *there*. St. Augustine preached:

> *Sing to the Lord a new song.* Look, you tell me, I am singing. Yes indeed, you are singing; you are singing clearly, I can hear you. But make sure that your life does not contradict your words. Sing with your voices, your hearts, your lips, and your lives. *Sing to the Lord a new song.*
>
> ...If you desire to praise him, then live what you express. Live good lives, and you yourselves will be his praise.[80]

Again Augustine said:

...As I have loved you.

This is the kind of love that renews us. When we love as he loved us we become new, heirs of the new covenant and singers of the new song.

...His object in loving us, then, was to enable us to love each other.[81]

The resurrection is not a past event, but it is a contemporary experience as we renew our lives and our love for one another. It is a continuous experience that cannot be confined to a single moment of time but that lasts throughout all generations.[82]

The Easter liturgy, then, provides the experience of a single mighty event: the dying and rising of Jesus Christ. We prepare to hear it again and learn it anew by hearing the Ash Wednesday reminder of our mortality and by the Lenten review of the benefits and obligations of baptism. We experience it as we commemorate the death, the resurrection, the ascension, and the sending of the Spirit, successively yet as parts of one single entity. And we experience that new life as we seek to obey the new commandment to love as we have been loved by Christ, whose work we celebrate and proclaim.

The paschal mystery of death and resurrection and giving the Spirit is paralleled in Holy Baptism, by which we drown in the water, emerge new people, and receive the anointing of the Spirit.[83] The mystery is set forth in the Holy Communion, in which we "proclaim the Lord's death until he comes" (1 Corinthians 11:26). And the Eucharist is the weekly celebration of the paschal mystery and our participation in it each time we "do this."

Baptism and Holy Communion, then, bind the parts of the mystery together and enable us to renew the experience daily and relive the experience of our forebears in the faith, Jewish as well as Christian. The Jerusalem Catecheses explain:

Let no one imagine that Baptism consists only in the forgiveness of sins and in the grace of adoption. Our baptism is not like the baptism of John, which conferred only the forgiveness of sins. We know perfectly well that baptism, besides washing away our sins and bringing us the gift of the Holy Spirit, is a symbol of the sufferings of Christ. This is why St. Paul exclaims: *Do you not know that when we were baptized into Christ Jesus we were, by that very action, sharing his death? By baptism we went with him into the tomb.*[84]

An ancient Easter homily proclaimed:

> Here then is the grace conferred by these heavenly myster-
> ies, the gift which Easter brings, the most longed-for feast of
> the year: here are the beginnings of creatures newly formed:
> children born from the life-giving font of holy Church, born
> anew with the simplicity of little ones, and crying out with
> the evidence of a clean conscience.... Through the repeated
> celebration of the sacred mysteries they receive the spiritual
> nourishment of the sacraments.[85]

And St. Basil teaches:

> There is in baptism an image both of death and of life, the
> water being the symbol of death, the Spirit giving the pledge
> of life.

> ...As a preparation for our life after the resurrection, our
> Lord tells us in the gospel how we should live here and now.
> He teaches us to be peaceable, long-suffering, undefiled by
> desire for pleasure, and detached from worldly wealth. In this
> way we can achieve, by our own free choice, the kind of life
> that will be natural in the world to come.[86]

So in the liturgy of Easter we learn of Christ and of ourselves, of
what is past and passing and to come. All this, the fullness of life
as God intends it and the price that was paid so that we might have
it, comes together in the paschal mystery. Small wonder, then, that
Easter is called "the queen of feasts."

The Culmination of the Year

Through the long stretch of Sundays after Pentecost, each Sunday
explores some aspect of the new life we are called to live. Then, in
the late fall, when in the northern latitudes of the temperate zone in
the Northern Hemisphere, the days grow short and a chill gloom
settles over the land, the final Sundays after Pentecost turn to a
consideration of the end of the world and the day of judgment.
This theme flows naturally and inevitably into the Sundays of Advent. There is no break. It is not as if the church's year begins again
looking to the birth of Jesus, for Christmas is properly understood
as coming not at the beginning but toward the conclusion of the
church's year. In liturgical understanding, Christmas functions as

the proclamation of the parousia, a confident declaration that he who came once in humility as an infant Jew and who comes to his people daily as Lord of the church, will come in glory at the end of time as King of creation. The fact of his first coming, remembered at Christmas, is the promise and guarantee of his final appearing.

There are certain striking similarities between the observance of Easter and of Christmas in the church's calendar. (1) In the medieval calendar the three pre-Lenten Sundays (Septuagesima, Sexagesima, Quinquagesima) corresponded to the last three Sundays after Pentecost (also counted after Trinity), which were seen as a unit focusing on signs of the end, the judgment of the world, and the parable of the wise and foolish maidens (Matthew 25:1–13), made memorable by the hymn *Wachet auf*, "Wake, Awake, for Night Is Flying."[87] (2) The days of Lent correspond to the days of Advent, two preparatory seasons, each with its own theme but each finding fulfillment in the feast for which it prepares. (3) The final week of Lent, Holy Week, corresponds to the final seven days of Advent, a less clearly defined time but identifiable nonetheless. Each of the last seven days of Advent has its proper antiphon to the Magnificat, the Gospel Canticle of Vespers. They are the wonderful "O antiphons," beginning on December 17 with O *Sapientia* ("O Wisdom") and continuing "O Adonai," "O Root of Jesse," "O Key of David," "O Dayspring," "O King of the nations," "O Emmanuel." The antiphons have been made familiar, although they are rearranged, in the Advent hymn, "O Come, O Come, Emmanuel." (4) The transitional Great Vigil of Easter corresponds to the transition from expectation to fulfillment on the Vigil of Christmas, Christmas Eve. Both vigils are times of intense preparation and anticipation, watching and waiting. Both reveal the heart of the celebration: the passage from hope to fulfillment. (5) Easter, the fifty-day season of rejoicing, corresponds to Christmas, the twelve-day season of rejoicing. (6) The fulfillment of Easter in the Day of Pentecost, followed by a green season of general time, corresponds to the fulfillment of Christmas in the Epiphany, followed by a green season of general time.

Yet there are differences. Lent, in medieval times, acquired a penitential character, and this somberness was applied to Advent also in such ways as restricting the use of flowers, forbidding the use of the organ, singing the litany in procession. Penitence centered on Christ's passion is the wrong mood for Lent; penitence is surely the wrong mood for Advent. Joy belongs to both seasons; both are times of serious preparation with an increasing intensity of renewal. Lent is a time of personal preparation, originally a preparation for baptism and now a renewal of baptism and life. Advent is a time of ecclesial preparation, having to do with the end, the consummation, which is celebrated at Christmas.

The life we know and live is unsatisfying. Advent therefore is characterized by a longing for deliverance from the built-in boundedness of human existence, from oppression and from repression, from persecution, from meaninglessness and emptiness, from frustration. This deep-seated longing that wells up in nearly every human life is the first characteristic of Advent.

A second characteristic of Advent is the mystery of the coming Deliverer. The season abounds in awe, fear, wonder, and, most of all, a deep and solemn excitement. The Song of Songs asks a question appropriate to Advent:

> Who is this coming up from the wilderness
> like a column of smoke
> from burning myrrh and frankincense
> of all the powdered spices that merchants bring?
>> (3:6 REB)

Another evocative expression of the mystery of God's coming is found in one of the finest responsories in the church's treasury, the responsory for Matins on the First Sunday in Advent.

> Watching from afar,
> I see the power of God coming,
> and a cloud covering the whole earth.
>> Go out to meet him and say,
>> Tell us if you are the one
>> who is to reign over your people Israel?
>
> All peoples of the earth, all children of dust,
> rich and poor alike,
>> go out to meet him and say,
> Shepherd of Israel, hear us,
> you lead Joseph like a flock:
>> Tell us if you are the one.
>
> Open wide the gates, you princes,
> let the King of glory enter,
> who is to reign over your people Israel.
> Watching from afar,
> I see the power of God coming,

and a cloud covering the whole earth.
Go out to meet him and say,
Tell us if you are the one
who is to reign over your people Israel.[88]

Here is the fearful hesitancy of a longing people to identify the mysterious advancing power as the Messiah they long for. Here is a careful desire not to be deceived by confusing what we want to see with what is seen. Here is a protective unwillingness to make hasty but mistaken identifications. It is a remarkable expression for inclusion in a liturgical rite. A characteristic attitude of Advent as of all authentic devotion is this scrupulous care not to claim too much too quickly. There is a hesitant restraint that will not let us too quickly declare, "Jesus is the Messiah," "Jesus is God," "Jesus is the one who is to come." If we are honest, we may admit that since the first Christmas and since the first Easter, the world, despite these wonderful stories, seems fundamentally unchanged. How then is it possible still to claim, "Jesus is the longed for King who is to reign"? Only when we first face unwelcome and disturbing facts with a determined honesty can we then move on to make our own the church's affirmations of faith. Surrounded by doubts, aware of the uncertainties, knowing all the reasons that militate against it, the church nonetheless can risk the bold claim that an infant born in Bethlehem is the mighty God.

It is such honesty that makes the liturgy worthy of attention. The church's liturgy is compelling because of the way in which it explores, re-creates, and seeks for the meanings in human experience of the divine.[89] It is valuable because it explores the diversity, complexity, and strangeness of that experience. It is valuable because it pursues its exploration without bullying or apologizing. It is valuable because it recreates the texture of that experience. In liturgy mortals look at human life with all the vulnerability, honesty, and penetration they can command and dramatize their insights in such a way as to invite others to share in the exploration and affirmation. The sense of coherence and unity that the liturgy achieves is accomplished not by ignoring but rather by acknowledging and expressing the complexities and apparent contradictions of human life before God. It is founded on the facts of experience. The liturgy does not deal primarily with ideas and events but rather with the way in which human beings may come to terms with ideas and events. It is to be evaluated not only by the doctrine it expresses but also by its coherence, sensitivity, depth, richness, and tough-mindedness.[90]

The Christian year, therefore, while setting before the church the model of the Christian life is not simply rehearsing familiar ideas. The goal to which the grand and continuing story points, its culmination, lies still ahead of us. The appearing for which we long and hope is not yet known completely. The old story is not yet old, for it is heard as promise.

The church year, in its presentation of the life of Christ is like an epic poem, and, like an epic, the church year must be retrospective, assimilating a vast amount of the relevant past, but if it is to maintain its life it cannot lack some essential power of anticipation as well. One of the features of an authentic masterpiece is its capacity to renew itself, to endure the loss of some kinds of immediate relevance while still answering the most important questions humans can ask, including new ones they are just learning how to frame.[91]

Advent builds toward Christmas. The first Sunday announces the theme: the king is coming. Only the Lutheran rite preserves (and only as an alternative) the medieval Gospel for this Sunday. It is a most interesting and significant selection. It is what we think of as the Palm Sunday story, the triumphal entry of Jesus into Jerusalem — and at first sight that story seems disconcertingly out of place here at the beginning of Advent. If the church year is a chronological re-telling of the life of Christ, this Gospel surely does not belong. But medieval people were not foolish, and they knew what they were doing when they appointed this Gospel for this Sunday. Its thrilling announcement stirs the church, 'Your king comes to you!" The cry gathers the themes of coronation from Ascension Day and the festival of Christ the King, the kingship theme pondered in the Passion Gospels for the Sunday of the Passion and Good Friday ("the king of the Jews," Pilate wrote), the assertion of Zechariah of the king's arrival (9:9), the personal emphasis in the relationship between this king and his people. The threefold coming which medieval devotion identified is gathered and presented in this announcement: your king comes to Bethlehem to be born in the humility of his incarnation; your king comes to you daily in word and sacrament and prayer and meditation and in other people; your king comes to you at the end of time to gather his own into the kingdom. The verbs need not be given in the past, the present, and the future tense ("came," "comes," "will come") for liturgy gathers all time into a contemporary experience. Bethlehem and today and the end become one experience.

The second and third Sundays in Advent focus on John the Baptist, the prophet of the Advent and the forerunner of the Messiah. The fourth Sunday focuses on the Virgin Mary in her expectation of motherhood. But these are not simply historical figures and moments. The gospel of the triumphal entry has taught us how to hear and read the other gospels of the season. The past is prologue to and promise of a greater appearing to come.

In the darkness of Christmas Eve light breaks forth. Like the Easter Vigil, it is a night of transition from darkness and fear to light and hope, from oppression to freedom. The promise of Christmas, that Christ will come again, is announced in the three-fold celebration of the birth: the mass of the angels at midnight, when the heavenly chorus that sang at creation is heard again amid the din of the world, announcing the new creation; the mass of the shepherds at dawn, when the first witnesses to the event, the poor and outcast shepherds leave their flocks (anticipating Peter and James and John who were to leave their nets to follow Jesus) and go to Bethlehem; and the mass of the world during the day, when the prologue to St. John's Gospel is read, unfolding the great mystery of the incarnation. The tripartite celebration ponders first the wondrous event itself, then the ethical dimension and demand of the event, and finally the theological reflection upon its significance.

The season of promise culminates in the Epiphany, the mystery par excellence. The mysterious magi bring their symbolic gifts and offer them to the holy child.

> Sacred gifts of mystic meaning:
> Incense doth their God disclose,
> Gold the king of kings proclaimeth,
> Myrrh his sepulchre foreshows.[92]

These shadowy astrologers, travelling vaguely "from the east" with their strange gifts, symbolize more than we can ever say, more than we can ever know. The fascination of this wonderful time is that we cannot know it all. Loose ends remain, questions are left unanswered, new questions are provoked. Here in these wonderful stories we find the size and the depth of the Christian mystery. Jesus Christ is not just a flat and familiar character from an old book. He is a living person. We understand that we can never know another human being completely; how much less can we comprehend one who is both Son of God and son of the Virgin Mary?

Thus the church year, like the liturgy and like Scripture itself, takes what is familiar, for example Christmas, turns it toward the future, and reveals unexpected depths of promise. What seems like the beginning, set long ago in the distant past, is in fact a promise and guarantee of what is to come. We live always on the horizon of divine promise, and that perspective casts doubt on all our comfortable security here. We learn anew that we are at most resident aliens in a foreign land, "strangers and foreigners...seeking a homeland" (Hebrews 11:13–16) where God had prepared a city for us, Zion, our permanent and abiding home.

Chapter Six

ARCHITECTURE
Hallowing Space

Since the beginning of the human race, time, both the cycle of night and day as well as the passage of the seasons, has awakened profound responses in humanity. Space also, particularly specific places, can be a powerful expression of the presence of the divine. Particular locations provide physical contact with the past, a place where continuity is honored. Each person, the nonreligious as well as the religious, recognizes and honors particular places of private significance: a birthplace, the scenes of one's first love, the school one attended. The community also honors certain places: Ellis Island, Independence Hall, Plymouth Rock, the plain at Runnymede. For sensitive people, space is not homogeneous. Such people experience breaks, interruptions in the expanse of space. Some parts are qualitatively different from the rest.[1] "Take off your shoes," God said to Moses. "This is holy ground" (Exodus 3:5). Space is not everywhere the same.

Temples are thresholds, as Frank Kermode observes, always liminal.[2] Such structures are boundary buildings, located symbolically on the border. They represent the edge of this world and an opening onto the next.

For a believer, the church shares in a different space from the street on which it stands. The door that opens on the interior of the church actually signifies a solution of continuity. The threshold that separates the two spaces also indicates the distance between two modes of being, the profane and the religious. The threshold is the limit, the boundary, the frontier that distinguishes and opposes two worlds — and at the same time the paradoxical place where those worlds communicate,

142

where passage from the profane to the sacred world becomes possible.[3]

Temples are the threshold of another dimension, a door opening into vast new areas of experience. This is not to say, however, that temples must be placed in remote locations, for the borderland they represent and define is not geographical. Their architectural space is so charged with power that it dissolves space. Holy places are therefore understood as located at the center of the world. They are the organizing focus, the center, by which experience can be ordered and understood.[4]

A sacred place, understood as the center of the world, represents an image of the cosmos. A multiplicity of temples implies a multiplicity of centers, but such multiplication raises no difficulty for religious thought. "For it is not a matter of geometrical space, but of an existential and sacred space that has an entirely different structure, that admits of an infinite number of breaks and hence is capable of an infinite number of communications with the transcendent."[5] A Byzantine church is traditionally round or square, rather than long and rectangular like Western churches. Such a round or square shape suggests clearly this understanding of the holy place as the center of the surrounding cosmos.

Sacred places imply a continuity of holiness. Many Israelite sanctuaries had previously served as Canaanite holy places. Gideon was commanded by God to pull down his father's altar to Baal and to cut down the sacred pole that was beside it and to "build an altar to the Lord your God on top of the stronghold here" (Judges 6:25–32). Jerusalem itself was a place of great sanctity long before David established it as his capital and site of the temple; Melchizedek of [Jeru]Salem, priest of El Elyon, received a tithe of Abraham's possessions (Genesis 14:18–20). The French cathedral of Our Lady of Chartres is built on the site of a Gallo-Roman temple, which was itself erected on the site of an ancient Druid center. Long before Christians consecrated the site to Mary, a central feature of the Roman temple was a statue of the mother goddess.

A sacred place is, at least on a profound level, not chosen by human beings. It is merely discovered or received by those to whom its sacredness has been revealed.[6] Every sacred place therefore implies a revelation, an epiphany of the sacred that results in detaching a territory from the surrounding space and making it qualitatively different.[7] The holiness of a place may be apparent to all or at least to many who visit it, or the discovery of such a place of revelation may be a surprise, as it was for the fugitive Jacob: "Surely the Lord is in this place — and I did not know it!" (Genesis 28:16). In the absence of a direct vision or apprehension of the divine, some sign may reveal the sacredness of a place. Here something that does not belong to this world has manifested itself.[8] The sign may determine a course of conduct for a seeker, or it may indicate an orientation, a place or object around which experience is organized. Such an orientation may focus on a tree or a spring that promotes unexpected healing. Elsewhere a pillar may mark the place where heaven and earth were once experienced touching each other.

Any orientation implies acquiring a fixed point. A sacred place is a break in the apparent but deceptive homogeneity of experience, an opening that reveals the fixed point, the cultural axis for future orientation.[9] A sacred place is an irruption into conscious experience of that deep reality that underlies the vast surrounding expanse of everyday life. It is an outcropping of the bedrock on which life and meaning is founded.

One such fixed point that gives orientation is a mountain.[10] A mountain can be seen as a microcosm of the universe, a small world revealing the mysteries of the greater world, and therefore a sacred place. What is now known as Mount Rushmore, with the faces of four presidents carved in its rock, was (and remains) a sacred mountain to the Native Americans from the region. Mount Zion remains a holy place to Judaism and to Christianity, and Mount Gerizim was for a time a rival holy place in the Northern Kingdom of Israel. For Christianity one mountain, in reality a low hill, towers above all the rest; it is Mount Calvary, the place of crucifixion.

Temples have been understood as replicas of the holy mountain, a link between heaven and earth. Their summits reach into the heavens and their foundations descend deep into the lower regions. Uniting the sky and the earth and the deep foundations under the surface of the earth, mountains and the temples that replicate them form an axis by which temples represent infinite possibility, defying description, refusing confinement in one image or understanding: they are at once a border, a threshold, a navel, a mountain — all of these and none of these.

Another focus for orientation, common in the Hebrew Bible, is a stone. Such a stone, charged with symbolic meaning and power, not only marks a holy place but is often itself regarded as a holy object that participates in the holiness of the place it identifies. The fugitive Jacob, fleeing from his brother Esau, whose birthright and blessing he had stolen, encountered God in a barren and stony place (Genesis 28:10–17). He used a stone of the place for a pillow, and as he slept he had a dream-vision of a staircase with angels ascending and descending. God stood beside him to promise to give to the fugitive the land on which he was lying. The unsuspecting Jacob woke up with the knowledge of what he had not realized before: "The Lord is in this place!" Holy fear overtook him, and, afraid, he confessed, "How awesome is this place! This is none other than the house of God, and this is the gate of heaven." This, he discovered through his vision, was a liminal place, the threshold of heaven, a door through which God had come down to the earth. The stone under Jacob's head was an integral part of the revelation. It served as a mediator between him and God.

In many parts of the world one encounters remarkable gatherings of stones. Stonehenge comes to mind at once, its full meaning apparently lost to us; so do Zen Buddhist stone gardens such as the one at the Ryoanji Temple in Kyoto, in which it is not possible to see all of the stone outcroppings at once, preserving the sense of the elusiveness of the world and a most refined spirituality. In the Original Testament, stones are set up as memorials. Joshua had the twelve representatives of the tribes who crossed the Jordan each take a stone from the river bed and set it in Gilgal as a memorial of the passage (Joshua 4:1–3, 6–7, 8b–20); another tradition understood that the twelve stones were set in the bed of the river where the feet of the priests bearing the ark had stood while the people passed over into the promised land (Joshua 4:4–5, 8a, 9, 15–19). Samuel set up a stone between Mizpah and Jeshanah and named it Ebenezer (that is, "stone of help") to declare by its wordless witness, "Thus far the Lord has helped us" (1 Samuel 7:12) in the war against the Philistines. The name of the memorial stone has become the name of countless churches, meaningless to many for several generations, and is sung with blissful incomprehension in the hymn by Robert Robinson (1735–1790), "Come, Thou Font of Every Blessing," set to the dancing rhythm of the tune Nettleton,

> Here I raise my Ebenezer,
> Hither by thy help I'm come;
> And I hope, by thy good pleasure,
> Safely to arrive at home.[11]

The reference was apparently readily understood in the eighteenth century.

In the Original Testament stones are also erected as witnesses to an agreement or solemn covenant. Jacob "took stones and made a heap," shared a covenant meal with Laban beside it, and gave it a name in Aramaic (Laban's language) and in Hebrew (Jacob's language), "heap of witness" (Genesis 31:44–52). The heap of stones or pillar called Mizpah ("watchpost") was a testimony to the covenant and a reminder that God would watch between the two untrustworthy characters, oversee the contract, and guarantee that both parties fulfill what they had promised. It was, in fact, as if the stone heard the terms of the covenant and by its enduring permanence kept their promises alive and effective.

More explicitly, Joshua united Israel in the covenant at Shechem, wrote the people's promise of fidelity to God "in the book of the law of God," set up a large stone under the oak in the sanctuary of the Lord, and declared,

> See, this stone shall be a witness against us; for it has heard all the words of the Lord that he spoke to us; therefore it shall be a witness against you, if you deal falsely with your God. (Joshua 24:27)

Altars, under the Original Covenant, if they were not made of a simple mound of earth, were made of unhewn stone; that is, the stones were used in their natural state, unaltered by human hands (Exodus 20:24–25). God solemnly warned, "If you make for me an altar of stone, do not build it of hewn stones; for if you use a chisel upon it you profane it." That is to say, the stones had to be living stones, the life of which has not been interfered with by human art or invention.[12] Moreover, the commandment implies that the sacred cannot be constructed; it makes itself. Further, a deep fear of idolatry lay behind the prohibition against hewing the altar. The carved images of Canaanite religion were forbidden: "You shall make for yourselves no idols and erect no carved images or pillars, and you shall not place figured stones in your land, to worship them; for I am the Lord your God" (Leviticus 26:1; see Exodus 34:13–14). Indeed, even the sound of working and dressing stone was so suspect that when the time came for Solomon to build the temple, "The house was built with stone finished at the quarry, so that neither hammer nor ax nor any tool of iron was heard in the temple while it was being built" (1 Kings 6:7).

But what has moved civilization the most in its long history are stones that have been worked and shaped by human hands and piled with such vision and skill that they define and give shape

to space. Even when we have long grown accustomed to building stones and take them for granted, a noble building continues
to elicit admiration. Perhaps more than all the other buildings of
Western civilization, the cathedral of Chartres inspires wonder and
religious awe.

> I do not wonder, stones,
> You have withstood so long
> The strong wind and the snows.

> Were you not built to bear
> The winter and the wind
> That blows on the hill here?

> But you have borne so long
> Our eyes, our mortal eyes,
> And are not worn — [13]

The modern poet, with a sophisticated knowledge of architectural
history, can still be so moved by the magnificence of a thirteenth-
century French cathedral that he, like his distant forebears since
the dawn of the race, does not find it unnatural to address with
religious wonder the very stones with which the great church is
built and to inquire of them their source of such perduring power.
His address breaks off (the lines above are the complete poem) as
human words fail to enclose and express the holy adoration.

A religious shrine, however, no matter how magnificent the external face of the building may be, gains its value by what it
encloses. Attention may be diverted for a time to the facade, the
outer walls, the images gathered and grouped on or within the
building, the furniture of the shrine. The principal focus, however, is the sense of enclosure and spiritual concentration in that
sacred space, the ability to pin down in brief compass a range of
convincing moments of feeling and experience. No architecture, no
building can create a sacred space. One can only design and build
a structure to explicate, proclaim, and elucidate the place. What
makes a particular place holy is its association with revelation, insight, clarification, an epiphany. Enclosed there in that space is the
totality of the world.

Thus some sort of enclosure surrounding a sacred space is
among the most ancient known forms of sanctuary. Only the spiritually imperceptive understand such enclosures as human efforts
to confine the holy by setting limits beyond which sacredness must
not pass. Rather, such enclosures mark off and make visible a

particular place where a revelation of holiness was received and
declare the continued presence of a revelation within its bounds.
This of course does not imply that the holy could not reveal itself
elsewhere in a thousand locations. Only the spiritually deprived
could imagine that the holy could be subject to human control.
Moreover, "the sacred is always dangerous to anyone who comes
into contact with it unprepared."[14] Certain "gestures of approach"
are required — Moses' taking off his shoes, for example; for those
who come to the holy without due care expose themselves to perhaps fatal danger. Uzzah, who recklessly reached out his hand to
steady the ark of God and who was therefore struck dead, is a vivid
biblical example of such imperceptive lack of reverence (2 Samuel
6:6–7).

By means of an enclosure a larger place such as a city was organized, made an image of the cosmos, given a center and a focus.[15]
So in times of crisis such as an epidemic or a siege, the whole
population would assemble to go around the city walls to renew
and reinforce the walls' power as ramparts marking the limits of
the force of the attackers, enforcing the separation of those out
side the walls from those safe inside. A basic symbol of enclosure,
used throughout the world, is the circle, a line without beginning
and without end, pointing to the ultimate wholeness of life. Such
symbols of wholeness answer deep yearnings in the human spirit.
The circle forms the basic ground plan of many sacred and secular
buildings in nearly all civilizations. Everywhere, habitation under-
goes a process of sanctification because it is an image of the world,
and the world is a divine creation.[16] According to Plutarch:

> Romulus, having buried his brother Remus, together with his
> two foster-fathers, on the mount Remonia, set to building
> his city; and sent for men out of Tuscany, who directed him
> by sacred usages and written rules in all the ceremonies to
> be observed, as in a religious rite. First, they dug a round
> trench about that which is now the Comitium, or Court
> of Assembly, and into it solemnly threw the first-fruits of
> all things either good by custom or necessary by nature;
> lastly, every man taking a small piece of earth of the country
> from whence he came, they all threw in promiscuously to-
> gether. This trench they call, as they do the heavens, Mundus;
> making which their centre, they described the city in a cir-
> cle round it. Then the founder fitted to a plough a brazen
> ploughshare, and, yoking together a bull and a cow, drove

himself a deep line or furrow round the bounds; while the business of those that followed after was to see that whatever earth was thrown up should be turned all inwards toward the city; and not to let any clod lie outside. With this line they described the wall, and called it, by a contraction, Pomoerium, that is *post murum,* after or beside the wall; and where they designed to make a gate, there they took out the share, carried the plough over, and left a space; for which reason they consider the whole all as holy, except where the gates are; for had they adjudged them also sacred, they could not, without offence to religion, have given free ingress and egress for the necessaries of human life, some of which are themselves unclean.[17]

In seeming contrast to this description of the marking out of the circular boundary of the city, Plutarch reports that in the argument between Romulus and Remus about where the city was to rise, "Romulus chose what is called Roma Quadrata, or the Square Rome."[18] Rome is thus at once round and square, both descriptions suggesting the wholeness and scope of the city and its empire. The circle is without beginning or end; the four sides or four corners of the square are related to the four points of the compass and suggest a preliminary orientation before the work on the city began. An Indian myth tells that Brahma, standing on a huge lotus, looked to the four points of the compass to take his bearings before he began the work of creation. The circular ground plan of Rome, repeated in so many other cities, transformed a secular construction "into an ordered cosmos, a sacred place bound by its center to the other world."[19]

Solomon prayed,

> You have given command to build
> a temple on your holy mountain,
> and an altar in the city of your habitation,
> a copy of the holy tent that you
> prepared from the beginning.
>
> (Wisdom of Solomon 9:8)

The temple in Jerusalem is understood as a copy, an approximate reproduction of the celestial model created by God from the beginning of time. Christian churches were from early times understood to continue such symbolism: the church building reflects the heavenly Jerusalem, it reproduces paradise, and it is itself a model of the cosmos. Such an understanding is particularly clear in a Byzantine church. There the church represents the universe. The altar is paradise, which lay in the East. The royal door in the center of the iconostasis leading to the altar was also called the Door of Paradise. During Bright Week (Easter Week) this door remained open throughout the entire service, for as the Easter Canon and also the Western collect for Easter declare, Christ has "opened to us the gate of everlasting life." The West, on the contrary, is the realm of darkness, grief, death, the realm of the mansions of the dead who await the resurrection. The middle of the building is the earth. The four parts of the interior of the church symbolize the four cardinal directions, and the whole is surmounted by a dome, as the earth lies under the dome of the sky.[20]

The first buildings constructed for Christian worship, such as the rebuilt house at Dura Europos (A.D. 241–242), were patterned after homes and private buildings: several rooms grouped around a central court. As congregations increased in size after Christianity became the religion of the Roman Empire in the age of Constantine, the basilica came into Christian use. Derived from public law buildings, these were the only monumental buildings in Rome in the early Christian years. The form was a large rectangle having a central nave bordered by side aisles separated from the nave by two or more rows of columns, all covered by a flat roof. Inside at one end was an elevated platform with a semicircular apse, the bishop's chair in the center. These buildings were oriented toward the East, that is, facing toward Jerusalem, toward paradise, toward the rising sun, carrying the thought and imagination of the worshipers beyond the building, beyond the city, toward the Holy Land and symbolically beyond life in this world toward the resurrection and the heavenly Jerusalem. This orientation remains an important key to understanding church buildings. It is, moreover, not only a Christian idea. All people recognize the symbolic significance of the sunrise in the east, and an eastward orientation is characteristic also of Hindu temples because, it has been explained, it is from the east westward that the gods come to mortals.[21]

In the fourth century, Constantine the Great (280?-337) chose Byzantium as the new capital of the empire (323), inaugurating it and renaming it (330) after himself, Constantinople, the City of Constantine. There he fused Roman energy with oriental character and culture. In the Eastern empire the church buildings were smaller, circular or square with an octagonal base, and surmounted with a dome beneath which was the altar. The building itself was a sign of the stability and centrality of religion under the dome of the sky, an outpost of heaven on this earth.

In the West after A.D. 1000 the Romanesque style adapted some features of the Roman monuments still standing in Italy and southern France. In England it was called the Norman style. With the collapse of the Roman Empire the Romanesque style was the product of monastic influence; only churches were built in this style. The plan was basically basilican, with massive walls and small round-arched windows and doors, towers in storied design. The exterior was remarkably plain and unadorned; the interior, however, was highly decorated with marble and mosaic. To this plan eventually transepts were added, and the choir was deepened yielding a cruciform plan. The effect of the Romanesque style was horizontal or dualistic — horizontal and vertical, earth-clinging, suggestive of confident majesty and strength.

In the twelfth century the wealth of monastic communities, the power of the bishops, the rise of great city-states, and the growth of craftsmen's guilds combined to contribute to a vast program of church building across Europe. The Gothic age was beginning, and architecturally it embraced secular buildings as well as churches. There was a desire to reduce the risk of fire and replace wooden roofs with stone. Vaulting wide naves and the desire to have loftier, airier, and better lighted buildings led to the introduction of the pointed arch and a system of piers and buttresses to support the walls and roof, making massive walls unnecessary. The walls were pierced with large openings, and these were filled with windows of stained glass that transformed the light that came through them, softening the light admitted to the church, producing a brilliant and instructive picture that told a story while the colors fused in the viewer's vision and in their mingling painted the cathedral air.[22] The solid masonry that had formed the enclosure of earlier buildings was transformed into a thin screen or skin, filled with glass, between which rose bundles of vertical shafts, thin flying arches, and webs of ribbing that appeared to be taking all the strain. The exteriors of the Gothic churches took on a beauty worthy of their interiors; Goethe called the facade of Strasbourg "frozen music."

> The spirit of the North was properly called Gothic, for it inherited the restless audacity of the conquering barbarians; it passed insatiate from victory to victory, and finally, with flying buttresses and soaring arch, laid siege to the sky. But it

was also a Christian spirit, appealing to heaven for the peace that barbarism had alienated from the earth. Out of those contradictory motives came the greatest triumph of form over matter in all the history of art.[23]

The effect is an exuberant vertical thrust. The lines of force flow in unified verticality suggesting lightness, height, mystery, lifting the soul to God.

Italy never fully adopted Gothic principles. The intensity of natural light in Italy suggested the use of small windows. Germany clung to the Romanesque, contributing lofty aisles, openwork spires, rich carving in wood and stone. In England the Gothic churches were lower than the French but were long and narrow, the choirs terminating in a square east end. It was in France that the Gothic found its most daring and original form, and it marked the high point of medieval culture. Above all the other majestic cathedrals of the Middle Ages the Cathedral Church of Our Lady of Chartres has been praised most highly.[24] The magnificence of the building makes us forget the squalor, the wars, the greed, the enormities of "the Age of Faith," and we marvel again at the patience, taste, and devotion of those who conceived and planned and dared and built and enjoyed these stupendous houses.[25] "The great cathedrals, and the multitude of abbeys and castles, are entirely and solely a product of the Middle Ages. The outstanding qualities of these people were their audacity and their trust, their sense of tradition and their sensitivity to the work of others."[26]

Every piece in the fabric of Chartres is evolved by the precision of geometry.[27] For people who believed they were building a representation of paradise, there was no room for visual adjustments to aid the eye, such as placing thicker columns against the corner with a narrower column next to it or tapering shafts with a swelling part way up to make the columns seem straight. The medieval cathedral was not built to be seen from the human point of view but from the pure and universal view of God.[28] It is therefore similar to the world itself and similar to each individual in that world, created for the pleasure and purpose of God. Function was not the only attribute of these buildings. Beyond the needs of the church for a house in which to celebrate its rites lay whole worlds of other beings and existences. Behind the superficial appearance of things lay a greater reality that gave meaning to what we see.

The two towers of Chartres, built at different times and of different design, are disconcerting to many viewers because they do not match one another, but in a more profound understanding they are "beyond sterile models of perfection" and represent

> the greatest event in art, when it goes beyond concepts of perfection to an unaccountable richness of life, embracing those complexities and contradictions...which shape the reality of things.[29]

Chartres lifts as if singing out of the wheat, within which grow the poppies, the blood of Adonis. "A Classical connection is indeed felt; we are dealing with a temple, above which two towers move like living bodies, the cone and the spire." The north tower rises to the point where the continuous cone of the other begins to diminish and then "leaps to its own spire so that the two act dynamically in relation to each other." Viewed from afar they shift position and engage in a stately dance against the sky. When we enter the town and approach the mighty building, "it begins to pivot toward us, turning on the cone, rising to the spire."[30]

In the cathedral of Chartres, the spaces are held together not in static rest but in a dynamic equilibrium, maintained because one part is kept in balance against another. If one thing is removed, the whole could collapse. It is secure only in its entirety.[31] So it is also with the body of believers. No one is self-sufficient; each is dependent upon the next. For those with eyes to see, such dynamic interdependence is a powerful proclamation of individual responsibility for the integrity of the whole in church as in society as well. The purpose of the Gothic style was "to enliven inert masses of masonry, to quicken spatial motion, to reduce a building to a seeming system of innervated lines of action."[32] The structure suggests that the architects believed that energy was immanent within the masonry itself and that those forces that inhabited every part of the building were rising as well as descending. "Thus there was a life which moved within the building, which was not inert stone, but being a cathedral, was also part of the Divine."[33] So was each person who entered that living space. Indeed, the very mortar that secures the stones participates in the life of the fabric. Many medieval buildings without their characteristic weak mortar would have collapsed. But as through the centuries the buildings settle and move, the weak mortars crack easily and then reset in the new position. "Alive and adaptable, the buildings would adjust themselves to the stresses placed on them to a surprising degree."[34] Chartres remains today as it was when it was built in the first decades of the thirteenth century.

Such cathedral building was more of a process than a project. It was a natural process that took a generation and more to evolve into its final form, an accumulation of historic events, an organism evolving toward a common image of the heavenly Jerusalem and reflecting something of each individual's vision as well.[35] Chartres

> is in its own way "our own dear Kore who is among us" [Plato, *Laws* 796]: always growing and breathing.... Its spires are the lances of France, outdoing the Norman towers in their continuous rush up out of the ground, out of the wheat that was the strength of France, as the olive was of Athens and the corn of the pueblos.
> Greater than Normandy, Chartres rises out of a richer earth, out of the very bread of mankind, and it rises integrally with its towers.[36]

The Middle Ages gloried in multiplicity, and Chartres shows us that we can be as deeply moved by a work created by many hands as we can by one created by the single genius.[37]

Even those most magnificent achievements of the human imagination know themselves to be but temporary, though they last a thousand years. They were often left deliberately unfinished, for as emblems of the restlessness of the imagination and the continuation of dreams they could never find complete repose. As symbols of the world they could never be completed until the consummation. As expressions of the life of individual worshipers they retained potential for growth and change until death completed the process. By their empty niches and unfilled spaces and uncarved blocks amid the finished statues of holy men and women, these sermons in stone continued to preach that the line of saints is not yet completed. It continues into the present and beyond until the last day.[38] And the message is also heard in a most personal way: there is room for each of us in the adornment of that temple, and there is room for us in the kingdom it represents.

St. Augustine in a sermon instructed a congregation, assembled for the dedication of a house of prayer, in the similarity between the building and themselves.

> This is our house of prayer, but we too are a house of God.
> If we are a house of God, its construction goes on in time so that it may be dedicated at the end of time.[39]

Those who first come to believe, he explained, are like the timber and stone taken from the forests and mountains. Their instruction, baptism, and formation are like the shaping, leveling, and smoothing of the stones and wood by the masons and carpenters. Their unity in love is like the fit of the timber and stones, supporting each other securely. God, who brought to a conclusion the process of the construction of the building, will likewise bring to a successful conclusion the work of its spiritual counterpart in the hearts of believers.

In the nineteenth century there arose in England a movement of remarkably far-reaching influence, the Gothic revival. It was far more than a romantic resuscitation of a long-dead architectural style, an attempt to bring the Middle Ages into the Industrial Revolution in England. It was nothing less than a serious and bold attempt to restore the Age of Faith. The Cambridge Camden (later the Ecclesiological) Society was dedicated to reviving and ensuring the purity of the Gothic style as a means of revitalizing the church after the ravages of rationalism. The work of the society is still to be seen on both sides of the Atlantic.

The late winter of 1990 in Pittsburgh witnessed the end of a melancholy demonstration of a protracted struggle between religion and commerce: the demolition of the oldest church building in the city, St. Peter's, designed by the distinguished architect John Notman (1810–1865), and one of "probably the two best examples of Gothic Revival in America."[40] The cornerstone of the church, Notman's only building in western Pennsylvania, was laid in downtown Pittsburgh April 15, 1851; the first service was held in the new church December 19, 1852. In 1901 the site was purchased by Henry Clay Frick for a building to be called by his own name to overshadow the neighboring Carnegie building. The church was taken down stone by stone and rebuilt at the edge of the emerging Oakland section of the city. By the fall of 1989 the now deconsecrated and abandoned church sat forlorn on its corner, its spire lifted in an empty prayer. To the end, the sign on the entrance door proclaimed "Welcome." It had become a place of broken dreams.

The door now stood open all day, and one by one the windows were removed. The enclosed sanctity of the sacred space was penetrated, an outward and visible sign of the deconsecration. The holiness of the place was dissipated, and the fabric became an eyeless shell. As the church windows came out, increasing light flooded into the darkened interior as it had not since the reconstruction of 1901. Not all was pleasant to see. In the increasing light the yellow walls (originally a cool off-white plaster) and the blue paint added to the arches and window frames and unfortunate purple and red elsewhere became clear in their inelegant intensity.

A further stage in the degradation of the building was the removal of the three stone crosses from the roof so that prospective buyers could examine them more closely. Without the crosses the building became less than what it had been, indecisive and incomplete. The iron finial of the spire had long since broken off so that for years the spire ended in a curious knob looking not unlike a shaving brush held against the sky.

A remnant of what must once have been a pleasant garden remained, hinting even in the decay that once there was here a sensitivity to landscape and living things and that once the beauty of the church had spread beyond its walls to grace its surroundings.

Monday morning, February 5, 1990, the demolition began. The sacristies on either side of the chancel were the first to go. Then the wrecker's clamshell bit into the roof of the chancel and ripped it open. It was the only part of the building with the original diamond-shaped slates still in place. As the roof opened, those outside could see what those who had been inside knew were there: on the ceiling of the chancel monograms of Jesus (IHS) alternated with crosses against a light green background. These signs of him whom the congregation had worshipped were rudely torn from their places and thrown down amid great black clouds of dirt that had accumulated through nine decades. The chancel walls were covered with a clashing turquoise with a gold fleur-de-lis design. (Which came first, one wonders, the decline of the vitality of the church, or the decline of its sense of wholeness and taste? Or did the two go together?)

As the church came down, the mighty jaws of the clamshell biting off great chunks of masonry, details otherwise overlooked became clear. The stone corbels that supported the ends of the roof beams against the walls were carved with a simple flowing design that made them from a distance look like cherubic faces with indented eyes, a sharp nose line, and round cheeks. These faces were echoed outside the building at the ends of the drip caps over each window and also in the details around the square tower over the double Gothic arches. Above them at the top of the tower were round knobs like bells or peony buds. As less and less of the majestic building remained, those parts not yet destroyed became more and more precious. Details seen only by the original carvers and by painters, like the scrolled ends of the knees of the roof beams and the angel heads with flowing hair at the top corners of the tower, were thrown to the ground, and spectators could admire the craftsmanship before the relics were carted away.

The tenacious pigeons, displaced from the tower while the building was being stripped, lined up on the ridge of the roof. When the roof disappeared, they returned to the tower, braving the noise and the dust.

The tower outlasted the church by a couple of weeks. It was surprisingly thick and solid, built for the ages, and it stubbornly resisted the wrecker's ball. But under the constant assault, which took place mostly on a Sunday when traffic on the busy corner was at a minimum, the tower eventually was smashed to the ground until only a stump remained surrounded by a pile of sandstone blocks. Notman's masterpiece was gone.

Perhaps it is just as well that the church was not preserved for conversion to secular use as some had hoped, for this was a serious building, sheltering and witnessing most serious events celebrated within a structure that continued the tradition of medieval English Christianity. Here in this place the prayers of generations had hallowed the blackened sandstone walls. Here the great transitional moments of individual lives were celebrated — baptisms, confirmations, marriages, funerals. Lives were begun and joined and completed in this building. Here an ancient story was passed on.

That much could be said even of an ugly church building. But in the understanding of the Gothic revivalists, supported by John Ruskin's view of Gothic architecture,[41] honesty of materials, soundness of craftsmanship, and even the attitude of the workers, like the materials they used and shaped, had to be worthy of a house of God. Everything done on that house was a holy work, and all irreverence was banned. Like an Eastern icon, the building and those who constructed it together contributed to the glory of God and in harmony together were an act of praise.[42] The church building was more than an isolated structure; the workers and the building, in this noble vision, continued what was believed to be the medieval pattern of harmony and unity of purpose, wholeness of enterprise, and the new church was an expression of a long and undying tradition stretching back beyond the time of Christ and ahead to the end of time. Here was tradition made tangible, a surrounding and all-enveloping memory and support and impetus for service within and beyond this house.

The cornerstone of St. Peter's seemed, as the building was being smashed to the ground, to become a grim irony: "St. Peter's Protestant Episcopal Church. Erected 1852 — re-erected 1901. Built upon the foundation of apostles and prophets, Jesus Christ himself being the chief cornerstone." But perhaps those who set that stone there to the left of the portal in 1901 knew more than may appear to the casual observer. This was not just a predictable and convenient selection of a familiar biblical text (Ephesians 2:20) used in the rite of laying the cornerstone. That text and inscription declare that the Christian church is a people, not a building, and that its cornerstone and foundation are not finally stone blocks but the founders of the community — apostles, prophets, and principally Jesus Christ. The people who made St. Peter's and who supported it are gone now. Their "house of the church" built to shelter a congregation of believers was no longer needed. The building, like all living things, ought to be allowed to die when the end has come.

Philip Larkin's poem "Church Going" ponders the abiding sanctity of a church visited by a speaker once he is "sure there's nothing going on." The speaker who began by feigning an irreverent attitude surprised and disturbed himself as well as the silence of the place by declaiming from the lectern somewhat too loudly, "Here endeth." After belief dies and superstition after it, he wonders, what remains in the ruins? In years to come will "the very last to seek / This place for what it was" be the speaker's representative, his vicar as it were, still "tending to this cross of ground"

> because it held unsplit
> So long and equably what since is found
> Only in separation — marriage and birth,
> And death, and thoughts of these — for which was built
> This special shell?

The building, any church, is "a serious house on serious earth," and there remains in others through the centuries as in the speaker himself a persistent "hunger to be more serious" that is stirred when one gravitates with that hunger to this ground, which past ages knew "was proper to grow wise in, / If only that so many dead lie round." The church and its churchyard with their message of life and death (or, in a more authentic biblical and Christian formulation, of death and life), even when the original crumbles and disbelief reigns, continues to proclaim its vision of comprehensive unity to those with ears to hear and eyes to see. And even when buildings decay and are demolished, an intangible but compelling sanctity abides. So it is when the individual dies; so it will be when the world is consumed at the last and dreadful day. The end is revealed as not the end after all.

A rejoinder to those who mourn the loss of a building (in the case of St. Peter's, the congregation died with the building) is that the church is not buildings; it is people. Indeed, the prevailing modern style of church architecture emphasizes exactly that. It is more than a new style; it marks a changed emphasis in theology. But as so often has been true in the long history of the church, what seems at first glance new and revolutionary is in fact a recovery of and a return to an old idea. The modern word is simplicity, enforced to be sure by economic constraints. As in the dissenting meeting houses in old and New England, beauty is revealed in plainness, authentic materials, and honest craft. The unadorned meetinghouse of 1787 that from its knoll dominates the village of Rockingham, Vermont, is a simple clapboard rectangular building without a steeple or other decoration, an impressive example of the beauty of stern simplicity. The straight-backed box pews match the restrained, clean lines of the severely plain exterior. It is not a place for liturgy but for intellectual discipline and spiritual attention to instruction and solemn praise. In such houses, with little decoration and elaboration of the simple space, the emphasis is not on the building but on the assembly, those who gather, the people who are the church and for whom the building is, in its ancient description, but "the house of the church." It is the people who supply color, movement, life. And yet, the building in its elegant simplicity helps form the faith of those who use the space.

In 1743, guided by Henry Melchior Muhlenberg, the Lutherans in Trappe, Pennsylvania (who called themselves "the Society of the Augsburg Confession"), built a small church in a simple rural style. It is in fact basically a stone barn, in harmony with its surroundings, especially in the mid-eighteenth century. The native brown stone flooring is laid directly on the earth. The interior walls are a plain white. All the timbers are hewn and framed with tenons secured with dowels, and without paint. Nails, hinges, and latches are hand-forged out of charcoal iron. There is a simple unadorned altar set in the midst of what in a grander church would be called the apse. The builders took care to see that their country church was properly oriented, with the altar to the east. There is a handsome imported pulpit of European red walnut on the Gospel (north) side of the church, with a sounding board. The building bears the name Augustus Lutheran Church in honor of Augustus Hermann Francke (1633–1727), the pietist and founder of the Halle Institutions, whose son persuaded Muhlenberg to come to America. It remains the oldest unaltered Lutheran church building in North America. The simple church is a clear expression of the importance of environment in Christian art and architecture. Honesty and authenticity are the means by which the building responds to its human and cultural surroundings. Here at Trappe, in an unassuming church, as at the far better known chapel of Notre-Dame-du-Haut at Ronchamp by Le Corbusier, the gifts of the earth and region are employed with integrity in their natural strength and beauty. At Ronchamp the use of color is sparing — the walls are white, the ceiling and external eaves are gray; the communion rails are of cast iron; the floor of cement paving. Le Corbusier's simple yet sophisticated pilgrim chapel, a small building set high on a hill, remains serene, silent, aloof, yet accepts and embraces the pilgrims who come to it.

Because, especially in modern buildings, the emphasis is placed on the assembly, what is important therefore is the way the relatively simple space is used. Indeed, the early church consecrated a church not by special rites of dedication but simply by celebrating the Holy Eucharist within it. In the building, if it is to be used for liturgical worship, there must be one object, the altar-table (both facets are equally important: a place of offering and a place of feasting). It (and not a reredos, pictorial window, or hanging cross) is the principal item of furniture, given elegance by its covering and by its use. There must be space for several ministers and servers to move freely around the altar and for the congregation to gather near it for the reception of the Holy Communion.

There needs to be a place for reading and preaching. A simple stand to hold the Bible is all that is necessary, for the focus here is intellectual and devotional as one reads, another preaches, and an assembly listens attentively and actively.

A church also of course requires a substantial and impressive font for baptism, appropriate to the sacrament accomplished in its waters. A still better idea, however, is for cooperative Christians of many denominations to have one font in a city or area for all to use, showing the foundational nature and function of the sacrament of initiation and rebirth by which one is made a Christian, a child of God, and an inheritor of the kingdom of heaven.[43]

Church buildings in the modern style may seem to have little to say by themselves apart from their use. They are shelters that await a gathering and a celebration that will give them meaning. And yet, for those with eyes to see, such sacred spaces, like all churches worthy of their name, may nonetheless be alive with an unseen but deeply felt presence. In some churches flickering candles tell of a living presence that inhabits the space and serve as a lingering sign of the prayer of those who have visited there earlier. In other churches the life is less visible, but earnest and continued prayer that has permeated the space and the very walls can be almost palpable. Whether one is alone or part of a congregation in such a space, something is happening.[44] A Christian is always a member of the body of Christ and is never alone. A single individual standing in an empty and silent church is surrounded by the unseen host of heaven.

Ancient church buildings were not perceived as static monuments. The church year, like the Christian life, is a pilgrimage through this world to the next, and medieval sacred places did not contradict that kinetic character of the faith. The very richness of the buildings and their ornamentation gave a sense of activity and motion. Processions moved through the alleys and aisles as a visible pilgrimage. The movements involved in the celebration of the mass by the several sacred ministers further enlivened the building and its use and formed an elaborate liturgical dance.

Christianity is a story, the history of salvation, that runs from separation in the garden to eventual reunion with God at the consummation. A great church embodies this progressive understanding. The pilgrim, like Nicodemus in John's Gospel, having turned from the darkness, enters from the west, leaving the world of shadows and death, through the royal portal on which were carved the basic truths of Christianity, and looks toward the altar and the rising sun in the east. Beyond the altar, invisible doors opened onto paradise.

As pilgrims to the cathedral of Chartres make their journey from door to altar, in the middle of the nave, the place of the people, they encounter a huge labyrinth of blue and white stones set in the pavement. Many of the churches of the time (Pavia, Lucca, Piacenza, Ravenna, Halingbro church on the island of Gotland in Sweden) and especially major cathedrals of northern France (Auxerre, Sens, Chartres, Rheims, Amiens) contain such patterns, nearly all of the same design.[45] The design is not a maze with deceptive false turns and dead ends. It is rather, and apparently significantly, unicursal, a path in which one cannot get lost or make a wrong turn. No matter how long it is with its repeated doubling back on itself, the correct path is laid out for us and we must but follow it patiently and diligently. One enters at the left of the center line and, with one detour, arrives rather quickly near the goal, the center, only to be led away again teasingly, deceptively close to the center and then away again until after a long circuit of half the circumference of the great circle, with one detour, the path leads at last, and with surprising ease, by a straight path to the center.

The meaning of the labyrinth is uncertain or more likely manifold. As is so often the case, pre-Christian ideas and practices lie not far beneath the surface. Entering a labyrinth was the equivalent of an initiation. The center could be a safe city, a tomb, a sanctuary or other magical-religious space that must be protected against the uninitiated.[46] Pilgrims who enter the church from the west and move unobstructed toward the altar in the east must pass over the labyrinth on the way. They are thus reminded that safe arrival at the goal, a place difficult of access and well defended, is by means of a trial in which not everyone may triumph. The way, straight and narrow, is arduous and fraught with peril, for it is a passage from the profane to the sacred, from illusion to reality, from the temporal to the eternal.

The labyrinths built into the pavement of churches may have been the place where Easter rituals involving dances and ball throwing took place,[47] for during the Middle Ages a number of dioceses practiced such Easter rituals. The most complete records are from the Cathedral of St. Stephen at Auxerre and indicate that the dance was accompanied by the early eleventh-century sequence *Victimae Paschali* by Wigbert (Wipo of Burgundy).[48] The dance apparently celebrated deliverance from the labyrinth of hell by the victory of Christ, foreshadowed in Greek myth by Theseus's defeat of the Cretan labyrinth and its Minotaur.[49] Moreover, at Chartres the labyrinth is inscribed on the floor of the church beneath which lies the crypt and under that the earth itself.

The labyrinth at Chartres, more than forty feet in diameter, spreads like a shadow cast by the great and admired western rose window, which is almost of the same diameter. The window and the labyrinth suggest the mystic correspondence of heaven and earth, declaring that what we know on earth, on our level, is but a reflection of a greater and higher and more splendid reality. The window in its center shows Christ the Judge of the world reigning in glory in heaven. It is a picture, painted with light, of heavenly order and perfection and peace. The rose window, simple in pattern but complex in its significance, is based on the circle, the most perfect of all shapes, and yet presents a multiple visual statement about the coherence, harmony, and mystery of the medieval view of the world.[50] The labyrinth also, like the rose window, combines simplicity and complexity. When the image of the rose falls on the pavement of the cathedral, when the image of heaven is cast on to the earth, it is seen as a labyrinth, a twisting and disordered path to the central flower with but six petals, one short of perfection. Earthly experience is inevitably incomplete. And yet, what seems at first sight, and especially in contrast to the rose window, disordered and even chaotic is in fact to God in eternity a vision of order, complete and meaningful. By the labyrinth pattern and its conjunction with the rose window we learn the limitation of human perception and perspective. "At the right time of the day and the year — perhaps at Easter? — the light from the window might illumine the maze, just as, at the harrowing, Christ as light entered the gates of hell."[51] The teeming chaos of the world and of our experience is enclosed and ordered, and if we keep to the path laid out for us we cannot go astray.

Another and more specific pilgrimage route is incorporated into many church buildings. It is the devotion called the way of the cross or the stations of the cross. The stations (stops) along the devotional way are marked with numbered crosses painted or inscribed or placed on the walls of the building. To aid devotion, pictorial representations are usually added to the crosses that mark each stop to assist pilgrims in imagining that they are walking the *via dolorosa* in Jerusalem, following the steps of Jesus from condemnation to the grave. The devotion came into use in the fifteenth century when pilgrims to the Holy Land identified sites associated with the passion of Jesus in Jerusalem. When the pilgrims returned to Europe they continued their devotion by erecting in churches or fields memorials of the pilgrim sites. The number of stations has varied through the centuries but in the eighteenth and nineteenth centuries it was fixed at fourteen, nine of which have a basis in the biblical account: (1) Jesus is condemned to death, (2) Jesus receives the cross, (3) Jesus falls the first time, (4) Jesus meets his mother, (5) The cross is laid on Simon of Cyrene, (6) a woman (Veronica) wipes the face of Jesus, (7) Jesus falls a second time, (8) Jesus meets the women of Jerusalem, (9) Jesus falls a third time, (10) Jesus is stripped of his garments, (11) Jesus is nailed to the cross, (12) Jesus dies on the cross, (13) Jesus is taken down from the cross, (14) Jesus is laid in the tomb.[52] The content of the devotion was private and was never fixed by any official church authority. The devotion is a way of walking with Jesus as he carries his cross from the judgment hall to Calvary. Then, with Mary and John, pilgrims stand by the cross, and with Joseph of Arimathea in imagination lay the body of Jesus in the new tomb. Finally, the devotion sometimes concludes before the altar, an ancient symbol of the living Christ, as a station of the resurrection, and the pilgrims glimpse the victory over death promised to them because of Christ.

Like the church year, which, because it is not a simple and straightforward presentation of the life of Christ, is constantly in motion, forming and suggesting ever new patterns, so temples continually subvert themselves. Sacred space was at first temporary, as for Jacob and Moses, and then it was made portable (and therefore tamed) in the Tabernacle, the "tent of meeting," which the Israelites carried with them in their nomadic time in the wilderness. On a deeper level, the whole earth is potentially an altar, and a holy place is always both a high place (a sacred mountain) and, while always facing eastward, the center (the navel) of the earth. For Solomon, in a classic presentation of the biblical view of holy places, the cosmos was God's temple. Standing before the newly constructed temple and the people, thereby declaring significantly both the locality and the universality of God's presence, the king spread his hands and prayed in dedication:

> Will God indeed dwell on the earth? Even heaven and the highest heaven cannot contain you, much less this house that I have built! Regard your servant's prayer and his plea, O Lord my God, heeding the cry and the prayer that your servant prays to you today; that your eyes may be open night and day toward this house, the place of which you said, "My name shall be there," that you may heed the prayer that your servant prays toward this place. Hear the plea of your servant and of your people Israel when they pray toward this place; O hear in heaven your dwelling place; heed and forgive. (1 Kings 8:27–30)

The king's prayer is echoed in the hymn of about the seventh century, *Angularis* [sometimes *Angulare*] *fundamentum.*

> To this temple, where we call thee,
>   Come, O Lord of hosts, today;
> With thy wonted loving-kindness
>   Hear thy servants as they pray,
> And thy fullest benediction
>   Shed within thy walls alway.
>
> Here vouchsafe to all thy servants
>   What they ask of thee to gain;
> What they gain from thee for ever

> With the blessed to retain,
> And hereafter in thy glory
> Evermore with thee to reign.[53]

It is also heard at the opening of William Cullen Bryant's hymn:

> Thou, whose unmeasured temple stands,
>   Built over earth and sea,
> Accept the walls that human hands
>   Have built, O God, to thee.[54]

Solomon's insightful prayer embodied an advanced theological concept that undermined the role of temples as houses of God, buildings that, in a debased view, confined their god to their space. The God of Israel, Solomon declared, fills the universe ("Heaven and earth are full of your glory," the church continues to sing in the *Sanctus,* joining the songs of the seraphim reported in Isaiah 6:3). And yet, despite their deep suspicion of the temples and the religion of their neighbors, Israel in the person of their king built their God a temple. It was a place of religious focus and concentration, a place of offering and sacrifice, a gathering place for Israel when prayer was required. In his extended and impressive prayer of dedication King Solomon united the view of God in the divine dwelling place of heaven, above and beyond the earth and mortal sight, and the temple where God's people come to encounter God and to pray.

> When your people Israel, having sinned against you, are defeated before an enemy but turn to you...then hear in heaven, forgive the sin.... When heaven is shut up and there is no rain because they have sinned against you, and they pray toward this place...then hear in heaven, and forgive the sin of your servants.... Whatever prayer, whatever plea there is from any individual or from all your people Israel, all knowing the afflictions of their own hearts so that they stretch out their hands toward this house; then hear in heaven your dwelling place, forgive, act, and render to all whose hearts you know...so that they may fear you....(1 Kings 8:33–40)

The temple made with human hands is nonetheless called God's house and is thus the universe in microcosm.

Later ages, yielding to a perennial temptation, often presumed that the presence of the temple guaranteed God's favor, and Jeremiah, standing in the gate of the Lord's house, thundered a

warning against such presumption. "Do not trust in these deceptive words: 'This is the temple of the Lord, the temple of the Lord,
the temple of the Lord' " (7:4). Only a thorough reformation of life
and action could assure God's presence in the holy place. St. Paul,
extending this prophetic insight that began to transform the idea of
a holy place, writing to the Greek Christians who lived in a country
with an abundance of deities and temples and who were unlikely to
be able to travel to Jerusalem to pray in the temple there, inquires
rhetorically, "Do you not know that you are the temple of God and
that the Spirit dwells in you?" (1 Corinthians 3:16). Sacred buildings are unnecessary, for the primary place where God is found is
within human beings. Each individual is a holy place, each body a
temple of the Holy Spirit. It is an insight that has comforted Christians in times of war and destruction. Nikolai Grundtvig's hymn
(1854) on this theme was rediscovered during the devastation of
the Second World War: "Built on a rock the church doth stand /
Even when steeples are falling."

> Not in our temples made with hands
> God the Almighty is dwelling;
> High in the heavens his temple stands,
> All earthly temples excelling.
> Yet he who dwells in heaven above
> Deigns to abide with us in love,
> Making our bodies his temple.[55]

The church is people, and even though churches are destroyed, the
church abides, perhaps stronger than ever, for its focus is redirected
toward what endures. "We are God's house of living stones," the
hymn says, and yet "in this house, an earthly frame," God is bestowing blessing. The building, although it is not the church but
only the house of the church, is not to be despised. It is rather to
be honored for what happens within its walls.

The location of God within each individual heart is an insight
not peculiar to Christianity, but it is used by Christians sometimes
with powerful effect in developing a sense of the divine within each
one of us and in sharpening the sense of ethical responsibility for
each other. We are to treat all people with love and respect because
each is a temple of God, a person for whom Christ died. In the
baptismal rite in the *Book of Common Prayer* the baptismal covenant that precedes the actual washing of baptism includes these
questions to the candidates, "Will you seek and serve Christ in all

persons, loving your neighbor as yourself?...Will you strive for justice and peace among all people, and respect the dignity of every human being?"[56]

But one need not choose the cosmos alone or the temple alone or the individual alone as the dwelling place of God. It is the property of an effective symbol to pin down in a brief compass a range of convincing moments of feeling, experience, and insight. The temple remains a powerful symbol, declaring even while subverting its own claims that it is the house of God. Christians are not afraid to build a house of God that is at the same time a house of the church, because the body, the temple, and the universe are analogous. The universe, the temple, and the human body each correspond to each other, and each reaches in six directions: the four cardinal points of the compass (north, south, east, and west) as well as above and below. So the earth, the floor of the temple, and the feet are the nadir; atmospheric space, the interior space of the temple, and the human trunk extend to the four quarters; the sky, the roof of the building, and the head are the zenith. The temple, the church building, is the world in a little space, a microcosm of the universe; and the temple, at the same time, is a representation of the self in harmony with the environment. The temple, itself a powerful symbol, is the world and also shows the individual self, calling for and encouraging the harmony of the three: temple, world, and self.[57] As God fills the cosmos, so God fills the temple; as God fills the temple, so God fills the individual soul, believer and unbeliever alike. Believers recognize the inner divine presence; nonbelievers are less aware of it.

The rite of dedication of a church as it is practiced in both East and West underscores the similarity of the church building and the individual human body. The dedication treats the building as if it were a living person undergoing baptism, sprinkling it with water and anointing its walls with oil.

The seventh-century hymn *Urbs beata Jerusalem*, translated by John Mason Neale, presents such a view of the church building, the temple, Jerusalem, heaven, and the individual as one:

> Blessed city, heavenly Salem,
>   Vision dear of peace and love,
> Who, of living stones upbuilded,
>   Art the joy of heaven above,
> And, with angel cohorts circled,
>   As a bride to earth dost move!

> From celestial realms descending,
>   Bridal glory round her shed,
> To his presence, decked with jewels,
>   By her Lord shall she be led:
> All her streets, and all her bulwarks,
>   Of pure gold are fashioned.
>
> Bright with pearls her portals glitter,
>   They are open evermore,
> And, by virtue of the merits,
>   Thither faithful souls may soar
> Who for Christ's dear name in this world
>   Pain and tribulation bore.
>
> Many a blow and biting sculpture
>   Fashioned well those stones elect,
> In their places now compacted
>   By the heavenly architect,
> Who therewith hath willed for ever
>   That his palace should be decked.[58]

In a striking way the hymn combines the vision of "the holy city, the new Jerusalem coming down out of heaven from God, prepared as a bride adorned for her husband" reported by St. John the Divine (Revelation 21:2) and the understanding of the church as built of "living stones into a spiritual house" (1 Peter 2:5; also Ephesians 2:19–22). As stones from the quarry are shaped by the sculptors, so the living stones, each individual, are shaped by the "heavenly architect" through discipline and even suffering, "pain and tribulation," into building blocks of the church of God.

As this hymn shows, the intention of the construction and the dedication of a church building is to carry our attention from the shadow, the visible temple built with hands, to the reality, the temple-city built of living stones in heaven, the foundation of which is made of apostles and prophets and the cornerstone of which is Christ.[59] "Sion" was interpreted by William Durandus, the thirteenth-century bishop of Mende, as the church militant on earth. (The word "Sion" was said to mean *speculatio*, "looking to the far-off.") "Jerusalem" was interpreted as early as Origen (died ca. 254) as *pacis visio*, "vision of peace,"[60] the church triumphant enjoying the beatific vision in heaven. In the Roman rite, the collect for the dedication of a church (said outside the dedicated church) prays, "God our Father, from living stones, your chosen people, you built an eternal temple to your glory. Increase the spiritual gifts you have given to your Church that your faithful people may continue to grow into the new and eternal Jerusalem."

Can we be sure that God, who is "beyond the farthest / Mortal eye can scan," will regard the songs of sinful humans? Francis Pott asks in his hymn "Angel Voices Ever Singing." The confident answer resounds:

> Yea, we know that thou rejoicest
> O'er each work of thine;
> Thou didst ears and hands and voices
> For thy praise combine;
> Craftsman's art and music's measure
> For thy pleasure
> Didst design.[61]

The ability to conceive, design, build, adorn, and use church buildings was conferred upon mortals by the Creator in order to give praise and pleasure to the great God, Father, Son, and Holy Spirit. John Greenleaf Whittier in his hymn "All Things Are Thine" declares that it is by human work that God's will is done on earth, even in building churches.

> Thy will was in the builders' thought;
> Thy hand unseen amidst us wrought;
> Through mortal motive, scheme, and plan,
> The wise eternal purpose ran.[62]

Le Corbusier wrote to the archbishop on the occasion of the dedication of the pilgrim chapel at Ronchamp on June 25, 1955:

Excellency: I give you this chapel of dear, faithful concrete, shaped perhaps with temerity but certainly with courage in the hope that it will seek out in you (as in those who will climb the hill) an echo of what we have drawn into it.[63]

Sacred space does more than simply provide an expression of holiness for those who will look for it and who have eyes to see. It probes our innermost selves, it challenges our very being until it discovers in us a response. It goes in search of and seeks out in each pilgrim a responsive echo, and in so doing it is an extension of the summons of the Gospel which, like the hound of heaven,[64] hunts us down and will not let us go until we give answer. Sacred space, Le Corbusier recognized, is not passive but vigorously active.

The angel who adorns the roof of great Gothic cathedrals is
Gabriel, trumpet ready to announce the end of the world. As the
church building represents the world and also a living individual, so the death of a congregation and its building corresponds
to the death of an individual. The angel who waits to make the
fearsome announcement puts the whole picture in perspective.
Over all creation, including the most magnificent monuments of
human creation and vision, hangs the threat of ultimate destruction, for everything in this world is temporary and transient —
the individual, the building, and the world itself. God alone is
everlasting.

A noble and enduring church building is a sign of the continuity
of the church, which can and of course will continue in the absence
of buildings. George Wallace Briggs presents the continuity in an
impressive way.

> Our Father, by whose servants
>   Our house was built of old,
> Whose hand hath crowned her children
>   With blessing manifold,
>
> For thine unfailing mercies
>   Far-strewn along our way,
> With all who passed before us,
>   We praise thy Name today.
>
> The changeful years unresting
>   Their silent course have sped,
> New comrades ever bringing
>   In comrades' steps to tread;
> And some are long forgotten,
>   Long spent their hopes and fears;
> Safe rest they in thy keeping,
>   Who changest not with years.
>
> They reap not where they labored,
>   We reap what they have sown;
> Our harvest may be garnered
>   By ages yet unknown.
> The days of old have dowered us
>   With gifts beyond all praise;
> Our Father, make us faithful
>   To serve the coming days.

> Before us and beside us,
> Still holden by thy hand,
> A cloud unseen of witness,
> Our elder comrades stand;
> One family unbroken,
> We join, with one acclaim,
> One heart, one voice uplifting,
> To glorify thy Name.[65]

Earlier Marcel Proust had written of the worn stones of the porch, the memorial stones, the windows and tapestries of his parish church in Combray:

> All these things and, still more than these, the treasures which had come to the church from personages who to me were almost legendary figures... because of which I used to go forward into the church when we were making our way to our chairs as into a fairy-haunted valley, where the rustic sees with amazement on a rock, a tree, a marsh, the tangible proofs of the little people's supernatural passage — all these things made of the church for me something entirely different from the rest of the town; a building which occupied, so to speak, four dimensions of space — the name of the fourth being Time — which had sailed the centuries with that old nave, where bay after bay, chapel after chapel, seemed to stretch across and hold down and conquer not merely a few yards of soil, but each successive epoch from which the whole building had emerged triumphant.... [66]

Such a long view is essential to a religious understanding of the world. It teaches gratitude for the contributions of the past and humility with regard to our own work. Such a view embodied in a church building presents a concrete expression of both tradition and promise, inheritance and hope, and it expands our horizon to a longer and broader and more inclusive view of the line of God's people through the ages. Our moment is but one section of a procession that stretches back to the beginning of the race and extends forward to the end of time. We enjoy what our predecessors have prepared and we plant what future ages will gather and sort out.

   D. H. Lawrence in *Etruscan Places* (1932) condemned ponderous church buildings, calling them "burdens on the face of the earth." He preferred the small wooden temples of the Etruscans, "charming instead of impressive," alive and flexible, which "won't last too long and become an obstruction and a weariness."[67] Lawrence's words sound quite modern. Nonetheless, in our hankering after simple, flexible, and multiuse spaces one might wonder whether what this age needs instead are some monuments of fixity in a world of change, a place that gives focus to the flux of our lives, a point that gives focus to the landscape. Churches can function like Steven's jar in Tennessee.[68] They can tell of permanence amid surrounding fluidity, order in the face of chaos, history for people without roots.

It is a continual temptation to overestimate the importance of our own time. Particularly for us who continue to be dominated by the idea of progress, the question of the utility and relevance of any specific past age arises — what has it done for us? — and if no such service can be found the age is dismissed as irrelevant and useless, something to be grown away from if not actually fled from. T. S. Eliot observed, "The notion that a past age or civilization might be great in itself, precious in the eye of God, because it succeeded in adjusting the delicate relation of the Eternal and the Transient is completely alien to us."[69] It is not a recent disease. Michel de Montaigne (1533–1592) noted our blindness to our own failings. In his essay "On Cannibals" he observed, "We are justified therefore in calling these people barbarians by reference to the laws of reason, but not in comparison with ourselves, who surpass them in every kind of barbarity."[70] He echoed the view of Pliny[71] that was inscribed on the beams of his library, "Presumption is our natural and original malady. The most vulnerable and frail of all creatures is man, and at the same time the most arrogant."[72] An overestimation of our own time and of ourselves and our own concerns leads us to require that what we inherit from the past speak to us directly rather than that we demand of ourselves the effort to address the past in its time and to listen attentively for what may be a compelling message but set out for us in an unaccustomed and indirect and subtle way.[73] People whose language and culture are different continue to read old books because old books can still speak, still teach, enlighten, and delight across the years and across generations and cultures. A classic contains more than any one interpreter or generation requires, for that is the very nature of a classic: it is an inexhaustible source of revelation and discovery. In it, no matter how familiar it may be, one can always find something new.

Sacred space, marked out and enclosed by a church building, is a declaration of the paradox of a timeless proclamation embedded in time, the Eternal born in mortal flesh at a specific moment and in a particular geographic area. It is a window of heaven and a door to eternity carrying our sight and spirit beyond the confines of this world and into the next as far as the human spirit can penetrate and understand. Temples are always liminal.

Chapter Seven

THE HOLY EUCHARIST
Hallowing Sustenance

Between the two natural cycles of days and seasons, both Judaism and Christianity have inserted a measure of time unrelated to the natural world: the week. Unlike the cycle of days that extends from sunset to sunset, the months that follow the cycles of the moon, and the years that follow the cycles of the sun and stars, the week is an entirely artificial measure. There is no necessity that requires a week to consist of seven days. There was, for example, a ten-day week in ancient China. In Nigeria in the twentieth century, in many of the smaller villages, the "week" was marked by the frequency of "market," and in some places market was held as often as every three days. The seven-day week is a human construct and only becomes a fixture in world reckoning in the second or third century after Christ. The seven-day week originated apparently in Mesopotamia and is thought to have been predicated on the concept of the influence of the planets, then understood to be the sun, moon, Mars, Mercury, Jupiter, Venus, and Saturn.

Nonetheless, the week has been accorded deep significance in Judaism and Christianity. In Judaism the week from Sunday through Saturday recapitulates creation, culminating in the sabbath rest. In Christianity the week from Sunday to Sunday more faintly echoes creation but more strongly signifies the new creation. As both the daily cycle and the yearly cycle may be understood as proclaiming the *Pascha,* so the mystery of the Pascha is repeated each Sunday, the Lord's Day. This day in Christian understanding is a unique day: it is a concrete period of time, and yet it is also outside of and beyond time, as in its patristic title, the eighth day. The Sabbath is an image of the perfection of the natural creation, the seventh day, the number seven suggesting completeness and wholeness. The

174

Sabbath is a day of rest and rejoicing in the completed creation, a time apart from work and human interference with the natural world, a time to explore and ponder the depth of life. The resurrection of Christ occurred the next day, "after the sabbath" (Matthew 28:1). The Lord's Day is thus understood not simply as another "first day of the week," a continuation in time, but the eighth day, the eschatological day of the new creation when the full story of Christ breaks out of its confines of space and time into a new dimension, the kingdom, reign, and realm of God, paradoxically begun and yet to come, now but not yet. It is the day of the Lord, of the Spirit (Pentecost), of the kingdom, of the church — all of which are in the world but also at the same time out of the world. Time thus becomes sacramental, a revelation of the realm and dominion of God.

The Christian church is characterized by its celebration of the Lord's Supper on the Lord's Day. The three realities — church, Holy Communion, and Sunday — come to their full flower when they are joined together. The eighth day is the day of the kingdom, the new creation, the Pascha. The Holy Communion is the celebration of the Pascha, the memorial of the death and resurrection of Christ so celebrated that it breaches the barriers of past and future, and the separation caused by time, is overcome. In the Eucharist, past, present, and future are transcended, and while still in this world we stand already in the kingdom of God. We are in possession of what we wait for. The church is the community that keeps and is formed by the celebration of the Lord's Supper on the Lord's Day. This Day is never complete without a celebration of the Supper; the Supper is never so full as when the church celebrates it on this Day.

The eighth day is not removed from time as if to render all other time profane, but it is rather a revelation of time redeemed. Sunday, beyond time, is celebrated in time and thereby gives meaning to all other days. So the bread and wine of the Holy Communion are not so separated from ordinary food and drink that they make all ordinary eating and drinking of less value and significance; rather, in their authenticity as real sustenance and in their richness as symbols, they reveal the depth of the meaning of a community meal.

The proper place of the Holy Communion is on Sunday, for it belongs not to the daily cycle but to the weekly cycle. On certain weekday feasts and the commemoration of saints, the Eucharist is a proper action but only because these find their meaning as paschal events rooted in Easter. The Eucharist and Sunday are inextricably joined.

There are two great patterns to the Eucharist as there are to Christian theology and spirituality. These are not, as one might at first think, Catholic and Protestant but East and West. The pattern of the West is exemplified by the principal ornament of most altars and churches, the crucifix (or the plain cross). The attention of the West — Roman, Anglican, Lutheran, Protestant of all kinds — is fixed on the crucifixion, the atoning death of Christ. Crosses abound in church decoration and on religious items. "Calvary" is a common name for churches of many denominations. (Curiously, the Hebrew name for the same location, "Golgotha," is never used.) The work accomplished on Calvary (atonement, reconciliation) is also the source of names for churches, as is the instrument of the work (holy cross) and the titles of him who did the saving work (Redeemer, our Savior). "We preach Christ crucified," declared St. Paul (1 Corinthians 1:23), and in a variety of ways, so have the churches of the West, from the simplest nondenominational Bible church to the churches that follow the richest liturgies of the Roman rite.

The attention of the East, on the other hand, focuses on the principal adornment of their churches, the image of the Pantocrator, the representation of Christ enthroned in glory reigning over the cosmos.[1] The Liturgy of St. John Chrysostom begins, "Blessed is the kingdom of the Father and of the Son and of the Holy Spirit now and forever." Forms of the lesser doxology sound again and again throughout the liturgy, "Glory to the Father and to the Son and to the Holy Spirit." The deacon's litany concludes, "For to you belong all glory, honor, and worship, Father, Son, and Holy Spirit, now and forever." The readings from the Bible are introduced with the cry, "Wisdom! Let us be attentive," announcing the presence in the readings of Christ, Holy Wisdom. The cherubic hymn at the Great Entrance calls on the congregation to "welcome the king of all, who comes invisibly upborne by the angelic hosts," and meanwhile the priest prays:

> O King of glory, no one is worthy to come to you, to draw near you, to perform a service for you when he is bound down by desires and pleasures of the flesh; for to serve you is something grand and awe-inspiring even for the heavenly powers themselves. . . .

After communion the people sing:

> We have seen the true light.
> We have received the heavenly Spirit.
> We have found the true faith,
>   worshiping the undivided Trinity,
>   who has saved us.

Throughout the Divine Liturgy of the Eastern churches runs a deep sense of awe in the presence of the holy and glorious ruler of the universe.

It is not of course that the two approaches of East and West are contradictory or mutually exclusive. Each partakes of the other. The crucifixion is essential in Eastern theology and liturgy, and Christ the King is a familiar figure in the West. But each tradition has its characteristic emphasis. From the two traditions together we learn that Christ who meets us in Holy Communion is crucified and risen. The ancient church always held the cross and the resurrection together as parts of one whole, and so it must always be. Without the resurrection, the cross is only tragic defeat, the place where a "young prince of glory died."[2] Without the cross, the resurrection is but a romantic dream of life without cost or ending. Cross and resurrection are each necessary for the understanding of the other, and together they describe the Christian life.

St. Paul said (1 Corinthians 11:26) that the intention of those who celebrate the Holy Communion is to "proclaim the Lord's death until he comes." To "proclaim the Lord's death" is a shorthand way of referring to the whole of Christ's work — life, death, and resurrection — by referring to the central action. We can proclaim his death only if we know the rest of the story, the resurrection. No one would "proclaim" the death of a friend or hero; but Christ's death was not the end of his story, and so it is proclaimed boldly and gladly by the church as the victory over all the forces arrayed against God. We proclaim the Lord's saving death "until he comes," and that makes clear that the saving victim cannot still be dead. Cross and resurrection, death and life are two sides of one event. That transforming and renewing event is to be experienced by us and lived by us as a testimony to what we believe, and we do so while looking toward the last day, the consummation of the whole work of Christ. Luther's version of the collect for Corpus Christi attributed to Thomas Aquinas is suggestive:

> O thou dear Lord God, who in connection with this wonderful sacrament hast commanded us to commemorate and

preach thy passion: Grant that we may so use this sacrament of thy body and blood that daily and richly we may
be conscious of thy redemption.[3]

The sacrament itself is a way of proclaiming and preaching the passion of Christ, whose death brought life into the world and deepens
our consciousness of our redemption.

Charles Wesley's powerful Advent hymn declares:

> Those dear tokens of his passion
> Still his dazzling body bears;
> Cause of endless exultation
> To his ransomed worshipers;
> With what rapture
> Gaze we on those glorious scars.[4]

Christ, who with his wounded hands and opened side met
St. Thomas after the resurrection, meets us in the sacrament of
Holy Communion with his victorious and unending life, which
vindicates the will of the Father, but he meets us with the holes
still in his hands and feet and side. The marks of crucifixion are
now also signs of victory and identifying marks by which we can
recognize him.

We have seen how the movement of night into day is basic to
daily prayer and the Vigil of Easter. Movement is also incorporated
in sacred space and temples. The Holy Eucharist too is characterized by movement. In both East and West, the celebration of the
Eucharist is primarily a series of actions. It is something that Christians *do,* and therefore to understand its dynamic one must sense
the movement, the progression, the actions that constitute the central liturgy of the church, even though the congregation for the
most part remains in one place.

The movement is both cyclical and linear. The Eucharist is properly celebrated every week; as the Lord's Day returns in the weekly
cycle, so does the Lord's Supper, "a perpetual memorial of that his
precious death and sacrifice, until his coming again."[5]

The eucharistic liturgy also has a linear movement, which progresses from entering the church to hearing the proclamation of
the word of God to sharing the visible word in the bread and wine
to departing for service in the world. Although this line turns in
a circle as the scattered congregation again assembles the following week, the linear movement of the Eucharist from entrance to
communion is a sign and foreshadowing of the movement of each

individual and of the pilgrim church through this world and into the fullness of joy in heaven.

Eight actions may be identified in the movement of the Eucharist. They summon each individual and all the church to (1) prepare, (2) assemble, (3) hear the living voice of Scripture, (4) intercede for all and on behalf of all, (5) offer their gifts and themselves, (6) give thanks, (7) eat and drink in communion with Christ and the church, and (8) scatter to serve the Lord in the world. These eight actions can be connected with eight of the many names Christians have applied to the Blessed Sacrament: the Holy Mysteries, the New Covenant, the Anamnesis, the Lord's Supper, the Sacrament of the Altar, the Eucharist, the Holy Communion, the Mass. The very multiplicity of names suggests the inexhaustible richness of what is often called simply "the Sacrament."

The sacred meal that is constituted by such actions is a rich feast of vision and reality expressed in deepest symbols.[6] The Lord's Supper is a meal that the followers of Jesus share with him and with one another. Such eating and drinking binds them together with each other and with him in Holy Communion. The sacred meal, which through the ages has been the center of Christian worship, keeps alive the memory of the saving acts that God has done in history, and in the wonderful magic of ritual makes them live again in the present. A thirteenth-century antiphon praises the Holy Eucharist, exclaiming in wonder and admiration:

> O sacred feast,
> in which Christ is received,
> the memorial of his passion is celebrated anew,
> our souls are filled with grace,
> and we are given a pledge of the glory which is to come.[7]

The Holy Communion gathers and gives shape to the past, while it points its celebrants always and ever forward to the work that must be done when the liturgy is completed and finally to the celebration of the consummation of the Eucharist in the unending heavenly banquet of perfect fulfillment and joy.

Preparation

This understanding is the background and basis for the first action of the Eucharist, *preparation*. If its manifold meanings are to be understood and loved and received with gladness, the abounding richness of this feast requires careful preparation by those who intend to share in it. An act of confession, whether in private as an individual confession or in public as part of the liturgy, is a common preparation for Holy Communion, but, as Luther teaches in *The Small Catechism,* those are worthy and well prepared who believe the words "for you" and "for the remission of sins." As by faith and repentance we prepare for Holy Communion, so by the reception of the sacrament we prepare for the feast to come by enjoying a foretaste of the heavenly banquet.

Echoes of Holy Baptism resound through the celebration of the Holy Communion, for these two sacraments shape the Christian life. Baptism, by which we are born anew and in which our Christian life begins, gives us confidence to approach the altar of God. The writer to the Hebrews explained:

> Therefore, my friends, since we have confidence to enter the sanctuary by the blood of Jesus, by the new and living way that he opened for us through the curtain (that is, through his flesh), and since we have a great high priest over the house of God, let us approach with a true heart in full assurance of faith, with our hearts sprinkled clean from an evil conscience and our bodies washed with pure water. (Hebrews 10:19–21)[8]

At baptism newborn Christians are often given a baptismal robe to show that they are now clothed in the righteousness of Christ ("Jesus, thy blood and righteousness / My beauty are, my glorious dress," a hymn by Zinzendorf sings) and that they now wear the radiant garments of a bride of Christ. The sacred ministers vest themselves to preside at the service, showing that what they are preparing to do is no ordinary activity. The ministers dress themselves in sacred clothing but do so on behalf of all, showing not only the requirements of clean and festive clothing but most of all the necessity of cleansed and prepared hearts.

Sometimes, especially in ancient writings, the communion meal of thanksgiving at the altar is called the Holy Mysteries, suggesting a communion in things beyond human comprehension by which we are lifted through the means of ordinary, earthly elements into God's presence. " 'What no eye has seen, nor ear heard, nor the human heart conceived, what God has prepared for those who love him' — these things God has revealed to us through the Spirit" (1 Corinthians 2:9–10).

> Let all mortal flesh keep silence,
> And with fear and trembling stand

the hymn translated from the Liturgy of St. James admonishes us.

It is not that one must necessarily first make a formal confession or pray a particular prayer before one is ready to participate in the holy mysteries, although that is not to be ignored. The act of joining with others is itself a work of God that cleanses and renews those who assemble. The very gathering is an occasion and a means of purification because it is the work of the Holy Spirit, who "calls, gathers, enlightens, and sanctifies the whole Christian church on earth."[9] The entire Eucharist thus depends upon the Holy Spirit, whose work it ultimately is.[10]

This priority of the work of the Holy Spirit and our dependence on the Spirit's aid does not, however, relieve us of the responsibility of careful preparation for worship. We cannot just sit back and let the Spirit go to work. The liturgy by definition is the work of the whole gathered congregation, all the people of God. Those who preside and those who assist in the leadership must give time not only to sermon preparation but also to ordering the entire liturgical action, including the choice of hymns and other music so that all the service is a coherent whole with point and direction. But even the most careful ministers cannot do it all. Everyone must prepare for worship. The people should be taught to read and think about the lessons before they get to church so that they will be able to listen intently, intelligently, and receptively to the readings (and so that they will be able to listen to the proclamation of the readings without having their faces buried in a book or leaflet). The people should also look over the other propers: the proper collect of the Day and the psalm, the proper Alleluia Verse and Offertory, if these are used. The day and the service should not be a surprise to the people when they get to church.

In preparation for receiving Christ in Holy Communion, an examination of conscience is necessary so the words and acts of forgiveness may be received. Moreover, before they come to church, the people need to think about their concerns, gathering intentions for the intercessions, knowing who and what they ought to pray for, so that they will have specific and particular things in mind as the prayer is offered; otherwise the intercessions cannot be the prayer of the church. Again, they need carefully to collect reasons and occasions for thanksgiving and celebration, both in the prayers of intercession and in the liturgy as a whole. Thus

individual needs and the needs of others are joined in this preparation. Such regular and continued examination of conscience in
preparation for confession and such regular and continued reflection upon the needs of others in preparation for the celebration of
the Eucharist are essential for deepened Christian living.

Assembling

The *assembling* is the second action of the Holy Communion.
A Christian congregation gathers in response to Jesus' promise,
"Where two or three are gathered in my name, I am there among
them" (Matthew 18:20). Rather than consolation for small numbers of worshipers, the point of this often-misunderstood saying
is that Christ's presence is to be found in the Christian assembly,
where people gather in his name. The emphasis in Jesus' promise is
on the gathering where he is to be found.

The celebration of the Holy Eucharist begins with the entrance
rite. In its narrowest sense, this is the entrance of the ministers
and servers into the assembly, making their way to their places by
the altar. The procession is commonly (but need not be) a grand
thing — led perhaps by incense and by cross and candles, joined
by the choir singing a stirring hymn. In a larger sense, however,
the entrance begins even before the entrance of the several members of the congregation into the church building to prepare for
worship. It begins when individual Christians wake and rise from
sleep. They do so on the Lord's Day to fulfill their obligations to
God, to themselves, and to others who expect and who are supported and encouraged by their participation in the services of
God's house. Getting out of bed on Sunday and preparing to go
to church and then making the journey is thus a liturgical act,
analogous to entering the portal of the building.

The action of assembling introduces once again the metaphor of
pilgrimage. We have encountered this image in the church year and
in the church building; now this basic image emerges in the shape
of the celebration of the Holy Communion by the pilgrim church.

In literature that makes use of the motif, two types of journey
may be distinguished.[11] One type is a circular movement of one
who sets out to accomplish a task and then returns. Such a journey
leads to the renewal and restoration of the traveller-hero. The most
prominent literary example is Odysseus, the Greek hero who left
his wife and son and home island to fight at Troy. The *Odyssey* is

the story of his ten-year journey home through trials, temptations, and tests until at last he returns to Ithaka, kills his wife's suitors, and reveals himself once more as husband and father. Christianity has described the movement of Christ the hero in similar terms. The Ambrosian Advent hymn sings of Christ,

> He leaves heaven to return;
> Travelling where dull hell-fires burn;
> Riding out, returning home
> As the Savior who has come.[12]

The circular movement of the Son of God is from heaven to earth and back to heaven again to resume his throne.

The other type of journey one finds in literature is a linear progression of the hero from a state of social or intellectual disorder toward a state of order often represented as a city. The prominent example of this kind of journey, also from the classical period, is Aeneas, who leaves the ruined Troy to found his own race in Italy and his own city, Rome. Christianity understands humanity by means of such a picture, moving from the disorder of sin to the perfect harmony of the heavenly city.

It is the achievement of the Eucharist to combine these two versions of the journey metaphor, joining renewal with order, restoration with the City of God. A collect originally by William Bright, in the *Book of Common Prayer* at Evening Prayer for Sundays, prays:

> Lord God, whose Son our Savior triumphed over the powers of death and prepared for us our place in the new Jerusalem: Grant that we, who have this day given thanks for his resurrection, may praise you in that City of which he is the light, and where he lives and reigns for ever and ever.[13]

The individual Christian may be said to make the second sort of journey, from disorder to order; humanity itself may be said to make the first sort of journey, from original perfection at the beginning in the Garden to the restoration of paradise at the end of the story. While each individual believer must appropriate the faith of the church, the Christian journey, unlike its literary analogies, is not made alone. It is made always in the company of others and of Christ himself. Such companionship is one of the consolations and encouragements of Holy Communion.

> In order to strengthen and encourage us... God gives us this sacrament, as much as to say, "Look, many kinds of sin are

assailing you; take this sign by which I give you my pledge that this sin is assailing not only you, but also my Son, Christ, and all his saints in heaven and on earth." Therefore take heart and be bold. You are not fighting alone. Great help and support are all around you.

This fellowship is two-fold; on the one hand we partake of Christ and all saints; on the other hand we permit all Christians to be partakers of us, in whatever way they and we are able. Thus, by means of this sacrament, all self-seeking love is rooted out and gives place to that which seeks the common good of all; and through the change wrought by love there is one bread, one drink, one body, one community. This is the true unity of Christian brethren.[14]

Thus the entrance rite is more than simply getting the ministers into the church and up to the altar. It is, as is the entire liturgy, the work of the people who rise and assemble to assume their place in the body of Christ. In their joyful fulfillment of their responsibility the words of the psalmist are renewed: "I was glad when they said to me, 'Let us go to the house of the Lord'" (Psalm 122:1).

This joy must be characteristic of the celebration of the Eucharist. John Ruskin tells of how on a Sunday in Turin, after an uninspired Waldensian service in the suburbs, he returned to the city the preacher had condemned and went into the gallery where Paul Veronese's *Solomon and the Queen of Sheba* "glowed in full afternoon light."

And as the perfect color and sound gradually asserted their power on me, they seemed finally to fasten me in the old article of Jewish faith, that things done delightfully and rightly, were always done by the help and in the Spirit of God.[15]

That experience marked a kind of conversion for him away from the cheerless religion of his upbringing and to an appreciation of the religious dimensions of the pleasure that art was able to provide. The first question in the *Westminster Shorter Catechism* (1648), "What is the chief end of man?" is answered, "Man's chief end is to glorify God and to enjoy him forever." Our obligation to praise God should be enjoyable for us, yielding pleasure deeper than laughter.[16] Isaac Watts has versified Psalm 147:

Praise ye the Lord! 'Tis good to raise
Your hearts and voices in his praise:

> His nature and his works invite
> To make this duty our delight.

Part of the preparation of the priest for the celebration of Mass in the Roman tradition was the recitation of Psalm 43:

> Send out your light and your truth
> that they may lead me,
>   and bring me to your holy hill and to your dwelling;
> that I may go to the altar of God,
>   to the God of my joy and gladness.

Gladness and joy mark those who approach the house of God and the altar.

Whenever we worship, the biblical stories come alive. The past lives again or, more accurately, lives still in us, and we are drawn on toward the goal of all creation. The entrance of the minsters at the beginning of the service, like all Christian ritual processions, is a dramatic portrayal of the pilgrim church, passing through this world toward that which is to come. We go in search of our true homeland in that heavenly country which God has prepared (see Hebrews 11:13–16). We follow in the company of Abraham and Sarah, the models for all the faithful who set out boldly in search of spiritual truth.

The entrance also portrays the hope of the prophet's vision of the nations streaming up the holy mountain to worship in God's temple (Isaiah 2:2–4; Micah 4:1–4). Those who enter this particular earthly temple to worship God, ideally a diverse company, are a sign and promise of the gathering of the nations, of people of all ranks and races and lands to share in the unity that lies ahead of us in the culmination of the kingdom. The gathering also instructs us in our responsibility as individuals and groups to open our hearts and minds to the diversity of humanity, who are all the recipients of God's love. Moreover, there are those whose faith and devotion are known but to God, who at the last day will also find their place prepared at the unending heavenly feast.

As the entrance rite of hymn or psalm, kyrie and/or canticle of praise concludes, the proper Collect of the Day is prayed. These mostly ancient prayers are remarkable achievements of compression, terse and epigrammatic, distilling in a few delicately crafted phrases a wealth of insight and devotion. The collect from the Gregorian sacramentary for Easter Day will serve as an example.

> Almighty God, through your only Son you overcame death
> and opened for us the gate of everlasting life. Give us your
> continual help; put good desires into our minds and bring
> them to full effect; through Jesus Christ our Lord.... [17]

In the view of Massey Shepherd, this collect from the Gregorian
sacramentary is "the key that unlocks the meaning of all our other
Collects for they but explain and comment upon it."[18] It teaches
us, even while we pray. In the subtle and understated manner
of collects, the prayer joins the risen Lord and the risen life. "If
with Christ you died to the elemental spirits of the universe," Paul
chided the Colossians, "why do you live as if you still belonged
to the world? ... Set your minds on things that are above" (Colossians 2:20; 3:2). Christ's resurrection lays ethical obligations on
those who would follow him. We learn in this prayer as throughout the New Testament that simply because Christ in his victorious
power is risen for us does not guarantee our rising in the likeness
of his resurrection to the enjoyment of eternal blessing. Something
is required of the believer.[19] Our life must be raised from the dead;
faith, if it is alive, must issue in a life of good deeds. But humanity, the Christian church maintains, is fallen, not just weak, and
therefore we require renovation and divine assistance if we are to
live the new life. Every good desire and each good work we accomplish are all due to God's surrounding and sustaining grace.
Through the victory won on the cross, triumphing over sin and
death, Christ has done for us what we could never do by ourselves.
So without God's continued support and assistance, we can neither
desire what is pleasing to God nor accomplish what we desire. The
Easter collect presumes and teaches our total dependence upon divine grace and goodness, but, it must be clearly understood, this
does not lead to dejection or paralysis. This total dependence has
two faces: without God we can do nothing, but with God we can
do all things. (See Philippians 4:13.)

The sacrifice of Christ for us established the New Covenant
between God and the people of God, which the words of institution proclaim: "This cup is the new covenant in my blood." Thus
the New Covenant becomes one of the names for the Eucharist.
In the Original Covenant, the Lord is portrayed as a God who
makes covenants as an expression of mercy. God in incomprehen-
sible grace chose to be bound to the people divinely selected to be
God's own.

> I passed by you again and looked on you; you were at the age for love. I spread the edge of my cloak over you, and covered your nakedness: I pledged myself to you and entered into a covenant with you, says the Lord God, and you became mine. (Ezekiel 16:8)

The covenant established on Horeb-Sinai was sealed in blood shed on the altar of sacrifice and sprinkled on the people (Exodus 24:3–8). For ancient Israel, blood was the seat of life. The spilling of blood in sacrifice showed the seriousness of the covenant: life must be given up in order to establish the covenant. And it also showed the life-giving property of the sacrifice and the covenant: the people are splashed with blood. A further sign of the covenant, which sealed it to the people in a still more intimate way, was the sacrificial meal in the presence of God (Exodus 24:1-2, 9–11). Despite the repeated faithlessness of the people, God remains faithful to the covenant and seeks to restore Israel to the original relationship.

> Return, O faithless children, says the Lord, for I am your master; I will take you, one from a city and two from a family, and I will bring you to Zion. (Jeremiah 3:14)

The prophets saw that the covenant carried with it the possibility of a legalistic understanding of the relationship with God, as if it could be maintained by external practices alone. They therefore looked for a time when the Lord would establish a new covenant, written on the hearts of the people.

> The days are surely coming, says the Lord, when I will make a new covenant with the house of Israel and the house of Judah. . . . I will put my law within them, and I will write it on their hearts; and I will be their God, and they shall be my people. (Jeremiah 31:31–33)

With all this in mind, Jesus at the Last Supper said of the chalice, "This cup is the new covenant in my blood." By this meal, which was to distill and proclaim Christ's death and resurrection until his appearing, God was initiating the new covenant promised through Jeremiah. This new covenant did not abolish the old one but grew out of it as the lifeblood of Christ replaced the lifeblood of sacrificial animals as the seal of the covenant.

In the biblical understanding, the covenant between God and the people bound them together: "I will be your God, and you shall be my people." Close, intimate, personal, and spiritually binding, the covenant tied God to human history in a way unheard of before in other religions of the world. The covenant was not made with individuals exclusively. The original covenant was made with Abraham and his descendants, a whole people although they were as yet in the loins of the patriarch. When Jesus instituted the New Covenant, he did so surrounded by the Twelve, who gathered at the table.

> That last night at supper lying
> Mid the twelve, his chosen band,
> Jesus, with the Law complying,
> Keeps the feast its rites demand;
> Then, more precious food supplying,
> Gives himself with his own hand.[20]

Throughout the Bible, God is gathering a people. Moreover, this New Covenant extends beyond Israel and Judah. Jesus said of the chalice, "This cup is the new covenant in my blood, shed for you and for all people for the forgiveness of sin." This New Covenant is for all and reaches out in a worldwide embrace to include the whole of humanity. The New Covenant enlarges our view of those who should and who one day will gather to worship the creator and redeemer of all.

Hearing

The procession that is the entrance rite makes a station at what was called anciently the ambo, the place for the readings and the sermon. Physical movement largely stops, but it is replaced by what at least ought to be an intense mental and spiritual concentration and action, for this third action of the Holy Communion is *listening* to the living voice of Scripture read and proclaimed in the midst of the church today. It is an essential section of the whole action, for here, in the power of the Holy Spirit (see Luke 4:18), the central stories of the faith are told again, the past renewed, the tradition passed on. The Reformation insistence that preaching be a part of the proclamation of Scripture is a way of saying that the ancient words of the Bible must be shown to have continuing importance and relevance today. The old stories retain their revolutionary power, for these words above all others are charged with living energy.

Words — written and read and spoken — are the medium of this part of the Eucharist most of all. And here lies a danger for modern participants. We are surrounded by such a surfeit of words in newspapers and magazines and radio and television and speeches and lectures that we find it difficult to receive words with attention. Moreover, so much of what we hear is intended to deceive that we seldom trust words to bear authentic and dependable meaning. We are surrounded by so much and so many varied forms of dishonest expression — "the false laughter of television, the fake enthusiasm of advertising, the commercial jollity and condolences of greeting cards, the lying assertions of politicians"[21] — that it is inevitable that some falsity will infect our language and thought. The disease has disastrous effects on a religion rooted in written Scripture that bears witness to one who is called the Word of God and that relies upon verbal proclamation to make its message come alive. There can be no hope of liturgical and spiritual renewal without a renewal of a sense of the majesty and wonder and power of language. Dante in the *Inferno* has the poet and guide Virgil say contemptuously of Nimrod:

> To him all speech is meaningless; as his own,
> which no one understands, is simply gibberish.[22]

The giant's babble prevents him from expecting and hearing the clarity and precision and possibility of language in himself and others. The lesson is important: if one's own language is enervated and flattened, one will have great difficulty responding to the richness of verbal craft, subtle and beautiful and spellbinding. If one's own language is unintelligible, the possibility of responding to the richness of language anywhere is fatally compromised. We speak (and think) gibberish, and because of that we assume that all other speech is as devoid of meaning as our own.

The proclamation of the Word of God within the liturgy of the word is an oral event. Language is spoken and heard. It is thus a mutual event in which one speaks and others listen. But the dialogue is deeper and greater than is experienced in ordinary life, for both reader and hearers are listeners to the Word that addresses them all, individually and collectively. The words read and spoken are intended to evoke a response in all who listen and hear, as Isaiah declared (Isaiah 55:10–11). We do more than receive information. We are challenged and stirred to the depth of our being by words that shake the foundations, that destroy and create, tear up and plant (Jeremiah 1:10).

The sort of reading that we are most familiar with may be called informative reading, reading for information. But the reading of the Scripture in the liturgy is *formative* reading — reading by which we submit to the author in order to hear, receive, and ponder. We are not in charge. We must surrender to the authority and power of the reading and let it form us as is its intention, so that we may grow into the image of God. So in the Eastern liturgies the readings are prefaced with the declaration, "Wisdom! Let us be attentive." It is more than the admonition of a teacher to pay attention to something that is important. It is a solemn declaration that in these readings Holy Wisdom himself is present and that we are to be receptive to these formative words. The reading of these central and normative words helps the church know itself as a coherent culture with a long tradition, and it also confronts the church with discomforting prophetic words that are a necessary part of its message.

By the readings from Scripture the church remembers the great things God has done to redeem the world. Such remembering gives rise to another ancient name for the Eucharist, the Anamnesis, a Greek word meaning "remembrance." The Anamnesis is the church's obedience to Jesus' command, "Do this in remembrance of me" (Luke 22:19; 1 Corinthians 11:24). Specifically it is that portion of the Great Thanksgiving that recalls and names before the Father the whole life and work of Christ, making those deeds a contemporary experience. But in the larger sense, the Anamnesis, the remembering, begins in the first half of the Eucharist, the ministry of the word, as the church reads again from the ancient record and the living word is again present among his people. What the church does to remember Christ is the celebration of the whole eucharistic action, the ministry of the Word as well as the ministry of the Sacrament, and there is a "real presence" of Christ throughout, but particularly in the climax of each of the sections: the reading of the Gospel and the eating of the meal. Remembering, in the deepest sense, makes present Christ and his work.

Outside of church, reading is usually done by oneself and is most often an intensely private mental activity. In the liturgy of the word, however, we move beyond the written word to a more dynamic and communal event. Gathered in the Christian assembly, we, together, hear the words addressed now to the present community from the community of the past. And yet we learn that in fact there is no separation and that we are all members of one community, the whole, undivided people of God living and dead, in heaven and on earth.

In the churches of the West, three lessons are read. The first reading (except during Easter when it comes from the Acts of the Apostles) is from the Original Covenant, telling of the mighty deeds done among God's people. The Old Original Covenant has not been abrogated, Christians are reminded by the source of this reading, and continues alongside the New Covenant, making Jews and Christians not two separate families but siblings, Judaism being the elder. As Jeremiah sang:

> The steadfast love of the Lord never ceases,
>   his mercies never come to an end;
> they are new every morning.
>   (Lamentations 3:22–23a)

The old stories continue to speak and to surprise; the power is undiminished.

Next, following a psalm that joins the two readings with scriptural comment on their themes, the Word of God is proclaimed through the Epistle, the Second Lesson, a reading from an apostle (usually St. Paul), read today in the Christian assembly as the apostle's letters were originally read in the churches of Asia Minor, Greece, and Rome. "I solemnly command you by the Lord that this letter be read to all," St. Paul wrote in his first letter to the Thessalonians (5:27). As these letters, not originally intended for the ages, continue to be read down through the centuries and far beyond the Mediterranean world that first saw the rise of the Christian movement, we have a convincing testimony to the power of tradition, the handing on of the stories and insights and testimonies of past generations. "So then . . . stand firm and hold on to the traditions which you were taught by us, either by word of mouth or by our letter," St. Paul admonished the Thessalonian church in his second letter (2:15).

Finally, the Word of God is proclaimed through a reading of the Holy Gospel of the Lord Jesus Christ. This reading is more than the third in a series. It is treated differently from the previous two readings. It is read not by a lay person but by one who has received ordination. It is welcomed by the Alleluia, and it is surrounded before and after by the Gospel acclamations, "Glory to you, Lord," "Praise to you, Lord Christ," addressed to Jesus Christ as to one actually present.[23] The ministry of the word comes to its climax as

the congregation, following an ancient practice, stands to receive
this reading, to listen to Christ speaking anew to his people now.

> When the gospel is read, let all the presbyters and all the dea-
> cons and all the people stand very quietly to hear the words
> of the King of kings.[24]

In this reading we have passed from the words of the servants of
God to the words of the Lord himself.

Following the three readings, the proclamation of the word
of God is continued through a statement in the language of the
present, the sermon. Readings and sermon together rehearse and
tell anew the saving revelation of God in Christ. The purpose of
preaching is so to open the Scriptures that attentive hearers will be
able to find themselves included in the continuing story of God's
presence and activity in saving the world. The preacher bears witness in contemporary terms to the truth of the ancient Scriptures,
receiving a particular idea from the readings, delivering the sermon
to the congregation, and the congregation in turn delivering the
message to the world.

Intercession

One of the ways this message from Bible to preacher to congregation is extended to the world is through the prayers of intercession
for the "whole state" (that is, the wholeness, health) of Christ's
church and the world. The ministry of the word is concluded with
the prayers of the people who, in the fourth action of the Eucharist,
make *intercession* for all and who give thanks on behalf of all.
There is no finer example of the responsibility of the church than
in this understanding of the purpose and scope of the intercessions.
The congregation, prompted by the Holy Spirit (Romans 8:27),
prays not for itself only but for all — in need, in joy, in grief, in
pain — and the congregation gives thanks not only for all that God
has done for them but for the good things that God has done for
and given to others, especially those who do not know the source
of these good gifts or whom to thank for them. The church of God,
knowing that all good things "are from above, coming down from
the Father of lights" (James 1:17), on behalf of all, especially those
who cannot or who will not express their gratitude, gives thanks
to the triune God, Father, Son, and Holy Spirit.

In Christ we learn of God's kingdom and will, and the pattern is set for our prayer. Christ, the eternal High Priest, continually intercedes for his church and the world (John 17:1; 1 John 2:1). When Christians pray, they join with their Lord in his intercession, asking for a continuation of God's gifts to all creation. By these prayers we reach out our arms, emulating Christ, whose arms were extended on the cross, to embrace the concerns of all humanity. The remarkable Anglican divine, Lancelot Andrewes, summed up the intent of all these prayers of intercession:

> Remember all your creation for good,
> visit the world with your compassion . . .
> and have mercy upon all, O Lord.[25]

The intercessions of the church make this noble summary specific by lifting up individual names and particular concerns (see 1 Timothy 2:8) before the throne of grace.

St. Paul wrote to the Romans (8:15b–17) that they have received a spirit of adoption:

> When we cry, "Abba! Father!" it is that very Spirit bearing witness with our spirit that we are children of God, and if children, then heirs, heirs of God and joint heirs with Christ — if, in fact, we suffer with him so that we may also be glorified with him.

Prayer, then, is more than a private transaction between the individual and God. Prayer is the work of the Holy Spirit, who joins with our spirit to give voice to the inarticulate groanings of the whole creation (Romans 8:22–23), binding us to the suffering and the needy, impelling us to service, pointing us beyond the present pain toward the fulfillment of the hope that has been planted in us. Those who pray have their vision expanded beyond themselves, beyond their own concerns and welfare, toward an ever-larger view of the church and the world, embracing others who pray on earth and in heaven, the needs and concerns of all the world, and the promised future of God.

Christians pray because they follow the example of Christ, who during his life on earth was regularly found at prayer (Luke 3:21; 6:12; 11:1–4). After the Ascension, Christ asked the Father to send the Holy Spirit to the waiting and praying church. "He always lives to make intercession" for those who approach God through him (Hebrews 7:25). Christians pray because they see their neighbors in need. They feel the pain of others and cry out to God for help, and by their prayer they offer themselves for service in meeting the needs of others, relieving pain, giving comfort, extending support. Christians pray also because they have glimpsed the future and because they treasure God's promise of re-creation (Isaiah 65:17; 66:22; Romans 8:19–21; Revelation 21:1–5). Longing for the completion and consummation of the cosmos, they are impelled to urgent prayer for consolation and wholeness and unity, looking forward in hope to that time when the kingdom is present in its fullness, the will of God is perfectly done, and, in that grandest vision of the Bible (1 Corinthians 15:28), God is all in all.

The Eucharist is called the Lord's Supper. In this meal we eat and drink with the Lord and with his disciples. Just as the Lord's Prayer prays with and for the community, "Our Father," so the Lord's Supper will not allow us to neglect the horizontal dimension of the community in heaven and earth with whom we share this meal. The Supper that permits us to share in the broken body of the Savior of the world involves us too in the broken world that caused his death. We bring to our celebration of this sacrament not only our own anguish but that of all the world. The Holy Supper is to "make us one body, one Spirit in Christ, that we may worthily serve the world in his name."[26]

After pausing to recount the old yet still fresh formative stories in Scripture, psalm, and sermon, the physical movement of the service resumes. The focus of attention moves from the ambo or lectern to the altar table, from the place of reading to the place of feasting, from the Book to the Meal.

Offering

In preparation, we do the fifth action of the Eucharist and make *offering* to God for God's use everything we have, for God's work in us cannot be effective until the ordinary, commonplace material of our lives, just as it is, is turned over entirely to God. In the presentation of our gifts of money and the bread and wine we offer representative samples of this world with all its sin upon them. We offer in the bread all that is necessary for life and in the wine all that makes life glad. We also spread before God what we have done with what we have received for good and for ill, including our corruption of God's good gifts. We present to God what we have first received, the grain and the grapes that God has provided and as human labor and commerce have worked upon them. The gifts stand not only for what God has given us; they also represent what we have made of God's gifts — the abundance and poverty, generosity and greed, moderation and excess.

In the sacrament of Holy Communion, God, who gives everything we have to offer, takes our offered gifts together with our lives represented in and by the gifts and blesses them and gives them back to us washed and transformed and made new, so that we may go confidently into the world to be God's people, to be what Luther called "walking monstrances," showing the splendor of God and doing the works of Christ who "went about doing good" (Acts 10:38). St. Paul appealed to the Romans:

> I appeal to you, therefore, brothers and sisters, by the mercies of God, to present your bodies as a living sacrifice, holy and acceptable to God, which is your spiritual worship. Do not be conformed to this world, but be transformed by the renewing of your minds, so that you may discern what is the will of God — what is good and acceptable and perfect. (Romans 12:1–2)

Such transformation is not an end in itself but is accomplished so that we may be worthy to offer a sacrifice of praise to God in words, songs, and deeds of self-sacrificing love.

> Through him, then, let us continually offer a sacrifice of praise to God, that is, the fruit of lips that confess his name. Do not neglect to do good and to share what you have, for such sacrifices are pleasing to God. (Hebrews 13:15–16)

Indeed, this offering is the work of Christ. Luther explained that

> we do not offer Christ as a sacrifice, but that Christ offers us. And in this way it is permissible, yes, profitable, to call the mass a sacrifice; not on its own account, but because we offer ourselves as a sacrifice along with Christ.[27]

It is an ancient insight. The Eucharist is the fulfillment of the pure offering of the Gentiles in the Messianic Age, the self-oblation of the church described by St. Augustine.[28] The true priest of this sacrifice is Christ himself, who "takes up our cause, presents us and our prayer and praise, and offers himself for us in heaven."[29]

The communion meal is shared around the holy table of the altar, that place in the church building where God and God's people meet, where the people place their offerings and their gifts, which signify the offering of themselves, and where they receive the most precious gift that God has to offer them. So the Eucharist is called the Sacrament of the Altar, the sacrament of meeting. It is the sacrament of encounter with God. We are offered to God, and God is offered to us.

Thanksgiving

The offering is preparatory to the sixth action of the Eucharist, *thanksgiving.* One of the names for the central prayer of the Eucharist is the Great Thanksgiving. In this prayer we — the entire congregation, although the prayer is spoken by the single voice of the presider — commemorate with high thanksgiving our perfect redemption through the mighty work of God in Christ, and we pray that God in Christ will come among us now in the power of the Holy Spirit to transform our lives through his deathless life.

In this great prayer, the past is renewed, the present is transformed, and the future is made already present. Thanksgiving is the generation of hope by the recollection of past mercies. What we know from the past of the power and love of God gives us confidence in the continued mercy of God despite the current circumstances of our lives. It is the work of the Holy Spirit in us to collapse time and its separations, and we are now one with the past and the future, and they are one with us. We are contemporary with Abraham and Miriam and Moses and Deborah and Ruth and David and the prophets and believing men and women of Christian history and with all who come after us until the end when all will be fulfilled in the kingdom of God. Past and present are gathered into one as together we look in anticipation for the dawn of the promised fulfillment of the kingdom of God. We receive this meal as "a foretaste of the feast to come."

It is no wonder, therefore, that the language as well as the spirit of the celebration of the sacramental meal is one of thanksgiving and that an increasingly common name for the meal is the Eucharist, "the thanksgiving." We can already thank God for the final and complete victory at the consummation, for it is assured, and we are even now given a taste of it in the sacramental meal.

The solemn proclamation of thanksgiving begins with the very ancient dialogue, which, with mutual regard and concern between clergy and people, lifts the united congregation to join with the church triumphant, joining heaven and earth and allowing us already in this life to take our part in the ceaseless worship by the citizens of heaven. In every church where these ancient words are exchanged and the venerable ritual is enacted, the vision of St. John the Divine becomes a present reality.

> After this I looked, and there in heaven a door stood open! And the first voice, which I had heard speaking to me like a trumpet, said, "Come up here, and I will show you what must take place after this." (Revelation 4:1)

> There was a great multitude that no one could count, from every nation, from all tribes and peoples and languages, standing before the throne and before the Lamb....And all the angels...fell on their faces before the throne and worshiped God. (Revelation 7:9, 11)

> > Day and night without ceasing they sing,
> > "Holy, holy, holy,
> > the Lord God the Almighty,
> > who was and is and is to come."
> > (Revelation 4:8)

We mortals do more than simply add our earthly and human songs to the chorus of angels. We dare to signify the cherubim whom Isaiah saw in his vision (Isaiah 6:1–3) and who surround the throne of the Holy One, and we take upon our mortal lips their thrice-holy hymn, the Sanctus:

> Holy, holy, holy, Lord God of hosts.
> Heaven and earth are full of your glory.

We are summoned to put aside all distraction and concentrate as completely as we are able on the stupendous mystery we are encountering. We are to see God, hidden in bread and wine, for mortal eyes cannot bear the direct, unmediated splendor of the Most Holy One, the Creator of the world. The Liturgy of St. John Chrysostom teaches and invites:

> > Let us, who mystically represent the cherubim,
> > and who sing the thrice-holy hymn
> > to the life-creating Trinity
> > now lay aside all earthly care
> > so that we may welcome the King of all
> > who comes invisibly upborne by hosts of angels.
> > Alleluia. Alleluia. Alleluia.

Ministers and people bow low before the presence. In the Chaldean liturgy of the Holy Apostles Addai and Mari, the priest, approaching the altar says:

> Before the glorious throne of your power,
>> the unattainable seat of your majesty,
>> the great place of your burning love,
>> the altar of forgiveness, set up by your mercy
>> and in which your glory dwells,
> we, O Lord, your people and the sheep of your pasture,
> join our voices with those of the unnumbered cherubim who
>> praise you
> and of the myriads of seraphim and archangels who sing your
>> holiness.
> We fall down in worship of you,
> to praise and glorify you for ever, Lord of all,
> Father, Son, and Holy Spirit.[30]

In a Swedish paraphrase of the Sanctus by Samuel Hedborn, the congregation sings,

> Holy Majesty, before you
> We bow to worship and adore you!
>> With grateful hearts to you we sing!
> Earth and heaven tell the story
> Of your eternal might and glory,
>> And all your works their incense bring.
> Lo, hosts of cherubim
> And countless seraphim
>> Sing hosanna!
> Holy is God, almighty God,
> All-merciful and all-wise God![31]

A Protestant expression of a similar reverence in the presence of the Holy God is the stately solemnity of Isaac Watts's paraphrase of Psalm 100:

> Before Jehovah's aweful throne,
> Ye nations bow with sacred joy:
> Know that the Lord is God alone,
> He can create, and he destroy.

Gerhard Tersteegen's hymn on the experience of Jacob in the wilderness of Paran admonishes:

> Lo, God is here! let us adore
> And own how dreadful is this place!
> Let all within us feel his power,
> And silent bow before his face.[32]

The Sanctus ended, the great Prayer of Thanksgiving continues, reviewing the history of salvation as a way of praising the God who saves. The central affirmations are summarized in the acclamation of the people:

> Thy death, O Lord, we commemorate,
> thy resurrection we confess,
> and thy second coming we await.[33]

In the power of the holy and life-creating Spirit, the work of God in Christ is remembered. The story of the salvation of the world is reviewed. The paschal mystery at the heart of the Christian faith is recalled and brought into the present as a living reality as the church remembers before the Father the saving deeds of the Son, who in fulfillment of his promises, makes himself present to the congregation. The Great Thanksgiving is concluded with the Our Father, the prayer our Lord taught his disciples, used here as the table prayer of the people of God.

Eating and Drinking

Now follows the seventh action of the Eucharist, *eating and drinking* the consecrated bread and wine. Christians affirm the presence of Jesus Christ in this meal but locate and explain the presence in a variety of ways. Properly understood, the terms used to explain the presence indicate the indefinable presence of the Savior of the world. The classical Lutheran formulation, for example, is that Christ is present *"under* the bread, *with* the bread, *in* the bread."[34] The effort is to avoid metaphysical speculation and to preserve the mystery of the eucharistic presence of Christ. God who is hidden and revealed in the read and preached word is likewise hidden and revealed in the visible word of the sacrament. As the reading and preaching of the Gospel has as its purpose the eliciting of a response from those who hear, so the communicant is called upon by the Holy Communion to respond in recognition and commitment as in the climax to the Fourth Gospel, "My Lord and my God."

Such feasting transforms us, for this meal is unlike earthly food. St. Augustine hears Christ say, "You will not convert me, like

common food, into your substance, but you will be changed into
me."[35] A future filled with promise is opened to us by the Spirit
whom we invoke and who is the presence of what is not yet. The
fulfillment of creation is anticipated and assured.

By this Supper we share a mystical union with Christ and he
with us. It is an intimate sharing, like that between two lovers.
So we call it the Holy Communion. The Apostles' Creed speaks
of the "communion of saints," which in the original Latin of the
creed could mean "communion (union) of the holy people," those
who believe in Christ; or it could mean the "communion in holy
things," the unity we have because we share in the sacrament that
makes us one, one with God and one with each other.

The moment of the holy communion is an intensely personal
encounter with the living Lord of the church. The medieval prayer,
Anima Christi is an example of such individual concentration.

> Soul of Christ, sanctify me;
> Body of Christ, save me;
> Blood of Christ, refresh me;
> Water from the side of Christ, wash me;
> Passion of Christ, strengthen me;
> O good Jesus hear me,
> Within your wounds hide me,
> Let me not be separated from you;
> From the malicious enemy defend me;
> In the hour of death call me,
> And bid me come to you
> That with the saints I may praise you
> through the ages of eternity.

The conclusion even of that intensely personal prayer of union
between Christ and the individual, however, expands beyond an
exclusively private concern. The goal of communion is union with
Christ and with all the saints. Even at the moment of communion,
receiving into our mouths the consecrated bread and wine, we are
reminded that we are eating this meal with all the church. It is indeed "the blest sacrament of unity"[36] binding together in intimate
union not only the congregation, not only all the churches of Christianity, but all the scattered and fragmented peoples of the earth
who are to be brought into the kingdom of God. In the ancient
prayer recorded in the *Didache,* a document from the first century:

> As this bread was once scattered over the hills and then
> was brought together and made one, so let your church be

brought together from the ends of the earth into your kingdom; for yours is the glory and the power through Jesus Christ for ever.[37]

The biblical allusion is to the grand vision of Matthew 8:11, "Many will come from east and west and will eat with Abraham and Isaac and Jacob in the kingdom of heaven."[38]

In the Eastern churches, while the people receive the Holy Communion, the choir sings to them, "Receive the body of Christ, taste the fountain of immortality," involving the whole congregation in the action of communion as each prays for the others. John Chrysostom preached:

> We communicate not only by participating and partaking, but also by being united.... For as the bread consisting of many grains is made one, so that the grains nowhere appear; they exist indeed, but their difference is not seen because of their union; so we are joined with each other and with Christ, there not being one body to nourish you and another to nourish your neighbor, but the very same for all. Wherefore the Apostle adds, "For we all partake of the one bread." Now if we are all members of the same and all become the same, why do we not also show forth the same love and in this respect also become one?[39]

The church comes to know itself in communion with its Lord. Augustine preached to his people:

> If therefore you are the body of Christ and his members, it is the sacrament of yourselves that is set upon the Lord's table, the sacrament of yourselves that you receive. Be what you receive, and receive what you are. You hear the words, "The body of Christ," and you answer, "Amen." Be a member of the body of Christ so that your Amen may be honest.[40]

If you have received well, you are that which you receive.[41]

Holy Communion goes beyond the personal action of reception, of eating and drinking, and involves the communicant with all those who receive the sacrament. Moreover, as the prayer from the *Didache* asks, communicants by their communicating are obliged to do their part, by prayer if in no other way, to bring the nations into the kingdom of God.

The Eucharist, like all works of art but intensified because it is more than a human creation, changes the way we look at the world. What we see with our eyes is not all that is there. Symbols, especially religious symbols, change how we see and therefore transform our relation to what we see, disclosing what is otherwise hidden. Words are often necessary to make clear what is happening and what is intended and to suggest what may not be obvious. Actions are necessary to dramatize and make vivid the energy of the word of God who brought the worlds into existence and who continues to call forth all that is. Words and actions are incomplete without each other. Words alone can give a distorted understanding of the Christian faith, suggesting that it is ethereal, otherworldly, spiritual. But in fact, Christianity, as Archbishop William Temple said early in the twentieth century, is the most materialistic of the world's religions. Liturgical churches are sacramental churches, taking seriously the created world that is capable of bearing the Creator to us. Sunsets, flowers, and mountain heights proclaim the divine beauty of the mighty Maker, but more importantly the Creator takes the elements of creation and uses them to come to us. In ordinary everyday actions, using the common elements of the world, God is present and acting. It is no pale memorial that we make, no merely symbolic action that we do. What is done in the sacraments is done by none other than God. Therefore we know that all creation can be the bearer of God's presence, and we go out from the sacraments with a new appreciation of the elements of nature — water and air and rocks and trees — and of the potential of all humanity. Horizons undreamed of are opened to our sight; further dimensions of reality are revealed; new unity, new responsibility, new opportunity are unfolded.

The sacrament builds unity while being at the same time a sign of unity, making real the unity for which Christ the High Priest is even now praying to the Father (John 17:11, 23). The sacrament is a gift of life to those in the shadow of death, grafting them on the true Vine, who is the life of all the living. It is the gift of strength to weary pilgrims and to the infirm or timid, directing them beyond themselves to others and empowering them for service, giving them strength and resolve to do the work of God.

Scattering

A brief expression of praise for the gift of communion concludes the liturgy of the Eucharist.

Finished and perfected, O Christ our God, so far as in us lies, is the Mystery which you have ordained. We have made the memorial of your death; we have seen the symbol of the resurrection; we have been enriched with your inexhaustible bounty and filled with your undying life; and of this count us worthy in the world to come.[42]

The final action of the Eucharist, therefore, is the *scattering* of those who have assembled, who, now that their work of prayer is done, depart to serve. It is an extension of the postcommunion thanksgiving, an enactment of the congregation's praise.

The old medieval name for the sacrament, the Mass, is still used by Roman Catholics, Anglicans, and Lutherans. The origin of the word is uncertain, but it probably comes from the dismissal at the conclusion of the rite (*Ite, missa est,* "Go, it is the dismissal"). The name Mass thus suggests that the sacrament has the intention of strengthening for service in the world. A prayer from the conclusion of the Syriac Liturgy of Malabar, translated into a hymn by Charles William Humphries and revised by Percy Dearmer, turns the communicants from the house of the church toward life in the world where their service, their liturgy in the larger sense, continues. For God, who is found most intimately in the Holy Communion, is also found in the needy of the world.

> Strengthen for service, Lord, the hands
> That holy things have taken;
> Let ears that now have heard thy songs
> To clamor never waken.
>
> Lord, may the tongues which "Holy" sang
> Keep free from all deceiving;
> The eyes which saw thy love be bright,
> Thy blessed hope perceiving.
>
> The feet that tread thy hallowed courts
> From light do thou not banish;
> The bodies by thy Body fed
> With thy new life replenish.[43]

As Holy Communion begins in the waters of baptism, so it ends there, with the obligation to live what we are, doing the work that makes us Christians.[44] The Liturgy of St. John Chrysostom concludes with the parting admonition, "Let us love one another, so that with one mind we may glorify the Father, and the Son, and the Holy Spirit, the Trinity one in essence and undivided." Love has been received, and so love must be shown.

The psalmist exclaimed in an odd phrase, appropriate to the Holy Communion, "Taste and see that the Lord is good" (Psalm 34:8). John Donne in his 1628 Easter sermon chose as his text 1 Corinthians 13:12, "Now we see through a glass darkly, but then face to face," contrasting now and then, our present partial knowledge and our coming perfect knowledge. In the course of the sermon, drawing upon St. Augustine and reflecting medieval anatomical ideas, Donne declares that "the sight is so much the noblest of all the senses as that it is all the senses"; therefore, according to Augustine, "all the senses are called seeing," as in Revelation 1:12 St. John turned "to see the sound" and in Psalm 34:8 we are invited to "taste and see that the Lord is good." Donne exhorts his congregation:

> Employ then this noblest sense upon the noblest object, see God; see God in everything, and then thou needest not take off thine eye from beauty, from riches, from honour, from anything.

So it is with the Holy Supper. In these "visible words" of the Sacrament we are enabled to "see the sound" heard in Scripture and sermon, and we who "taste and see" are given the promise that we who taste the bread and wine will, when time is done, see the reality of God who comes to us in this holy sacrament and whom we find everywhere in creation.

This sacrament of Holy Communion in its never-ending richness has been given to console us in distress, to bind us to God and to one another, and to strengthen us for doing the work of the kingdom so that at last the entire world may join in the praise of God, the maker and redeemer of all. Then, at the last, even the richness of sacraments will give way to clear and direct sight.

Chapter Eight

HYMNS
Hallowing Song

☩

Hymns have played a significant, often decisive role in the life of the church from its early years. St. Ambrose had his followers sing hymns proclaiming the orthodox faith to counter the claims of the Arians. Hymns were added to the breviary. Sequences were inserted into the Mass. Hymns accompanied extraliturgical devotions. Through the centuries, popular devotion, often theologically unrefined, has been fed by vernacular hymns. Dwight L. Moody (1837–1899), a shoe salesman who gave up business for missionary work, met Ira B. Sankey in 1870 and together campaigned in many American cities and in Great Britain. Moody said the schools he founded in his hometown of Northfield, Massachusetts — Northfield Seminary for girls (1879) and Mount Hermon School for boys (1881), now united as Northfield Mount Hermon School — were "sung up." The funds for the schools were raised by his revivals that were in large measure singing-assemblies.

It is practically impossible to imagine the Christian church without hymns, so intertwined are they with Christian life and thought and worship. Although song has seemed natural to human beings everywhere, however, increasingly we seem uncomfortable with public song. Children continue to make up fragments of melody for themselves before they learn to speak their thoughts, but as we grow in years we sing publicly less and less. In a culture in which many are so inept with language that we distrust our own speech and stuff it with indications of our insecurity and the tentativeness of our expression, smothering our speech with "like" and "you know," it is no wonder that our words seldom rise to song. We listen to the songs of others, but ever fewer of us take songs into our mouths in public and let the words flow over our lips. Instead, we are hesitant, afraid, ashamed of song as it comes from us. Nonetheless, hymns are practically essential to Christianity. To explain the helpful and necessary role of hymns in the spiritual life to hesitant moderns, it may be observed that hymns serve a twofold function: they give us a voice and they are instruments of instruction.

Giving Us Voice

First, hymns can speak for us. We are often dumb to tell what we think or feel, but the words of a hymn, joined to its tune, can express feelings and emotions we feel but for which we have trouble finding words. Hymns can serve as our surrogate voice. Here, indeed, is a significant difference between hymns and poetry. When we read a poem with pleasure we may agree with the speaker. We may say, "Yes, Robert Frost is right. That is how it is; I have known people like that.' Or we may say, "That is a terrifying idea. I have never thought of it that way before, but now I see how someone might feel that way." When we read poetry we read someone else's thoughts. No matter how completely we may agree with the poem, it is still heard as the voice of another. But when we sing hymns, the distinction between the hymn writer and us evaporates, and the voice in the hymn becomes our voice, the thoughts expressed in the hymn are experienced as our thoughts. I appropriate words written by someone else for my own use to express my own thoughts and feelings. Those who teach poetry insist on maintaining a distinction between the poet who composed the poem and the speaker whose voice we hear in the poem. When, for example, Robert Herrick writes of a delectable mistress, that chaste priest of the Church of England is not (or at least is not necessarily) expressing his own experience; when John Donne writes in the voice of a woman he is not speaking for himself. When we sing a hymn, however, we do not much care who wrote the words.[1] When I sing,

> Good Christian friends, rejoice and sing!
> Now is the triumph of our King![2]

I am singing those words to the people around me in the congregation and to the whole church on earth and in heaven. When I sing,

> Judge eternal, throned in splendor,
>   Lord of lords and King of kings,
> With thy living fire of judgment
>   Purge this land of bitter things,[3]

Henry Holland's words become mine as I implore the Judge of the nations to purge and purify this land of its hatred and poverty and violence and whatever particular evil gave rise to the choice of this hymn for this particular day. Hymns give us songs to sing, but, most of all, they give us words to use as if they were our own.

In times of bitter quarrel hymns can give expression to our longing for an end to the "night of doubt and sorrow" and for the time when shadowed grief will give way to the "morn of song." When the schism at Concordia Seminary in St. Louis took place in February 1974, those who went into exile to form Seminex marched off singing not a stirring Lutheran chorale but "The church's one foundation is Jesus Christ her Lord." In the name of pure Lutheran theology the protesters sang an Anglican hymn. The choice of an English hymn by a largely ethnically German denomination suggests the ecumenical role hymns play in the life of the church; hymns move easily from one situation to another as new groups find old words appropriate to their situation. Individuals and churches do more than merely continue the use of songs derived from and representative of their own denomination. Hymns reach across the boundaries and unite peoples and times and causes.

"The Church's One Foundation" was written in 1866 by Samuel John Stone, a young Anglican priest, in protest against the protracted controversy occasioned by a book, *The Pentateuch and the Book of Joshua Critically Examined* by John William Colenso (1814–1883), the first (Anglican) Bishop of Natal, South Africa. In the book, Colenso, who had already been accused of tolerating polygamy, questioned whether any of the Pentateuch had been composed in Moses' time, doubted that Moses ever lived, and declared that Joshua and the Books of the Chronicles were entirely fictitious. Forty-one bishops urged Colenso to resign. When he refused, he was deposed by Bishop Gray of Capetown, who claimed jurisdiction as metropolitan in South Africa. Colenso maintained that he held office under patent from the crown and stood by his claim. An unhappy, involved, and prolonged struggle followed in which the original issues faded into the background, and the question became one of the degree to which the church was subject to the state. Stone, deeply troubled by the bitter quarrel, wrote of the church,

> Though with a scornful wonder
> Men see her sore oppressed,

> By schisms rent asunder,
>   By heresies distressed;
> Yet saints their watch are keeping,
>   Their cry goes up, "How long?"
> And soon the night of weeping
>   Shall be the morn of song.[4]

The Lutheran controversy in twentieth-century St. Louis, although it was between two conservative positions, in some ways resembled the Anglican struggle in the nineteenth century in South Africa. The choice of Stone's hymn was remarkably apposite.

When our hearts overflow with joy and gratitude we find our voice in the language and sound of hymns. "The Lutheran *Te Deum*," Martin Rinkhart's "Now Thank We All Our God," gives us appropriate words to sing at weddings, baptisms, funerals, and countless other occasions, to praise the Triune God who has cared for us since birth and who is asked to continue that care throughout this life, freeing us "from all ills / In this world and the next." Moreover, the hymn reminds us that we are to do more than sing words. We are to thank God also with our hearts and with our hands as well, doing the gestures of devotion, celebrating the Great Thanksgiving of the Lord's Supper, extending our hands to those in need. The General Thanksgiving in the *Book of Common Prayer* prays:

> Give us that due sense of all thy mercies
> that our hearts may be unfeignedly thankful;
> and that we show forth thy praise,
> not only with our lips, but in our lives,
> by giving up ourselves to thy service,
> and by walking before thee
> in holiness and righteousness all our days....[5]

With attractive understatement, Rinkhart's hymn commits us to a life of gratitude and thanksgiving.

Joseph Addison's hymn "When all thy mercies, O my God, / My rising soul surveys" asks rhetorically:

> O how shall words with equal warmth
>   The gratitude declare,
> The glows within my ravished heart?
>   But thou canst read it there.[6]

It is a startlingly bold image. To describe the heart as "ravished" carries sexual overtones, not uncommon in Christian devotion.

(*The Hymnal 1982* has weakened Addison's vigorous word "ravished" to "fervent," shifting the focus from the assault to the response of the individual heart.) The experiences of human interaction are overturned in this daring hymn, and what between human beings is repulsive and intolerable becomes disconcertingly desirable in our relationship with God who is Spirit. The heart, having been burned by the fire of God, glows in such gratitude for the assault that words cannot equal the heat of the experience. Words fail as we attempt to praise adequately the goodness of God, but God can "read" in the grateful heart what cannot be expressed in words. They can never be equal to the task, but words help us to see and to say their inadequacy, reminding us of the limits of language. When combined with a noble and stirring tune, however, the words take on renewed power and flight.

Johann Mentzer's splendid hymn "Oh, that I had a thousand voices / To praise my God with thousand tongues"[7] recognizes the poverty of the single human voice adequately to render thanks to God and the need to join both soul and body to praise the creator by singing with attention, joining spirit and voice, and also perhaps by adding bodily actions to what we are saying — folding the hands, bowing the head, genuflecting, making the sign of the cross. The hymn asks the help of forest leaves, meadow grasses, flowers and all creatures that "throng the earth, the sea, the sky" to praise the mighty Maker, for a thousand human tongues would be insufficient.

Sometimes the words that hymns provide do not say that they are insufficient; instead they show themselves to be inadequate. The Easter sequence "Christ the Lord is risen today" will not let us sing more than a brief phrase before the ecstatic song of heaven, "alleluia," breaks in; then another brief phrase and an interruption again by "alleluia."

> Christ the Lord is risen today; Alleluia!
> Christians, haste your vows to pay; Alleluia!
> Offer ye your praises meet, Alleluia!
> At the paschal victim's feet. Alleluia![8]

It happens over and over through six stanzas as the hymn in its unhurried, joyful way makes its proclamation of the resurrection.

When our hearts are overwhelmed with grief, hymns can articulate what we cannot express in our own words. We can fling even in the face of our last enemy, death, the bold countervailing assertion of Johann Lindemann's "In thee is gladness / Amid all sadness." The hymn teaches us to see our immediate and overpowering grief in proper perspective:

> If he is ours,
> We fear no powers,
> Not of earth or sin or death.
> He sees and blesses
> In worst distresses;
> He can change them with a breath.[9]

With its ringing tune *In dir ist Freude* the hymn is a magnificent song for funerals. Frederick Lucian Hosmer's most careful and convincing lines,[10]

> O Lord of life, where'er they be,
> Safe in thine own eternity,
> Our dead are living unto thee.
> Alleluia,[11]

express confidence in God's care of the faithful beyond the bounds of death, but it asserts no more than we can know. Whatever our views of where exactly the dead are (and there are diverse Christian traditions regarding their state), we can be sure that they are safe in the eternity of God and that, wherever they are, they are living to God's praise.

Hymns foster and express a sense of deep awe in the presence of the Holy One. Frederick William Faber's "My God, How Wonderful Thou Art" gives us words to praise the wonder, majesty, and beauty of God. Samuel Hedborn's "Holy Majesty, before you / We bow to worship and adore you" helps us to express what the Sanctus declares, "Holy, holy, holy Lord, God of power and might" as worshipers bow low before the awe-inspiring majesty of the thrice-holy One. Gerard Moultrie's translation from the Liturgy of St. James has us implore, "Let all mortal flesh keep silence," for Christ our God descends "our full homage to demand." The solemn and stately sound of the sixteenth-century tune *Old Hundredth,* especially in slow, almost ponderous whole and half notes, supports the splendidly restrained text by Isaac Watts, "Before Jehovah's aweful throne, / Ye nations bow with sacred joy." John Wesley's excellent translation of Gerhard Tersteegen's superb hymn "Lo, God Is Here! Let Us Adore," sung to *Winchester New,* is drawn from the shattering and transforming experience of Jacob the fugitive who found that even in the wilderness he was not beyond God. In such hymns we may in part be recipients of the

exhortation "Let us worship God," but most of all we join with
the whole church to speak on its behalf to "all mortal flesh" and
to the nations of the world, telling them what they need to know
and do to fulfill their obligation to the sovereign Lord of all.

Hymns can put into words warm aspiration to a richer and
fuller devotional life. Charles Wesley's "Love Divine, All Loves Excelling" is surely one of the finest Christian hymns. Its unlikely
inspiration was in part John Dryden's lines in *King Arthur* (1671):

> Fairest isle, all isles excelling,
> Seat of pleasures and of loves,
> Venus here will choose her dwelling
> And forsake her Cyprian groves.... [12]

But Wesley's hymn has us pray:

> Love divine, all loves excelling,
>   Joy of heaven, to earth come down,
> Fix in us thy humble dwelling,
>   All thy faithful mercies crown.
> Jesus, thou art all compassion,
>   Pure, unbounded love thou art;
> Visit us with thy salvation,
>   Enter every trembling heart. [13]

This divine love, excelling all loves, has a name, Jesus, who is himself pure, unbounded compassion, the joy of heaven who has come
to earth to live among us and in us. His presence not only strengthens trembling hearts but has as its purpose the transformation of
each of us into his own likeness.

> Finish then thy new creation;
>   Pure and spotless let us be;
> Let us see thy great salvation
>   Perfectly restored in thee:
> Changed from glory into glory,
>   Till in heaven we take our place,
> Till we cast our crowns before thee,
>   Lost in wonder, love, and praise.

The hymn abounds in biblical references and allusions. The glorious final stanza gathers the new creation (2 Corinthians 5:17;
Galatians 6:15; Revelation 21:1, 5), its spotlessness (Ephesians
5:27; 2 Peter 3:14), the perfection of salvation (Colossians 1:28;
Hebrews 5:9; 1 John 2:5), our change from glory into glory

(2 Corinthians 3:18), and the casting of our crowns before God (Revelation 4:10).

William Cowper has spoken for many pilgrims in their longing desire, enabling then to sing "O for a closer walk with God" and to pray for strength to tear our dearest idols from the throne and to worship the only God. Then we can live and walk close with God in calmness and serenity and "purer light shall mark the road / That leads me to the Lamb."

Hymns can give expression to our fear of the end of the world and of what comes afterward. Many medieval and Reformation hymns on this theme continue to speak with compelling force.

> The day is surely drawing near
>   When Jesus, God's anointed,
> In all his power shall appear
>   As judge whom God appointed.
> Then fright shall banish idle mirth,
>   And hungry flames shall ravage earth,
> As Scripture long has warned us.[14]

This hymn by Bartholomäus Ringwaldt has made the old images of the end still live with disturbing power. The most terrifying of the late medieval hymns telling of the Four Last Things (death, judgment, heaven, or hell) is the thirteenth-century *Dies irae* attributed to Thomas of Celano. It is indeed the classic expression of the frightening end of all things, deriving from the fearsome depiction of the Day of the Lord in Zephaniah 1:14–16 and 2 Peter 3:10–13. In the translation by William Irons the hymn sings in part:

> Day of wrath! that day of mourning!
> See fulfilled the prophets' warning,
> Heaven and earth in ashes burning!
>
> Wondrous sound the trumpet flingeth,
> Through earth's sepulchers it ringeth,
> All before the throne it bringeth.
>
> Death is struck, and nature quaking,
> All creation is awaking,
> To its Judge an answer making.
>
> Righteous Judge of retribution,
> Grant thy gift of absolution,
> Ere that Day's dread execution.

> Thou the woman gav'st remission,
> Heard'st the dying thief's petition;
> Hopeless, else were my condition.
>
> Worthless are my prayers and sighing,
> Yet, good Lord, in grace complying,
> Rescue me from fires undying.[15]

Such scenes of the Last Day are out of fashion now. No modern hymnal includes the hymn, but the advent of nuclear weapons has made medieval pictures of the final crash of the universe remarkably contemporary as the world enters the twenty-first century.

Hymns can give words with which to confront and endure the anguish that tears at individual lives. By providing words to sing, hymns supply a measure of control over a chaotic and distressing world that seems to have little regard for us and our needs. Jane Borthwick has translated Paul Gerhardt's *Ich bin ein Gast auf Erden:*

> A pilgrim and a stranger,
>   I journey here below;
> Far distant is my country,
>   The home to which I go.
> Here I must toil and travail,
>   Oft weary and oppressed,
> But there my God shall lead me
>   To everlasting rest.[16]

Such images have through the centuries helped innumerable afflicted Christians through the sickness and pain of this world toward home.

By giving us words to sing, a hymn can redeem an imperceptive and irreverent service. When the liturgy is done in a careless and off-hand way, replete with jokes by the presider and with seemingly endless announcements by sundry members of the congregation, as if the assembly were merely a club meeting, the words of a solid hymn, perhaps by Isaac Watts, can bring a distressed congregant back again into the more noble tradition of the church in which depth of thought and feeling are honored. The words of a modern hymn by one such as Fred Pratt Green can show how sensitive use of contemporary English can revitalize worship and praise.

Instruments of Instruction

Hymns do more than provide us with a voice and songs to express what we have difficulty articulating. They have a second characteristic. Sir Philip Sidney (1544–1586), defending poetry against the puritans who had no time for it and echoing an idea that goes back at least to Horace (65–8 B.C.), declared that poetry has a dual purpose: to teach and to delight.[17] So it is with hymns. They too provide delightful instruction and are, to use Sidney's phrase, characterized by a "virtue-breeding delightfulness." Some two hundred years after Sidney, Samuel Johnson, commenting on *Paradise Lost,* continued the idea, declaring, "Poetry is the art of uniting pleasure with truth, by calling imagination to the help of reason."[18] Without the pleasure of a delightful imagination, poetry that instructs us cannot rise above the level of didacticism, and few of us enjoy being lectured to.

Hymns teach us in a pleasant and memorable way. St. Augustine wrote of his experience at his baptism:

> The tears flowed from me when I heard your hymns and canticles, for the sweet singing of your Church moved me deeply. The music surged in my ears, truth seeped into my heart, and my feelings of devotion overflowed, so that the tears streamed down. But they were tears of gladness.[19]

So it is still: as we sing hymns truth seeps into our hearts. An observation by Schleiermacher expresses a similar understanding of the great purpose of church music.

> There is so much discussion as to how one can again revive the common expression of the religious life; but it scarcely occurs to anyone that the best results could most easily be achieved if one would again place song in a more correct relation to the word. What the word has clarified, the tone must vivify, must transport straightway as a harmony into the innermost recesses of one's being, and there must hold it fast.[20]

Such vivifying, such transporting, and such tenacity in holding fast demand the very best in hymn text and tune.

Hymns by delighting teach us. They teach doctrine first of all. One thinks of the hymns that Ambrose had the orthodox Catholics sing against the Arians. Luther's catechetical hymns have taught people since the Reformation. "From Heaven Above to Earth I

Come" is a devotional instruction on the meaning of the incarnation and our appropriate response to God's coming to us. "To Jordan Came the Christ Our Lord" similarly is a presentation of the meaning of Christ's baptism and of the necessity of Christian baptism. Frederick William Faber's "Most Ancient of All Mysteries" is perhaps the finest hymnic presentation of the doctrine of the Holy Trinity we have. It portrays the Trinity not in specific doctrinal formulations, as in the Athanasian Creed, but as the "most ancient of all mysteries" who is "simply God." Ancient hymns can correct and deepen our understanding of the mystery of Christmas. Prudentius's hymn "Of the Father's Love Begotten" teaches us that he who is Alpha and Omega, begotten before all worlds, promised by the prophets, is the source and goal of all that has been and is and will be, and is therefore to be praised by all the angels and by every tongue on earth. Ancient hymns unfold to us the meaning of the passion. Fortunatus's hymns "Sing, My Tongue, the Glorious Battle" and "The Royal Banners Forward Go" tell the paradox of the cross on which the redeemer of the world as a victim was victorious over the death that claimed him. This tree, the cross, with its precious life-restoring fruit replaces the tree in Eden with its forbidden fruit that brought death into the world. Hymns like Martin Schalling's "Lord, thee I Love with All My Heart" can teach us how to live and how to die by declaring the absolute necessity of God's presence to give meaning — "Yea, heaven itself were void and bare / If thou, Lord, wert not near me" — and by asking that when the end shall come the angels may carry the singer home to Abraham's bosom to await the resurrection when "these mine eyes with joy may see / O Son of God, thy glorious face."

Second, hymns teach us ideas. John Ellerton's hymn "The Day Thou Gavest, Lord, Is Ended" describes the never-ending praise of the church "as earth rolls onward into light."

> The sun that bids us rest is waking
>   Our brethren 'neath the western sky,
> And hour by hour fresh lips are making
>   Thy wondrous doings heard on high.[21]

Henry Hallam Tweedy's hymn "Eternal God, whose power upholds / Both sun and flaming star" (despite what in Great Britain could be taken to be an oath, "flaming star") teaches that our love of the beautiful is a love of God and that ugliness is an offense to God, whose characteristic properties include beauty.

O God of beauty, oft revealed
In dreams of human art,
In speech that flows to melody,
In holiness of heart;
Teach us to ban all ugliness
That blinds our eyes to thee,
Till all shall know the loveliness
Of lives made fair and free.[22]

By such words we learn that the good, the beautiful, and the true are one. Hymns teach the glory of Christ the King. In a text of wonderful richness by Matthew Bridges and Godfrey Thring, "Crown Him with Many Crowns," Christ is extolled as the Lamb on the throne; the virgin's Son; God incarnate; the fruit, stem, and root of the mystic rose; the baby of Bethlehem; the Lord of love, of life, of peace, of time. The grand song concludes:

Crown him the Lord of peace,
Whose power a scepter sways
From pole to pole, that wars may cease,
Absorbed in prayer and praise.
His reign shall know no end,
And round his pierced feet
Fair flowers of paradise extend
Their fragrance ever sweet.

Crown him the Lord of years,
The potentate of time,
Creator of the rolling spheres,
Ineffably sublime.
All hail, Redeemer, hail!
For thou hast died for me;
Thy praise and glory shall not fail
Throughout eternity.[23]

Hymns teach us why a church building is a sacred place. A Latin hymn first found in a manuscript of the ninth century, *Christe cunctorum* [sometimes *sanctorum*] *dominator alme,* in Maxwell Julius Blacker's translation sings to the "Only-Begotten, Word of God Eternal":

This is thy temple, here thy presence chamber;
Here may thy servants, at the mystic banquet
Humbly adoring, take thy Body broken,
Drink of thy chalice.[24]

> Here for thy children stands the holy laver,
> Fountain of pardon for the guilt of nature;
> Cleansed by whose water, springs a race anointed,
> Faithful to Jesus.[25]

> Hallowed this dwelling where the Lord abideth,
> This is none other than the gate of heaven;
> Strangers and pilgrims, seeking homes eternal,
> Pass through its portals.[26]

Hymns such as the splendid Icelandic hymn translated by Charles Pilcher as "How Marvelous God's greatness"[27] teach the praise given by the natural world to the creator. Flowers, snowflakes, dawn, evening, mountains, valleys, oceans, winter waves, stars all point beyond their own beauty to the transcendent beauty and power of the one who made them.

Hymns can extend our view of the church and teach us a broad and inclusive view of who the faithful are. Those who belong to God may be far more in number than we are able to recognize. Johann Heermann's hymn O Jesu Christe, wahres Licht (in Catherine Winkworth's translation, "O Christ, Our True and Only Light") prays:

> O make the deaf to hear thy Word,
> And teach the dumb to speak, dear Lord,
> Who dare not yet the faith avow,
> Though secretly they hold it now.[28]

Christ is asked not only to enlighten those who are lost in error, to seek those who have strayed, to heal the wounded conscience, but also, in this stanza, to open reluctant ears and to strengthen those who will not or who cannot express the faith that resides in their inmost being, a faith that may not be known even to them, but only to God.

Hymns can exemplify the gift of reticence and so teach humility in not professing more than we ought, not asserting more than is accurate. In the version in *Lutheran Book of Worship* a familiar Advent hymn from the sixth century begins:

> Hark! A thrilling voice is sounding!
> "Christ is near," we hear the cry.[29]

The earlier version, however, is more circumspect. In Edward Caswall's translation of 1848 as revised in 1852 it was:

> Hark, a thrilling voice is sounding:
> "Christ is nigh!" it seems to say.[30]

There is indeed a voice that is heard; that much, the hymn declares, is undeniable. But the import of its message is not entirely clear. We believe that we have understood it correctly, but there is, we recognize, the possibility that we have misunderstood. We who think we know what the voice is saying may be mistaken; so the most that we can accurately sing is what "it seems to say." Some may be reminded of St. Augustine's report of his conversion by hearing a voice, "whether a boy's voice or a girl's voice, I do not know," and, interpreting that incident as "a divine command to open my Bible and read the passage at which I should open," found Romans 13:13 ("not in reveling and drunkenness, not in debauchery and licentiousness, not in quarreling and jealousy. Instead, put on the Lord Jesus Christ, and make no provision for the flesh, to gratify its desires"). Reading that passage from Romans, Augustine enjoyed the sudden calm of conversion.[31] We may remember also the concluding lines of George Herbert's poem *The Collar*:

> Methought I heard one calling, Child.
> And I replied, My Lord.

The speaker is scrupulous not to claim too much, not to boast in the insufferable way of some that "God said to me." The reticent speaker thinks that he has heard a voice, and he believes that it spoke the harsh and chiding word, "Child!" But he allows that in his rebellious pride he may have been mistaken. There is no doubt in the mind of the reader of the poem that there is a voice and that the voice is the voice of God, but that is the conviction of the reader, not the assertion of the humiliated speaker.

Hymns, teaching and delighting, enrich our understanding of language. It was in the hymn "Art thou weary, art thou languid / Art thou sore distressed?" that I first encountered the word "guerdon."[32] I had to look it up, and my vocabulary was enriched. Isaac Watts's "Before Jehovah's Awful Throne" uses the original meaning of "awful," a word once inhabited by terror, and Watts's use, reminding us of the origin of the now transformed and too familiar word, restores some of its original vigor. *The Hymnal of the Moravian Church* (1969) replaced the troublesome word and rendered the opening line, "Before Jehovah's glorious throne." *Lutheran Book of Worship* (1978) changed the word "awful" to "awesome," a word, however, cheapened by fad use. *The Hymnal 1982* has rewritten the line, "Before the Lord's eternal throne."

What the original makes clear is that awe is the only proper attitude before the throne of the Holy One, who holds the power not only of creation but also of destruction. We cannot presume upon the goodness of such a God.

> Before Jehovah's awful throne,
> Ye nations bow with sacred joy;
> Know that the Lord is God alone;
> He can create and he destroy.[33]

The characteristic Calvinist emphasis on the absolute sovereignty of God, who is utterly beyond human presumption and manipulation, is clear.

John Ellerton's translation of St. Ambrose, "O Strength and Stay, Upholding All Creation," a magnificent apprehension of the nature of God apart from the revelation in Christ, reminds us that "stay" need not always be a verb; here it is a noun. Robert Bridges's translation of Ambrose's "O Splendor of God's Glory Bright" has

> Morn in her rosy car is borne,
> Let him come forth, our perfect morn,[34]

reminding us that "car" need not always mean automobile. The hymn broadens our understanding of the development of language and familiarizes us with older forms of usage. There is the pleasant fastidiousness of "Come, Ye Faithful, Raise the Strain," praising God, who

> Led them with unmoistened foot
> Through the Red Sea waters.[35]

We learn the rotund archaism of John Mason Neale's translation of "Jerusalem the Golden,"

> They stand, those halls of Zion,
> Conjubilant with song.[36]

The German "leisen hymns" preserve the Greek cry from the old Mass, Kyrie eleison, and teach the congregation two useful words of Greek. Isaac Watts's familiar hymn "When I Survey the Wondrous Cross" originally contained a stanza that was dropped from hymnals in the eighteenth and nineteenth centuries because it was thought too gory.

> His dying crimson, like a robe,
> Spreads o'er his body on the tree;

> And I am dead to all the globe,
> And all the globe is dead to me.

The language of the stanza, however, is remarkably restrained and therefore powerful. "Dying crimson" (not the more obvious word "blood") suggests the setting of the sun as well as the death of the young Prince of glory. The nakedness of the Prince being intolerable, the crimson silently "spreads" like a robe over the body on the tree (rather than "cross"), recalling the fall caused by the fruit of the forbidden tree in Eden, and the silence makes yet more appalling the death of this young man. As he dies, we die to the world in order to be reborn with him to a new allegiance and a transformed life. Isaac Watts's hymn "Nature with Open Volume Stands" in its original form had

> O the sweet wonders of that cross,
> Where Christ my Savior loved and died!
> Her noblest fruit my spirit draws
> From his dear wounds and bleeding side.

"Her" refers to the soul of the speaker and reminds us that traditionally in devotional writing and thought, the soul, whether of a male or a female, is consistently perceived as female, making possible marriage metaphors when the soul is joined to Christ or to God when God is described with masculine imagery.

Hymns moreover can be read as devotional poetry, and as such hymns teach us form and meter, especially when we use a text edition of a hymnbook. Older hymnbooks, especially in the Lutheran tradition, were available in a text-only format, but that is no longer the case. It is an indication that hymns are being used less and less in private devotion and are being used exclusively in public congregational activities. Moreover, American hymnals characteristically place several stanzas between the staves of music. This shows the interaction between text and tune but prevents either the text or the tune from standing on its own as an independent composition. The shape of a text on a page undistracted by music shows clearly that hymns are a kind of poetry and shows how lines are balanced, shortened or lengthened, indented or not, calling attention to the poetic shape and sound. In Samuel Crossman's passion hymn "My song Is Love Unknown" the last four lines of each stanza (usually printed as two) are abbreviated and given a different rhyme scheme, making the last four dimeter lines, rhymed *cddc,* respond to the situation presented in the first four trimeter lines, rhymed *abab:*

> My song is love unknown,
> My Savior's love to me;
> Love to the loveless shown
> That they might lovely be.
>   O who am I
>   That for my sake
>   My Lord should take
>   Frail flesh, and die?[37]

The delightful galloping meter of Peter Abelard's hymn is most clearly seen when the text, translated by John Mason Neale, is printed apart from the splendid seventeenth-century tune, O *quanta qualia.*

> O what their joy and their glory must be,
> Those endless sabbaths the blessed ones see;
> Crown for the valiant, to weary ones rest:
> God shall be all, and in all ever blest.[38]

There is the unusual truncation in Reginald Heber's "God, Who Made the Earth and Heaven" and more noticeable in Fred Pratt Green's text in the same meter:

> For the fruit of all creation,
>   Thanks be to God.
> For his gifts to every nation,
>   Thanks be to God.
> For the plowing, sowing, reaping,
> Silent growth while we are sleeping,
> Future needs in earth's safe-keeping,
>   Thanks be to God.[39]

The shortened lines stand out by their very brevity. The two most famous "shaped verses" in English are George Herbert's *The Altar,* in which the shape of the lines on a page suggests a pedestal table altar, and *Easter Wings,* in which the shape of the lines, when rotated a quarter-turn, reveals two winged angels side by side. That technique is found in hymn texts also, most notably in the grand hymn by Philipp Nicolai:

> O Morning Star, how fair and bright!
> You shine with God's own truth and light,
>   Aglow with grace and mercy!
> Of Jacob's race, King David's Son,
> Our Lord and Master, you have won

> Our hearts to serve you only!
> Lowly, holy!
> Great and glorious,
> All victorious,
> Rich in blessing!
> Rule and might o'er all possessing![40]

The lines here as in the original printing of the text are so arranged to suggest the shape of a chalice.

Hymns teach us, and they do so by providing pleasure, teaching and delighting at once. There are of course the comical aspects of hymns, such as singing "Stand Up, Stand Up for Jesus" while sitting down. There are hymns that make us laugh, such as Percy Dearmer's missionary hymn, "Remember all the people / Who live in far-off lands" with the lines

> Some work in sultry forests
> Where apes swing to and fro.[41]

It is no surprise that the hymn is not found in current hymnals. There is the Episcopalian favorite "I Sing a Song of the Saints of God" with the delightful declaration concerning saints:

> You can meet them in school, or in lanes, or at sea,
>   In church, or in trains, or in shops, or at tea,
> For the saints of God are just folk like me,
>   And I mean to be one too.[42]

But there are deeper instructive pleasures in hymns too.

Robert Schumann, reflecting on the impression of hearing Mendelssohn play Bach's chorale prelude on the tune *Schmücke dich, O liebe Seele* in Bach's church, St. Thomas in Leipzig, recalled in a letter to Mendelssohn:

> About the *cantus firmus* hung golden garlands, and it was transfused with such a bliss, that you confessed to me that if life had deprived you of all hope and faith, this one chorale would restore all anew.

A noble text wedded to a stirring tune can give the congregation a memorable and encouraging companion to accompany them throughout the week.

There is pleasure in the rhythm of hymn tunes. There is the delightful syncopation of *Ein feste Burg* in its original isometric form with its cross accent.[43] There is the pleasant dancing rhythm of the tune *St. Clement;* the quiet flowing of the incomparably exquisite *O Welt ich muss dich lassen (Innsbruck);* the noble and stately *Tantum ergo;* the most versatile chorale *Wie schön leuchtet,* "the queen of chorales," used in Germany for both weddings and funerals; the rollicking *Monkland;* the vigorous and sturdy *Cwm Rhonda;* the seductive *Sandon,* beloved by Canadians, like a vocal dance; the lively gallop of *Marion;* the bright and dancing *Land of Rest;* the sound of the late Middle Ages in the Agincourt hymn *Deo gracias.*

There is the pleasure of sound, rhyme, alliteration in hymn texts. Hymns make their impact upon us in part through their metrical form, making their statement memorable and indeed memorizable while teaching us by example important lessons about poetry as well as lessons in Christian doctrine. Edward Grubb's "Our God, to whom we turn / When weary with illusion" finds a proclamation of God in

> The line of lifted sea,
> Where spreading moonlight quivers.[44]

The alliteration of "line of lifted sea" and the light of the rising moon quivering on the waves exemplify by sound and sight the beauty that speaks of the Creator. In Coelius Sedulius's fifth-century Christmas hymn, "From East to West, from Shore to Shore," angels in the sky sing above a silent field, and on that field shepherds in their poverty learn the incomparable news of the Good Shepherd. The silence of earthly fields is broken by the angels' songs, and the shepherds' poverty is enriched by the heavenly knowledge imparted to them of the Good Shepherd. The passion hymn "Glory Be to Jesus" contrasts two victims, two gentle sons slain by violence, whose blood stained the earth. Abel's blood cried out for vengeance (Genesis 4:10–11); Jesus' blood cries for our pardon. The whole hymn turns on the contrast between the world and the church, between what comes naturally in our fallen state and what is given in the redeemed creation.

All of these examples of instructive pleasures found in hymns are the result of the control humanity has learned to exercise over sound and breath. By their very nature as song hymns provide instruction in the spiritual life by showing the results of discipline and order that convert mere sound into song, unrestrained emotion into controlled power. Robert Frost in his playfully profound poem *The Aim Was Song* presents the pleasant idea that humanity taught the wind how to blow properly so as to achieve song. The wind, "Before man came to blow it right," blustered violently day and night "in any rough place where it caught." (Note the rough rhythm of the line.) Humans discovered the miracle of control, discipline, conversion, measure; the result of such discipline was song, "The wind the wind had meant to be." The aim was song, and the means of achieving song was discipline and restraint, which gave point and beauty to what otherwise was only loud and harsh noise. Like a child with a new trumpet, the wind untaught "blew too hard." Power must be harnessed to be of service. Growth must be controlled to be strong and luxuriant. The strength of the Christian life is shown in a paradoxical way: in the apparent weakness of humility and submission. God, who said my "power is made perfect in weakness" (2 Corinthians 12:9), demonstrated that perfection of power on the cross in the passion and death of Christ and summons disciples to learn and share in that power by walking in the way of the cross, until our will is so transformed that we can pray gladly with the Savior in his passion, "Not my will but yours be done" (Luke 22:42).

Uniting Us

There is one further function that hymns have in Christian devotion, and this returns us to where this chapter began. The distinction between the hymn writer and the singer of the hymn collapses as we use the words of another as our words. We are united with the author and the author with us. When a congregation sings a hymn, the process of identification is expanded. Each individual is united with the others in the assembly as they join in their common enterprise, and a unity is fostered and expressed by singing the hymn together. Hymns unify a congregation and can be a sign pointing to the unity of the whole church.

St. Augustine in his *Confessions* notes that "the Church at Milan had begun to seek comfort and spiritual strength in the practice of singing hymns, in which the faithful united fervently with heart and voice."[45] The practice of singing hymns fires fervor and fosters unity. The entire liturgy is of course the "work of the people," the common expression of the prayer of the church, shared with others in our own time and of ages past. But singing hymns gives the assembly a task that is more clearly unifying than many other parts of the liturgy. Hymn singing is the one thing that the congregation does, besides listening to the sermon, for an extended period of time. There are liturgical responses that the congregation sings or says ("And also with you," "Hear our prayer," "We lift them to the Lord," "Amen"), but these responses are just that — responses — and they are (or ought to be) brief if a body of people is to sing or say them together as one voice. It is the hymns, including the psalmody and the canticles such as "Glory to God in the Highest," that bind the congregation together in an audible unity. These are the parts of the liturgy assigned to "all," the entire assembly, ministers and people together. Such common song inspires the congregation as each of us supports and is in turn supported by the voices of others. In this way, hymns remind us of our responsibility as members of the body of Christ and as members of society. In Christian song, churches can forget their quarrels and mortals lose their limitations, because in rising above divisions they have attained that "higher ground where the soul is content to affirm and adore. The hymns of Christendom show more clearly than anything else that there is even now such a thing as the unity of the Spirit."[46]

Hymns echo an even grander sound, the cosmic harmony, the pervasive order that is basic to creation. This fundamental harmony of being is a unity that is more than mere uniformity, for it makes use of variation and difference, blending them into one harmonious order that is an image of universal love. So Clement of Alexandria could refer to Christ as the "New Song" who replaced all the music of antiquity. The Christian affirmation of the triune God is a declaration that in God's own being there is a social harmony and that creatures are coherent only with and by such a God in whom we live and move and have our being, who wills that others join the melody until all is gathered into the harmony.[47] The final reality will therefore be perfected music.

Vigorous congregational song is a thrilling experience, as a diverse collection of believers comes together to join in their common task and privilege. The unity shown and heard in congregational hymn singing is a sign of the promised unity of the entire broken and scattered family of God, who will all one day, as some do occasionally already, sing with one heart and mind and voice to the God of all creation, the source and focus and goal of unity, in whom, as the Epistle to the Colossians teaches (1:17), all things hold together.

Chapter Nine

BAPTISM
Hallowing Life and Death

✢

In an eloquent meditation on the many facets of the sea, *The Great Deep: The Sea and Its Thresholds,* the British fiction writer, poet, and explorer James Hamilton-Patterson observes that the very words "the Deep" exert a tidal pull on our emotions. Tennyson's childhood on the Lincolnshire coast left the imprint of the sea and its imagery on his poems.[1] Speaking of the effect of the sea on Tennyson, but not only Tennyson alone surely, Hamilton-Patterson writes, "Stately, funeral, mysterious, it spoke ultimately of loss: a steep, dark bulk, time's liquid correlative which gulps down objects, lives, and all that was and will be." By comparison, Hamilton-Patterson notes, " 'heaven' is blank and thin, even faintly unserious."[2]

The Deep, utterly solemn, haunts us with the strange power of its cosmic chill and isolation, the eternal and absolute darkness, and yet we are drawn to it.[3] It fills our language with its metaphors. The salt that is in sea water is also in our blood and tears and sweat. "The satisfaction for certain people of walking back down a beach and into the sea is akin to that of a long-postponed homecoming."[4] (The walk home is not always entirely pleasant. I remember as a child hearing my parents speak solemnly of how a friend of my father's "walked into the ocean" to end his life. It remained for me a haunting phrase.) Such a view of the sea with its profound depths and all-encompassing power can help us understand baptism.

Holy Baptism, like the Deep, will not let us forget the "unavoidable aspect of death which lies at the heart of the mystery of life."[5] Primal people understood this harsh but undeniable truth, and the mystery religions celebrated it in various guises — the Syrian Adonis, the Asiatic Attis, the Egyptian Osiris, the Persian Mithras —

and focused on the ritual representation and repetition of the death and resurrection of a god and hence of the god's initiates. The promise of Christianity is that the kingdoms of the world will "become kingdom of our Lord and of his Messiah, and he will reign forever and ever" (Revelation 11:15) and that the church will be marvelously united with Christ the bridegroom. This transformation and consummation can be accomplished in no other way except through the cross.

Writing of the necessity of all things to be conformed to Christ by way of the cross, Louis Bouyer has observed,

> Nothing is in the city of God which has not come from the city of this world. But nothing can go to the city of God without leaving the city of this world; and such a transition always means, in some way or other, to die. The city of this world cannot simply become the city of God. All that it can do is be broken to pieces in order to provide the city of God with its building stones — and this means death for the city of this world also.[6]

Death consistently throughout the Bible is seen as a curse, the consequence of the fall, a corruption introduced into God's good creation, imported into paradise from the outside. Moreover, in the Bible as in most other ancient stories, death enters the newly created world by way of a murder: in the Genesis account, Cain kills his brother Abel. It is an imposed and interposed violence, alien to the original intention of the Creator.

By the self-offering of Christ, himself both priest and victim, he made our death his own, giving himself with his own hand into death for us. The curse of death is thus transformed into a blessing by means of the death of Christ on our behalf, reversing the effect of the forbidden tree in Eden by means of the tree of the cross on Calvary. The preface of the cross and passion praises God the holy Father through Christ the Lord,

> who set the salvation of the human race upon the tree of the cross, so that, whence death arose, thence life also might rise again, and that he, who by a tree once overcame, might likewise by a tree be overcome.[7]

Satan, whose name the church does not deign to use as the holiest part of the Eucharist begins, who by the forbidden tree in Eden once overcame humanity, was defeated outside Jerusalem by the tree of the cross. As a result, human beings by going "the way of all the earth" (1 Kings 2:2) to "the house appointed for all living" (Job 30:23) are joined intimately to the paschal mystery, are absorbed into it, and are given a share in its final fulfillment.[8]

The sea swiftly and powerfully puts things on a mortal footing, and the seaside, the edge of things, exudes impermanence.[9] It is in the Deep rather than in the more pleasant echoes of running brooks and watercourses that the profundity of Holy Baptism is to be sought. It is here in the sea, the great Deep, that all the rivers and streams of the earth flow and are swallowed up. The regular, dependable turning of the tides is a deep rhythm that throbs through our life as the irregular babbling of a stream can never do. The moving water of the sea is both lulling and imperative. The constant flux of waters, ebbing and flowing, speaks of human origins and of individual destiny as well.[10] Life came from the water, and it is to the great silence that we must each return.

Death as a voyage is a common trope, and the sea invites embarkation.[11] It is not only sentimentality that impels many who preside at funerals to choose to read Tennyson's "Crossing the Bar." The poem, once a staple for memorization, gives in a memorable way the ancient image of death as a voyage aboard a silent ship leaving with the ebbing tide. In an earlier tale, as King Arthur neared death he was carried down to the seaside and there placed aboard a ship tended by three veiled queens who carried him mysteriously out to sea and "brought him to his burials." At the beginning of English literature, *Beowulf* tells how the companions of Scyld the courageous, when "he went away into the protection of the Lord," carried him down to the sea-currents, laid him with great treasures in the hollow of a ring-prowed ship, and "let the water take him, gave him to the sea." No one can truthfully say, the poet bard admits, who received that cargo. The image is deep in the psyche of the peoples of northern Europe and elsewhere: death is like a voyage. The correlation works the other way around also: travel is like death in that it requires separation and, indeed, mourning.[12] And travel by sea, unlike the far more rapid air travel, gives time for mourning, separation, and loss as one sees space slowly open between ship and shore and watches the coastline recede and eventually disappear.

Holy Baptism offers to each individual the opportunity to participate in the mystery of the Pascha, to make with Christ the passage from death to life, to reach life by means of death. This passage — through the cross to the resurrection — is the deepest reality of the Christian mystery.

For the ultimate reality to which the sacramental order is leading us finally is the reality of the mystical but perfectly real identifying of us with Christ, of our lives with His life.[13]

Such a passage is no simple journey. It is like the crossing of the Atlantic that the ancestors of many of us made in the eighteenth and nineteenth centuries aboard old, frail ships. The condition of those who chose to make the crossing was often so desperate that they dared to risk all they had on a perilous passage through unknown dangers to a new world and a new life.

The great biblical example of such a passage is the exodus, the definitive experience of ancient Israel, moving from slavery to freedom, from death to life, by passing through the sea. That same water, which opened to welcome them safely across its sea bed, closed over the pursuing army, annihilating those who threatened Israel's life and sealing off any return to the house of slavery. Only one path was now available to them: the perilous way of freedom, which took them through the howling wilderness (Deuteronomy 32:10) for forty years and then at last across the Jordan into the promised land. The Christian sacrament of Holy Baptism echoes the exodus, delivering from slavery and setting toward the promised land, the heavenly country promised to God's people, those who undergo the experience of a pilgrimage through resistance and struggle and temptation.

But Christianity finds an even greater source of symbolism for baptism in an even earlier event, the great flood. What the Bible describes as "all flesh" was destroyed, except for eight people — Noah, his nameless wife, and their three sons and their nameless wives — who were preserved in the ark. So preachers have commonly declared that those who are safely inside the ark of the church are preserved from the destruction that rages outside. "See round thine ark the hungry billows curling," Philip Pusey's adaptation of a hymn by Matthäus Apelles von Löwenstein pleads to the "Lord of our life and God of our salvation," for "Thou canst preserve us."[14]

Behind the exodus and the flood lies the most ancient of all archetypes, the creation itself. In the beginning, when God began to create the cosmos, "the earth was a formless void and darkness covered the face of the Deep, while a wind from God swept over the face of the waters" (Genesis 1:2). The desolate emptiness is emphasized. The void is without shape or form and is veiled in the mystery of darkness to ensure that nothing is discernable, and all the while an eerie wind sweeps across the watery abyss. The primordial deep (*tehom* in Hebrew) retained its mystery: God challenged Job (38:16):

> Have you entered into the springs of the sea,
> or walked in the recesses of the deep?

Moreover, the threat of the primordial deep was always terrifying in its dark and silent desolation. The Lord God says to Tyre,

> When I make you a city laid waste, like cities that are not inhabited, when I bring up the deep over you, and the great waters cover you, then I will thrust you down with those who descend into the Pit. (Ezekiel 26:19–20)

The abyss was an emblem of the great silence and "deep darkness" (Job 38:17) of death, the nonbeing that preceded creation and that will succeed it.

But that mighty wind, which swept the face of the deep, was, in the wonderful ambiguity of the Hebrew *ruach,* also the breath and the Spirit of God. And it is that Holy Spirit, whose symbol in the Fourth Gospel is water, who brings creation into being and who sustains all that is.

In the baptismal rite, the Thanksgiving over the water, praising God for the gift of water and most of all for baptism, reviews the Old Testament patterns, joins them to Jesus' baptism, death, and resurrection, and calls upon the Holy Spirit to move anew over the water in this font to give life to those who are cleansed in it.

> We thank you, Almighty God, for the gift of water. Over it the Holy Spirit moved in the beginning of creation. Through it you led the children of Israel out of their bondage in Egypt into the land of promise. In it your Son Jesus received the baptism of John and was anointed by the Holy Spirit as Messiah, the Christ, to lead us, through his death and resurrection, from the bondage of sin into everlasting life.

> We thank you, Father, for the water of Baptism. In it we are buried with Christ in his death. By it we share in his resurrection. Through it we are reborn by the Holy Spirit. Therefore in joyful obedience to your Son, we bring into his fellowship those who come to him in faith, baptizing them in the Name of the Father, and of the Son, and of the Holy Spirit.

> Now sanctify this water, we pray you, by the power of your Holy Spirit, that those who are here cleansed from sin and

born again may continue for ever in the risen life of Jesus
Christ our Savior.

To him, to you, and to the Holy Spirit, be all honor and glory,
now and for ever.[15]

This central prayer of the baptismal rite joins the life of the candidates to the history of salvation, making that history their history,
and incorporating them into that story so that they may perceive in
their lives a continuation of the mighty acts of God. Each candidate
can therefore say, "I plunge into the Red Sea, and I will emerge in
the promised land. I die to sin and death, and I will be born again
to new life." Each candidate is given a new, longer, more inclusive
history: what God has done in the past and what God promises
for the future.

Baptism is the door to life, life pictured with such promise and
fullness that it is a worthy counterpart of the Deep. Baptism is the
gate of heaven seen in the wilderness by the fugitive Jacob fleeing the wrath of his brother Esau (Genesis 28:17), and it is the
door opened in Jesus' side out of which flowed water and blood
(often understood to refer to the sacraments of baptism and the
Eucharist). The prayer over the water in the Roman baptismal rite
therefore includes a reference to this opening of the side of Jesus,
and the Easter collect in the Gregorian sacramentary, discussed earlier in this study, in its initial clause alludes to this opening of the
door to life:

Almighty God, through your only Son you overcame death
and opened for us the gate of everlasting life.[16]

The opening of the gate of heaven was made literally in Jesus'
body,[17] and that wound becomes an interpretation of the meaning
of this life-giving sacrifice.

The New Testament references to baptism provide many images
for the one reality of new life.[18]

1. Baptism is a participation in the death and resurrection of
   Christ.

   Do you not know that all of us who have been baptized
   into Christ Jesus have been baptized into his death?
   Therefore we have been buried with him by baptism
   into death, so that, just as Christ was raised from the
   dead by the glory of the Father, so we too might walk
   in newness of life. For if we have been united with him

in a death like his, we will certainly be united with him in a resurrection like his. (Romans 6:3–5)

...when you were buried with him in baptism, you were also raised with him through faith in the power of God, who raised him from the dead. (Colossians 2:12)

2. Baptism is pictured as a washing away of sin.

But you were washed, you were sanctified, you were justified in the name of the Lord Jesus Christ and in the Spirit of our God. (1 Corinthians 6:11)

3. It is a new birth corresponding to the new creation.

...no one can enter the kingdom of God without being born of water and Spirit. (John 3:5)

4. It is, drawing on another Old Testament story, an experience of salvation from the flood.

[Christ] went and made a proclamation to the spirits in prison, who in former times did not obey, when God waited patiently in the days of Noah, during the building of the ark, in which a few, that is, eight persons, were saved through water. And baptism, which this prefigured, now saves you.... (1 Peter 3:19–21)

5. Baptism is an exodus from bondage, foreshadowed in the time of Moses.

I do not want you to be unaware, brothers and sisters, that our ancestors were all under the cloud, and all passed through the sea, and all were baptized into Moses in the cloud and in the sea. (1 Corinthians 10:1–2)

6. It is a renewal by the holy and life-giving Spirit.

God our Savior...saved us, not because of any works of righteousness that we had done, but according to his mercy, through the water of rebirth and renewal by the Holy Spirit. (Titus 3:5)

7. It is an enlightenment by Christ, recalling Isaiah 60:1 and made vivid by the practice of giving a lighted candle to the newly baptized.

> Sleeper, awake!
> Rise from the dead,
> and Christ will shine on you.
> (Ephesians 5:14)

The writer to the Hebrews, reflecting the characteristic view of that treatise, warns,

> It is impossible to restore again to repentance those who have once been enlightened, and have tasted the heavenly gift, and have shared in the Holy Spirit ... (6:4)

and then gives the encouragement,

> But recall those earlier days when, after you had been enlightened, you endured a hard struggle with sufferings.... (10:32)

8. Baptism is a reclothing in Christ, enacted by the custom of robing the newly baptized in white garments as they come out of the water. The baptismal robe is a bridal garment, a symbol of purity, forgiveness, new life, and becoming a new person.

> As many of you as were baptized into Christ have clothed yourselves with Christ. (Galatians 3:27)

9. It is a liberation into a new humanity.

> ... you ... were baptized into Christ.... There is no longer Jew or Greek, there is no longer slave or free, there is no longer male and female; for all of you are one in Christ Jesus. (Galatians 3:27–28)

The images overlap and reinforce each other, building up with their accumulated power a picture of the richness and depth of the understanding of baptism in the ancient church.

The rites of baptism were correspondingly rich and powerful. In the ancient church the candidates, after what often was years of preparation, at last were stripped of their clothing and all that it represented, descended into the water, and disappeared completely. When they emerged they were no longer what they were; they were now a new people, born anew. The image of Adam that they had borne was blotted out; the stains of earth were washed away. They were dead with Christ to the mortal life that had been spoiled by Satan. Washed of their sins, they were new people, newborn, bearing the image of the new Adam, Jesus Christ. The priest marked their forehead with oil, engraving there as it were the image, the icon, of Christ, who is himself the icon of the Father. The newly baptized were clothed in white garments as they emerged from the water, for they had regained the garment of immortality that had been lost by Adam, and were clothed as brides of Christ. A lighted candle was put in the hand of each as a token of their enlightenment, for they were no longer children of darkness but children of light. They no longer lived for themselves; it was Christ who lived in them. By water and the Spirit the divine pattern revealed in Christ had been imprinted on them. Now that they had been born again, brought into God's family as adopted children, and now that the Spirit lived in them, they could pray with full meaning, "Our Father."

Even a summary of the powerful and manifold actions of the rite of baptism suggests that "bath" does not comprehend the essence of this sacrament. For baptism is not over and finished when the washing is done and one emerges from that water, reborn. It cannot and indeed must not be repeated, as is the washing of the physical body.

> It is therefore indeed correct to say that baptism is a washing away of sins, but the expression is too mild and weak to bring out the full significance of baptism, which is rather a symbol of death and resurrection. For this reason I would have those who are to be baptized completely immersed in the water, as the word says and as the mystery indicates.... The sinner does not so much need to be washed as he needs to die, in order to be wholly renewed and made another creature, and to be conformed to the death and resurrection of Christ, with whom he dies and rises again through baptism. Although you may say that when Christ died and rose again he was washed clean of mortality, that is a less forceful way of putting it than if you said that he was completely changed and renewed. Similarly it is far more forceful to say that baptism signifies that we die in every way and rise to eternal life, than to say that it signifies merely that we are washed clean of sins.[19]

Holy Baptism is thus a process by which we are made part of the body of Christ, the church. This incorporation takes a lifetime to achieve.

A person at birth has only begun the process of growth and maturation. A marriage is only the beginning of a lifetime of growth and exploration of each other. So it is with baptism. This chapter might appropriately find its place immediately following the Easter Vigil, the premier occasion for the celebration of Holy Baptism, and before the Holy Communion, for which it prepares and to which it leads. But the role of baptism in the Christian life is deeper and more long-lasting than an initiation, an entrance through a door or a gate. It is therefore still more appropriate to place it near the end of this study, for baptism tells not only of the beginning but of the continuation and of the end of the Christian life.

Luther taught us not just to remember our baptism but to glory in it.[20] The action of baptism is quickly accomplished: water is applied to a candidate three times while calling upon the name of the triune God by whom and in whom the candidate is being baptized. Even the most elaborate celebration, replete with full ceremonies — many candidates, processions to and from the font, psalms and hymns, oil and robes and candles — can be accomplished in an hour. But, as Luther taught in his catechisms and elsewhere, the effects of the celebration last a lifetime and beyond. Baptism is a forward-looking action, characterized first of all by promise. "The first thing to be considered about baptism is the divine promise, which says 'He who believes and is baptized shall be saved' [Mark 16:16]."[21] This promise moreover is made at baptism by none other than God. "There is great comfort and a mighty aid to faith in the knowledge that one has been baptized, not by man, but by the Triune God himself, through a man acting among us in His name."[22] The exact formula of baptism pales into relative insignificance — East and West use different formulas, Luther notes — for the essential assurance is that baptism is administered not in the name of human beings but in the name of the Lord. Even the character and worthiness of the minister of the sacrament is irrelevant to the validity of the action, for baptism is God's work in us. In baptism, therefore, every Christian has enough to study and to practice a lifetime.[23]

Luther preferred immersion as a complete and perfect sign of baptism as the twofold action of dying and rising, being plunged beneath the water and being lifted up out of it.[24] For him, as for much of the church, the sign and what the sign signifies are inseparable. The sign is no mere object lesson, a picture representing a great truth. In Luther's understanding, Word and Spirit, sign and that which is signified, belong together. Whenever one is present, there is also the other. The sign is not limited to the moment of the administration of baptism, and that which is signified is not projected into the distant future of adult years. For baptism is properly understood not as an act but as a process extending throughout the life of the baptized. Sin is not drowned at once, nor are its consequences escaped in a moment. The sacrament of initiation is therefore but the beginning of a constant struggle against sin that ends only with the close of life.[25] Life is perpetual baptism.

Holy Baptism undergirds the whole of the Christian life with the solid foundation of the assurance of God's grace and favor; baptism "is an expression of the open arms of the Father"[26] welcoming not only infants and others who come for the first time, but welcoming all "who with hearty repentance and true faith turn unto him"[27] throughout their lives. For the process of baptism is not always onward and upward. Baptism declares us free from sin and death, but it does not make us free *of* sin and death. At the time of baptism sin does not completely die nor does grace completely rise. "For as long as we are in the flesh, the desires of the flesh stir and are stirred."[28] As soon as we begin to believe, we begin to die to this world and to live in God in eternal life. But throughout our life in this world after baptism we remain at once sinful and justified. We continually relapse, breaking the baptismal covenant from our side.

> It will therefore be no small gain to a penitent to remember above all his baptism, and, confidently, calling to mind the divine promise which he has forsaken, acknowledge that promise before his Lord, rejoicing that he is still within the fortress of salvation because he has been baptized.[29]

> Understand that this is the significance of baptism, that through it you die and live again. Therefore, whether by penance or by any other way, you can only return to the power of your baptism, and do again that which you were baptized to do and which your baptism signified. Baptism never becomes useless, unless you despair and refuse to return to its salvation.[30]

We make use of our baptism daily as we seek forgiveness, consolation, and strength. "To appreciate and use baptism aright, we must draw strength and comfort from it when our sins or conscience oppresses us, and we must retort, 'But I am baptized!' "[31] Confession is nothing else than a return to our baptismal covenant, returning, like the prodigal son in Jesus' parable (Luke 15:11–32), to the astonishingly generous welcome waiting at home. Baptism turns away despair with its ringing affirmation, "But I have been baptized!" Jerome spoke of penance as "the second plank after shipwreck";[32] baptism, the ark in which we are saved, is, in this understanding, wrecked and sunk by sin, and penance is a plank to which we cling for life. But Luther objected, "The ship remains one, solid, and invincible; it will never be broken up into separate 'planks.' In it are carried all those who are brought to the "harbor of salvation." Even if there are those who rashly leap overboard into the sea and perish, "the ship itself remains intact and holds its course unimpaired."[33] So Blandina, one of the martyrs at Lyons in A.D. 177, an example cited by Luther,[34] in every time of temptation made baptism her defense, saying simply, "I am a Christian." It is baptism that gives us protective clothing to wear when our last hour comes and we face the great mystery of death and after it the judgment.

In the psalms the waters of the Deep are a powerful symbol of punishment for human sin. Psalm 69:15 prays:

> Do not let the flood sweep over me,
> or the deep swallow me up,
> or the Pit close its mouth over me.

The Deep is a place of horror, shame, and despair. Yet faith finds the promise of Easter in the depths of sin and the grave, because baptism has made the Deep a place of life and hope. Baptism confronts the unfathomable depths of our sin, which descend far below our comprehension, with the boundless depths of mercy. Psalm 42 declares:

> Deep calls to deep at the thunder of your cataracts;
> all your waves and your billows have gone over me.

The psalm prayer to this psalm in the Roman *Liturgy of the Hours* and in *Lutheran Book of Worship* picks up the image and in a strikingly apt phrase prays, "Lord God, never failing fountain of life, through the saving waters of baptism you called us from the depths of sin to the depths of mercy." Thus the great Deep is doubly appropriate in connection with baptism, telling of both sin and mercy.

Baptism, like the Deep, speaks powerfully to us of the transitory and the dependable, of impermanence and eternity. Like Richard Henry Dana Jr., the author of *Two Years Before the Mast* (1840) who like many others went to sea in an effort to improve his eyesight, we who are plunged into the waters of baptism have our sight corrected by training our eyes on the far horizon where what is seen leaves off and what is unseen begins. We learn from this sacrament that the world we see is not all there is and that the visible things amid which we live will all pass away, and so will we with them. Ash Wednesday, the first day of Lent, in a dramatic and powerful annual repetition of baptism, marks with an ashen cross the heads of all who come to the altar. Young and old, aged and infants, all have the cross that was engraved on their foreheads when they were baptized solemnly redrawn with ashes accompanied by the sobering reminder, "You are dust, and to dust you shall return." The water of life is suspended, and the desiccated remainder, ashes, speaks of the inevitable death and decay in all that is cut off from God. And yet, ashes are an ancient cleansing agent, and, learning again our mortality, we are cleansed of pride and illusion and enabled to see ourselves as we truly are. The clarification begins on Ash Wednesday with the cross drawn with ashes, and it culminates in the renewal of baptismal vows and sprinkling with Easter water at the Great Vigil. We move from dust to water, from a dead end to hope, from the grave to life.

Baptism gives shape to the season of Lent as it does to all of our lives. For Lent is a preparation for the baptism of new Christians and a renewal of baptism for those who have already been made members of the church by "the water of rebirth" (Titus 3:5). Baptism is our personal appropriation of the crucifixion and resurrection. By this yearly focus on baptism we are annually conformed to the passion of Christ whose sign we bear on our foreheads if not yet in our hearts, and so we are prepared for a worthy celebration of his resurrection, not least in the lives of each of us who belong to him. We who have been baptized are called to holiness of life. "As he who called you is holy, be holy yourselves in all your conduct; for it is written, 'You shall be holy for I am holy'" (1 Peter 1:15–16). In the Sermon on the Mount Jesus put it in a more startling way: "Be perfect, therefore, as your heavenly Father is perfect" (Matthew 5:48). We may try to dismiss such language as hyperbole, but other New Testament writers keep us from underestimating the seriousness of the command. St. Paul wrote, "Do not be conformed to this world, but be transformed by the renewing of your minds, so that you may discern what is the will of God — what is good and acceptable and perfect" (Romans 12:2). He wrote to the Corinthians, "Let us cleanse ourselves from every defilement of body and of spirit, making holiness perfect in the fear of God" (2 Corinthians 7:1). James, however, may be more helpful: "Let endurance have its full effect, so that you may be mature and complete, lacking in nothing" (James 1:4). The word "perfect" brings to mind something or someone faultless, unspotted, unblemished, and it thereby suggests the impossibility of the requirement, for one small sin and perfection is made forever an impossibility. The verb "to perfect," however, brings us closer to the dynamic New Testament idea: to fulfill, realize, develop, mature.[35] The baptized are called to such perfecting growth in holiness by the work of the Holy Spirit within them, until one day they stand complete in the image God has of each of them and that is shown in the life and person of Jesus Christ.

The First Sunday in Lent, the Sunday of the temptation of Christ, shows us the life of struggle to which our baptism commits us. Jesus, coming out of the Jordan after his baptism, was immediately led (Mark with his characteristic energy says "driven") by the Spirit into the wilderness for his contest with Satan. That battle between good and evil "rages within and around us, and our ancient foe tempts us with his deceits and empty promises."[36] Our defense in that battle is our baptism. The next Sundays in Lent make use of traditional New Testament images of water, life, renewal, and baptism, anciently focused in the stories of the woman of Samaria at the well, the man born blind, and the raising of Lazarus.

Thus during Lent we make our annual spiritual pilgrimage to Jerusalem, where during Holy Week we will watch the great events of the passion, death, and resurrection. We go on our journey, like our spiritual ancestors the Israelites, in the wilderness, for forty days, to be cleansed, purified, and renewed by discipline. What we are intensely during Lent we are throughout our lives: we are the pilgrim people of God on our way home.

Lent is a time to emphasize the faithful living of a life of pilgrimage, learning what is of lasting importance and what is passing. It is a time to live more faithfully our baptismal covenant, to explore the implications of what it means to be a child of God, to draw strength from our incorporation into God's family.

Holy Week begins with the Sunday of the Passion and its intense contemplation of the sacrifice of the Son of God, the culmination of the life of Christ and his people and intimately joined to its fulfillment in the resurrection, without which it is incomplete — and all of which is made ours by baptism. The culmination of the Lenten discipline and the transition to Easter occurs at the Easter Vigil, the unified commemoration of the passion-death-resurrection of Christ the Lord, the most appropriate time in all the year for baptism and the renewal of baptismal promises as the church learns year by year what it means to be brought into the ancient covenant, to be grafted onto the ancient stock of Israel, to be bound to the formative events of creation and the Red Sea and the Passover. The proper emphasis of Lent is baptism, for it is baptism that makes the cross and crown our own.

Baptism intensifies our sense of ourselves and our sense of community, for it is in relation to others that we learn our identity and our responsibility. Jesus taught us to pray "Our Father," and anciently one of the final gifts of the church to its new members before their baptism was to teach them the words of this prayer. Baptism joins us to the family of God, the church, and from that time forward we are part of a whole body. On his sick bed John Donne wrote of hearing a bell tolling to announce the passing of someone in the parish from this world to the next and to invite the prayers of all who heard the solemn sound of the "passing bell."

> The *Church* is *Catholicke, universall,* so are all her *Actions;*
> *All* that she does belongs to *all.* When she *baptizes a child,*
> that action concerns mee; for that child is thereby connected
> to that *Head* which is my *Head* too, and engraffed into that
> *body,* whereof I am a *member.* And when she *buries* a *Man,*
> that action concerns me: All *Mankinde* is of one *Author,* and
> is one *volume....* The *Bell* doth toll for him that *thinkes* it
> doth.... Who bends not his *eare* to any *bell,* which upon any
> occasion rings? but who can remove it from that *bell,* which
> is passing a *piece of himselfe* out of this *world?* No man is an
> *Iland,* intire of itself; every man is a peece of the *Continent,* a
> part of the *maine;* if a *Clod* be washed away by the *Sea, Eu-*
> *rope* is the lesse, as well as if a *Promontorie* were, as well as
> if a *Mannor* of thy *friends* or of *thine owne* were; any mans
> *death* diminishes *me,* because I am involved in *Mankinde;*
> and therefore never send to know for whom the *bell* tolls.
> It tolls for *thee.*[37]

The individual and the community are inseparable.

We use our baptism daily. Jesus taught us to pray, "forgive us our sins as we forgive those who sin against us." His story of the unforgiving steward (Matthew 18:21–35) is a warning to those who receive forgiveness that they are expected to show to others the same undeserved and unexpected mercy that they have received. We learn from the gift of baptism that if we have been so graciously accepted into the family of God without any deserving on our part, then we must learn to treat others as we have been treated, looking upon them with our hard hearts softened by grace.

> *Affliction* is a *treasure,* and scarce any man hath *enough* of it. No man hath *affliction* enough that is not matured, and ripened by it, and made fit for *God* by that *affliction.* If a man carry *treasure* in *bullion,* or in a *wedge* of *gold,* and have none coined into *current Monies,* his *treasure* will not defray him as he travells. *Tribulation* is *Treasure* in the *nature* of it, but it is not *current money* in the *use* of it, except wee get nearer and nearer our *home, Heaven,* by it.[38]

The work of baptism, Luther wrote, is suffering and death. "For in the easy life no one learns to suffer, to die with gladness, to get rid of sin, and to live in harmony with baptism."[39] So we spend our lives learning what it means to be baptized.

Then when death overtakes us, baptism finds its fulfillment. No one has written more powerfully and eloquently of the eternal significance of baptism than Martin Luther. The principal glory of Lutheran theology is its profound understanding of the nature, power, and duration of Holy Baptism. Baptism consists of preparation, presentation, thanksgiving, renunciation of evil and profession of faith in the triune God, baptism in water, laying on of hands and signation with the cross, welcome into the congregation and church, instruction in the mysteries of the faith, living, confessing and receiving forgiveness, dying, sharing in the resurrection. For, as Luther wrote in his gleaming essay *The Holy and Blessed Sacrament of Baptism* (1519), baptism is not fulfilled completely in this life. The physical baptism is quickly over, but the spiritual baptism, the drowning of sin, which it signifies, lasts as long as we live and is completed only in death. Then it is that a person is completely sunk in baptism and that which baptism signifies, the death of the old nature, comes to pass.

> Those who are baptized are condemned to die, and therefore this whole life is nothing else than a spiritual baptism which does not cease till death.[40]

> Therefore the life of a Christian, from baptism to the grave, is nothing else than the beginning of a blessed death.[41]

The drowning, the dying of baptism lasts as long as we live. So too the rising from the water, the spiritual birth, continues until death, indeed until the last day. Then at last we shall rise from death to live eternally.

Then shall we be truly lifted up out of baptism and be completely born, and we shall put on the true baptismal garment
of immortal life in heaven.[42]

The purpose of the work of Christ and therefore the purpose of
baptism is to raise us with Christ and in Christ to the heavenly
places (Ephesians 2:6). Athanasius summarized in a striking sentence the purpose of the work of Christ: "He was humanized so
that we might be deified."[43] A Christmas collect from the oldest
sacramentary, the Leonine, puts that idea in the form of a prayer.

O God, who wonderfully created, and yet more wonderfully
restored, the dignity of human nature: Grant that we may
share the divine life of him who humbled himself to share
our humanity, your Son Jesus Christ.[44]

When the work symbolized by our rising from the baptismal water
as a new person is completed, we will rise from this life to the fulfillment of God's promises in the new life of the heavenly kingdom,
purified and perfected. Then our sanctification will be complete.

So the saints, those in whom we can already see the fulfillment
of baptism, have been precious to the church. Their examples encourage us who are still on the way, who are sometimes unsure
whether we can complete the arduous journey. A young Jewish
woman was made the birth-giver of God, *Theotokos,* and became
in bearing her Maker "more glorious than the seraphim."[45] A mortal became the mother of God, and she is therefore preeminent
among the saints of God. The martyrs, beginning with Stephen
the deacon and protomartyr, followed their Lord into death and
beyond, walking the way of the cross, willing to sacrifice even
their very lives so that the church might live and grow. Confessors
gave their testimony, risking their security and their lives. Saints,
holy men and women, were called from every land and people and
station in life. These exemplars surround us with their cloud of witness, and they support us on our way and strengthen us with their
testimony to the unbroken line of witnesses from the beginning
until now, a line that will stretch to the end of time.[46]

The collect provided by the *Book of Common Prayer* since 1549
for All Saints' Day impressively acknowledges the unity of all the
baptized, living and dead, in this world and the next.

Almighty God, you have knit together your elect in one communion and fellowship in the mystical body of your Son
Christ our Lord: Give us grace so to follow your blessed

saints in all virtuous and godly living, that we may come to those ineffable joys that you have prepared for those who truly love you; through Jesus Christ our Lord....[47]

Despite its many lamentable earthly divisions, there is only one church, here and there, militant and triumphant, one body of Christ our Lord. Not even death divides it.

The Burial of the Dead, therefore, is properly seen in relation to Holy Baptism. It is the completion of the process, the other end of what happens in baptism, the culmination of the work of the Holy Spirit, who calls, gathers, enlightens, and sanctifies the whole church. So the Burial of the Dead is itself, like the service of Holy Baptism, a progressive rite, a procession from station to station.

The burial service is a stational liturgy, a procession that moves through the church as each of us moves through life in this world, making stops occasionally, but always moving on toward our final rest. Like baptism itself, the Burial of the Dead is a passage into a new life. After the preparatory ministrations of the church at the place of death, in the home and at the funeral establishment, the Burial of the Dead begins at the entrance of the church as the ministers meet the coffin and perhaps cover it with a pall, recalling the baptismal clothing. The church in the person of the ministers goes to meet its departed member and one last time welcomes that member into its earthly assembly. Then the procession enters the church, often accompanied by singing, as the coffin, mourners, and ministers move toward their places before the altar of God. The Liturgy of the Word follows with words of consolation, strength, and hope. The Prayer of the Day is said, lessons are read with a hymn or a psalm sung between them, culminating in the Gospel. The sermon applies the words of Scripture to the individual situation of this family and this newly departed servant of God. The Apostles' Creed, the baptismal creed, is said, and the prayers of intercession conclude the Liturgy of the Word. The Liturgy of the Table follows with the actions of the Great Thanksgiving: taking, blessing, breaking, and distributing the eucharistic elements, moving the congregation out of their pews, past the coffin, to come to the altar to be fed with the living bread from heaven. The celebration of the Eucharist and the reception of the Holy Communion is particularly appropriate at a funeral, for the Eucharist provides a personal participation in the paschal mystery, the transition from death to life, of Christ and thus of those who belong to him. Holy Communion, the birthright of the baptized, is the culmination of the celebration of Holy Baptism, the meal to which the sacrament of entrance leads. When we make use of our baptism by repentance and confession of sins we do it fittingly in the sacrament of bread and wine.[48] And so when baptism finds its fulfillment in death, the Holy Communion continues as the appropriate celebration.

Then, after the communion, the ministers move again to the coffin and there commend the newly departed to the care of the merciful Savior and to the "company of the saints in light." The procession moves out of the church to the cemetery, and there the procession goes to the grave. The coffin is lowered into its place in the earth with the words of committal. The final dismissal turns the mourners from the grave to the rest of their lives in the world, to life without the newly departed, to the new horizons bright with promise that open daily before God's people.

The Burial of the Dead, like a procession, pauses at various locations in the church and graveyard to mourn the loss of a loved one, to hear God's words of consolation and support, to eat the foretaste of the heavenly banquet, and to commend the newly departed to God's never-failing care and love. Then life goes on. The accent throughout falls on actions, on movement, and that very progress itself is a proclamation of the vigorous, forward-driving energy of life that is the gift and promise of God.

The Burial of the Dead is a baptismal liturgy. The fundamental action underlying the rich complex of rites that together constitute the way the church sends one of its members from this world to the next is Holy Baptism. Holy Baptism is surrounded by supporting actions and rites: enrollment of candidates and instruction before the baptism, after it the gradual incorporation into the life of the church, and confession and forgiveness. The Burial of the Dead is likewise given context by the preparatory rites: the visitation of the sick with lessons and prayers, confession, anointing, Holy Communion, the commendation of the dying, the wake. Like life itself, the Christian liturgy has a restless energy that may pause from time to time but that cannot rest "until all is fulfilled in the kingdom of God" (Luke 22:16).

As baptism brings us into the church and the communion of saints, so when we die no one can doubt that we are not alone but are still surrounded and supported by a great company. The Christian, as Luther preached,

can be certain, as the sacraments point out, that a great many eyes are upon him: first, the eyes God and of Christ himself, for the Christian believes his words and clings to his sacraments; then also, the eyes of the dear angels, of the saints, and of all Christians. There is no doubt, as the Sacrament of the Altar indicates, that all of these in a body run to him as one of their own, help him overcome sin, death, and hell, and bear all things with him. In that hour the work of love and the communion of saints are seriously and mightily active.[49]

The Christian community, established in baptism, is unbroken by death, and those who have been made part of it can never be isolated from the others. Baptism is the assurance that when death comes, it is not the end. For at the end there is not death; at the end there is God.

Chapter Ten

THE SOURCE OF RENEWAL

In northwest Mesopotamia at a place called Haran a family had been marked by tragedy and loss. A son had died before his father, and later at a great age the father died. Into that sad scene God enters abruptly to divide further the already broken family. Without warning, God says to Abram:

> Go from your country and your kindred and your father's house to the land that I will show you. I will make of you a great nation, and I will bless you, and make your name great, so that you will be a blessing. I will bless those who bless you, and the one who curses you I will curse; and in you all the families of the earth shall be blessed. (Genesis 12:1–3)

With that sudden act, the whole sweep of biblical history begins, continuing down to the present day — spiritually in our synagogues and churches and in our hearts, politically in Israel and the Middle East. God called Abraham into service, and Abraham in bold obedience set out, not knowing where he was going but only that God was leading and supporting him. In that dramatic call, not just one man but a whole people — Israel, Abraham's descendants — is chosen to play a decisive role in God's purpose in history. Christians also claim in their own way to have Abraham as their father too. It was the beginning of an epic journey.

That momentous call of Abraham becomes the pattern for all earnest seekers who set out in quest of religious meaning. He becomes the model for us all, as the writer to the Hebrews understood.

> By faith Abraham obeyed when he was called to set out for a place that he was to receive as an inheritance; and he set out, not knowing where he was going. (Hebrews 11:8)

That act of daringly obedient faith inspired the splendid prayer of Eric Milner-White:

O Lord God, who hast called thy servants to ventures of
which we cannot see the ending, by paths as yet untrodden,
through perils unknown: Give us faith to go out with a good
courage, not knowing whither we go, but only that thy hand
is leading us and thy love supporting us; to the glory of thy
Name.[1]

Like our forebears millennia ago, we are still the pilgrim people
of God, strangers and foreigners on the earth seeking a homeland
(Hebrews 11:13–14).

We, like our ancestors, are on pilgrimage. We are familiar
with processions, the ritual indications of pilgrimage. There is the
sometimes extended procession with palms on the Sunday of the
Passion, beginning perhaps outside the church building or going
from the church outside and then back into the church again.
There is the procession with the cross on Good Friday that invites us to adore our crucified God. In the Easter Vigil there is
the procession into the darkened church, led by the paschal candle, the light of Christ. Later in the vigil the ministers, sponsors,
and candidates for baptism process to the font, and after the baptism those who are no longer candidates but now are numbered
among the baptized process back to the altar for the celebration
of the Eucharist. Every Sunday there is the entrance of the ministers, sometimes joined by the choir. Physical movement is desirable,
for liturgy is a kind of drama, an enactment of the history of salvation. Things happen; people move about, and at least our eyes
must follow the movement. Processions are a sign of a people on
the move who have no fixed or permanent place for worship or for
living. Processions are little pilgrimages that we take in and around
a church building. They point us to the larger procession on which
we are venturing, the journey of life, and a still larger procession,
the journey of the faithful through the centuries. The concave stone
steps of ancient churches have been worn with the feet of centuries
of pilgrims who have gone before us on the pilgrimage. We learn
by that silent witness that we have company, largely unseen, on the
journey. We join in a long procession. Dante in the *Divine Comedy*
declares in astonishment, I "had not thought death had undone so
many."[2] A pilgrimage is not only a journey with intention, a direction, a goal, even though we, like Abraham, may not know where
or what that goal is. It is also a journey with a promise of meaning
and connection. The traveller is required to abandon the familiar.
It may mean leaving home; it may mean learning to do old things

in a new way or learning to do new things. But those who make the pilgrimage are required to subject themselves to the risk of discovery. The result may be a challenge to their understanding and satisfaction, as the pilgrimage of the Magi was for those seekers, as T. S. Eliot describes them in his poem *The Journey of the Magi.*

The first characteristic of the life of faith that the pilgrimage teaches us therefore is impermanence. The pilgrimage reminds us of an aspect of our physical life, the process of aging, which we would often like to ignore because it cannot be changed or helped. We are all growing older, for that is a part of life and growth. The familiar evening hymn has us sing, "Change and decay in all around I see,"[3] and we see the change not only around us, out there, but also, when we reach a certain age, in ourselves. We are part of the change and decay. Processions remind each of us of our passage through this world. There is nothing here that will last to which we can cling; there is nothing into which we can settle too comfortably. Processions remind us again and again of the impermanence of all that we see, including ourselves.

We may look back longingly at what we sometimes call the Age of Faith, the age that with great vision and daring skill built the great churches and the monumental cathedrals, which still awe us jaded and cynical moderns. Those splendid, overwhelming monuments of the soaring human spirit have lasted these many centuries in their massive solidity. But there is a disconcerting traditional decoration that adorns the roofs of those great monuments: an angel. One sees the tradition continued in New York City in the Cathedral Church of St. John the Divine and on Riverside Church. Both churches are graced with an angel on the apse. I was walking around Riverside Church one day on my way from a class at Union Seminary, pleased to see the angel up there, a pleasant decoration looking up the Hudson valley. Suddenly I saw it for what it was: not a pleasing relic of a past age that thought it could find angels everywhere, but a reminder of the end of time. Those angels on the apse have trumpets, and on churches that like St. John the Divine are oriented in the traditional direction with the altar toward the east, the angel on the apse looks eastward toward Jerusalem, toward the rising sun, trumpet ready, looking vigilantly for signs of the Second Coming. An angel on the apse says silently but convincingly that all this solid splendor we delight in here, the mighty blocks of granite and limestone, the massive Gothic "pile," as the English are fond of calling a great church, all this is only temporary, though it last a thousand years. The immense building itself, a representation of the cosmos, looks for its own destruction when time itself is done, when the heavens are rolled up like a scroll, as Isaiah warns (34:4), and when the new heaven and new earth appear. The church's worship — its liturgy, its Scripture, its houses — preaches against permanence and security. The temporary may serve for centuries, like the Gothic cathedrals, but it is temporary nonetheless. The impermanence of all we see, including ourselves, is the first lesson that the pilgrimage teaches us.

With those great but temporary buildings we come to a second characteristic of the life of faith that the pilgrimage teaches us, and that is continuity. As we make our journey, we stimulate an awareness of the past out of which we have come. Ours is a long history, and the permanent buildings of ages past tell us of that. They give us a sense of rich continuity. We have come from somewhere; we are a people with a history. We move today with centuries of tradition and discovery behind us.

This sense of continuity recalls us to the sources of our faith. Because we are on our way, we cannot settle into the present as if we have always been here where we find ourselves today. We cannot become too comfortable here. We are reminded that we have come out of a long history, and during that long history we have learned many things. We have as a people accumulated a great variety of experiences by which we have learned about God and the world. And all the past that lies behind us is not obsolete or out of touch with modern life. If there seems to be little connection, it may not be the past but our own time that is out of touch. In his remarkable book *Orthodoxy,* written in 1908, G. K. Chesterton makes a provocative observation about Christian creeds.

> I have alluded to an unmeaning phrase to the effect that such and such a creed cannot be believed in our age. Of course, anything can be believed in any age. But, oddly enough, there really is a sense in which a creed, if it is believed at all, can be believed more fixedly in a complex society than in a simple one.

> The complication of our modern world proves the truth of the creed more perfectly than any of the plain problems of the age of faith.... That is why the faith has that elaboration of doctrines and details which so much distresses those who admire Christianity without believing in it. When once one believes in a creed, one is proud of its complexity, as scientists are proud of the complexity of science. It shows how rich it

is in discoveries. If it is right at all, it is a compliment to say
that it's elaborately right. A stick might fit a hole or a stone a
hollow by accident. But a key and a lock are both complex.
And if a key fits a lock, you know it is the right key.[4]

We pilgrims are part of a tradition that is "rich in discoveries,"
and we can rejoice in its complexity. The complex richness of that
noble tradition is enshrined in the liturgy, preserved for our benefit,
for our use and exploration and discovery.

When we worship, we are thus called to be faithful to the broad
Christian tradition that flows like a mighty river out of the discoveries of the past. But here is the paradox: the tradition to which we
are called to be faithful is a tradition of growth. Ours is a long history, but it is always growing and changing and developing. This
tradition out of which we come and that we carry with us and in
us therefore invites us to explore. It not only calls us back; it not
only encourages us to keep on doing what we have done; it sends
us out now, and it sends us on. It does not beguile us into content-
ment with what we now have. It urges us to further discovery and
exploration, for there is more to be sought and more to be found
and more to be made ours.

The continuity of the tradition will not let us rest in what has
been accomplished so far. There is a rest promised to the people of
God, the writer to the Hebrews assures us, but it is still ahead. "A
sabbath rest still remains for the people of God" (Hebrews 4:9).
The sabbath rest is promised, and the promise is sure. But the rest
is not yet our possession. "Let us therefore make every effort to enter that rest." As we look expectantly and even impatiently to the
future, we learn, as we move through this world on our pilgrimage, that although things change, not everything is in flux. We are
on a pilgrimage to a goal: the promised rest of God. St. Augustine
prayed at the beginning of his *Confessions,* "You have made us for
yourself, and our hearts are restless until we find our rest in you."[5]
That perfect rest is found not in this world but in God.

We are inescapably children of tradition, and because of that we
are children of hope, for our tradition is one of growth toward the
goal God intends for creation. Hope, then, is the third characteristic of the life of faith that the pilgrimage teaches. Impermanence,
continuity, and hope: these three are related to the time through
which our pilgrimage passes — past, present, future. But when we
worship the past lives again, and we are present then. The barrier
of time is collapsed, and the past and present flow into one an-

other without distinction. Our tradition is alive now, here, in us as we worship. And as we worship here and now, we not only participate in the past, we participate also in the future, which we glimpse and share and taste now, already. When we worship, past and future are gathered into the present, and we experience beforehand the perfection of eternity that has no past or future but that is always the eternal present.

T. S. Eliot in *Little Gidding* speaks of returning to a place and knowing it for the first time.

> We shall not cease from exploration
> And the end of all our exploring
> Will be to arrive where we started
> And know the place for the first time.[6]

We move in a circle that is not finally a circle. In Holy Communion we return week after week to that familiar family meal and are often surprised by new insights given to us there. We return to the Lord's Supper and know it for the first time. We return to the liturgy again and again and yet find it ever new, discovering new things we never knew before, finding new depths to our experience. When in the liturgy we remember, we call to mind again the familiar stories of the past and know them for the first time, exclaiming to ourselves (at least sometimes), "So that's what it was like; so that's what it meant." We do it with respect to the future too and find excitement even there, although by anticipation we have known and seen and tasted it before. We find in ourselves when we worship new depths and new possibilities we had not dreamed of. Because of what we have seen and heard and learned and done in the Holy Communion we return to the world as if for the first time and see it with new eyes, with a new compassion, with a love we did not have before. So our relationship to the liturgy, to ourselves, and to the world is deepened and renewed; and worship, specifically the Holy Communion, becomes the center and source of our renewal, for in worship we meet God, who makes all things new.

It is that encounter with God that commands our attention. Worship summons us to change because our encounter with God convinces us that God cannot be content with things as they are. Worship challenges us to grow because our encounter with God cannot leave us untouched. When we are confronted with God's life-giving power, our lives cannot remain the same. Worship does more than simply suggest or teach or urge. Worship in fact requires our renewal because we cannot worship the living God and not be made new. We cannot be washed in God's holy water and cannot eat God's life-giving meal and remain as we were. We are inevitably changed by our encounter with God. Our relationship to God is changed; our relationship to each other is changed; our relationship to the world is changed. We are changed by that encounter precisely because it is an encounter with *God.*

St. Paul exclaims:

> O the depth of the riches and wisdom and knowledge of God! How unsearchable are his judgments and how inscrutable his ways! (Romans 11:33)

The concluding words of the chapter,

> For from him and through him and to him are all things. To him be the glory forever. Amen (Romans 11:36),

are echoed in the concluding doxology of the Great Thanksgiving,

> through Christ, and with Christ, and in Christ, all honor and glory are yours, Almighty God and Father, in the unity of the Holy Spirit, for ever and ever. *AMEN.*[7]

From whom, through whom, to whom; Source, Guide, and Goal; the beginning, the middle, and the ending. The triune God is the place from which our pilgrimage begins, the guide along the way we travel, and the end toward which we constantly move. Yet the Source is that which draws us on, and the Goal is that which we now glimpse and taste, and, as in the mystery of the Holy Trinity, the three are one. This vision of God unifies and expands at the same time, so that the three are one and the one is three. Worship, the encounter with almighty God, heightens our perception so that we see beyond the immediate, so that we see through the immediate, to still more, to ever new visions of grander things to come, new possibilities of which we have not even dreamed.

One day in the heat of the afternoon, Abraham the pilgrim was sitting in the shade of his tent, and some visitors appeared in front of him (Genesis 18). In a dreamlike and mysterious sequence of events he sees three men approach; then the three seem to be only two, and then they are only one. And they are not actually humans but angels and perhaps not angels but God or God and two angels. That is what happens to us when we worship. We have our eyes opened to new horizons; the familiar becomes strange and the unfamiliar is made known.

Abraham's journey, which we are to imitate, is as the Bible understands it not a nomadic wandering, not an aimless drifting across the ancient Middle East at the whim of pasture and weather. It is a pilgrimage: it has a definite purpose and goal. It is a journey that is going somewhere, across time, moving from the past through the present into the future, from then, through now, toward what will be. The end is yet to be revealed, but we are confident that God is leading, and that God knows where we are going into the veiled way of the future.

We fare forward like medieval pilgrims going to a shrine of which they have heard but that they have never seen. They are quite sure the destination is there, but they are not sure exactly what it will be, nor are they sure what they will encounter on the way. So the invitation to join the pilgrimage is a call to adventure and risk, but it also promises great reward, not least of which is the company with whom we travel. We join a company like Chaucer's pilgrims in the *Canterbury Tales,* real people who laugh and jest and shock and annoy and teach and inspire.

With such a high calling before us and with such a realistic faith stirring within us, we cannot stay in one place. We must constantly be moving on until we find our perfect rest in God, who is our Source, our Guide, and our Goal. Then the praise that sounds throughout the church of God will be taken up and purified and combined with the praise of all the universe hymning God who will at last be all in all.

With that vision held before us by the liturgy of the church, we recognize with St. Augustine, in words familiar to many from the General Thanksgiving in the *Book of Common Prayer,* that we must show forth that praise "not only with our lips, but in our lives, by giving up our selves to your service, and by walking before you in holiness and righteousness all our days."[8] For it is only in such lives of perfect service that we can begin to declare the praise of the God of justice and of love, who created the universe and who still sustains us and all things. Thus our encounter with God in worship is the constant source of our continuing renewal.

NOTES

✠

Chapter One: Toward a Definition of Spirituality

1. The collect in *The Book of Common Prayer* (New York: The Church Hymnal Corporation and the Seabury Press, 1979) for Proper 25 and in the Roman Sacramentary for the 30th Sunday of the Year. In *Lutheran Book of Worship* (Minneapolis: Augsburg Publishing House; Philadelphia: Board of Publication, Lutheran Church in America, 1978) it is the prayer of the day for the twenty-third Sunday after Pentecost.

2. Bernard Häring, "A Modern Approach to the Ascetic Life," *Protestants and Catholics on the Spiritual Life*, ed. Michael Marx (Collegeville, Minn.: Liturgical Press, 1965), 72. Reprinted from *Worship*, December 1995.

3. The text is that of the *Church Book* (Philadelphia: General Council Publication Board, 1891), the *Common Service Book* (Philadelphia: Board of Publication of the United Lutheran Church in America, 1918), and the *Service Book and Hymnal* (Minneapolis: Augsburg Publishing House; Philadelphia: Board of Publication, Lutheran Church in America, 1958). A German text of this formula appeared as early as 1842 in the United States as one of several formulas for confirmation. The form is a gathering of 2 Peter 3:18, 1 Peter 2:20, Philippians 3:10, and Titus 2:13. The formula has been revised in *Lutheran Book of Worship*.

4. See *Salvation in Christ: A Lutheran-Orthodox Dialogue*, ed. John Meyendorff and Robert Tobias (Minneapolis: Augsburg Fortress, 1992), 24.

5. Louis Bouyer, *Introduction to Spirituality* (Collegeville, Minn.: Liturgical Press, 1961), 2.

6. Bouyer, 4.

7. F. P. Harton, *The Elements of the Spiritual Life: A Study in Ascetical Theology* (New York: Macmillan, 1932), 6.

8. Bouyer, 15.

9. Martin Luther, Explanation of the Third Article of the Apostles' Creed, *The Small Catechism*, in *The Book of Concord*, ed. Theodore G. Tappert (Philadelphia: Muhlenberg Press, 1959), 345.

10. *Salvation in Christ*, 31.

11. Abraham Heschel, *Man's Quest for God: Studies in Prayer and Symbolism* (New York: Scribner's, 1954), xii.

12. *The Book of Concord*, 365.

13. *Salvation in Christ*, 22.

14. *Book of Common Prayer*, 339.

15. Bouyer, 11.

16. Margaret R. Miles, *Carnal Knowing: Female Nakedness and Religious Meaning in the Christian West* (Boston: Beacon Press, 1989), 9.

17. Bouyer, 14.

18. *Salvation in Christ*, 32.

19. Harton, viii.

20. The image is used in the medieval office for travellers, the Itinerarium, which prays, "God, who led your servant, Abraham, out of Ur of the Chaldeans, and kept him safe in all his wanderings; may it please you, we pray, also to watch over us, your servants. Be to us, Lord, a help in our preparations, comfort on the way, shade in the heat, shelter in the rain and cold, a carriage in tiredness, a shield in adversity, a staff in insecurity, a haven in accident; so that under your guidance we may happily reach our destination, and finally return safe to our homes." Cited in Philip T. Weller, *The Roman Ritual* (Milwaukee: Bruce, 1964), 748. The office is preserved in Lutheran use in a prayer in *Lutheran Book of Worship*, 167, and in the full form in Herbert Lindemann, ed., *The Daily Office* (St. Louis: Concordia, 1965), 690–693.

21. "Only-Begotten, Word of God Eternal," *The Hymnal 1982* (New York: The Church Hymnal Corporation, 1985), no. 360, 361, stanza 4, trans. Maxwell Julius Blacker.

22. George Steiner, *Real Presences* (Chicago: University of Chicago Press, 1989), 142.

23. Nikolaus Decius, "O Lamm Gottes unschuldig," trans. Joel Lundin, *Lutheran Book of Worship*, no. 111.

24. Margaret Miles, *Carnal Knowing*, 1–8.

25. Tertullian, *On the Resurrection of the Flesh* 15, in *Ante-Nicene Fathers*, vol. 3 (Grand Rapids: Eerdmans, 1963), 555.

26. Athanasius, "On the Incarnation" 54, *Christology of the Later Fathers*, ed. Edward Rochie Hardy (Philadelphia: Westminster Press, n.d.), 107. Archibald Robertson's translation is "he was made man so that we might be made God."

27. Douglas V. Steere, "Common Frontiers in Catholic and Non-Catholic Spirituality," *Protestants and Catholics on the Spiritual Life*, 43.

28. Steere, 52.

29. Mary Ward, *Till God Will*, in *English Spirituality: The Little Gidding Anthology of English Spirituality* (Nashville: Abingdon, 1987), 86.

30. *Service Book and Hymnal*, no. 508; *The United Methodist Hymnal* (Nashville: The United Methodist Publishing House, 1989), no. 421; *The Presbyterian Hymnal* (Louisville, Ky.: Westminster John Knox Press, 1990), no. 378.

Chapter Two: The Source and Summit of Faith

1. Frederick W. Robertson, *Sermons Preached at Brighton*, new ed. (New York: Harper and Bros., n.d.), 62.

2. It is perhaps not surprising to learn that Tersteegen was later drawn to mysticism.

3. *Didache* 9.4.

4. Henri Frankfort, *The Birth of Civilization in the Near East* (Garden City, N.Y.: Doubleday, 1956), 57–58.

5. *The Hymnal 1982* (New York: The Church Hymnal Corporation, 1985), nos. 165, 166. The translation is by John Mason Neale (1818–1866).

6. Horton Davies, "The Puritan and Pietist Traditions of Protestant Spirituality," *Protestants and Catholics on the Spiritual Life,* ed. Michael Marx (Collegeville, Minn.: Liturgical Press, 1965), 36.

7. John Keats, *Lamia*, lines 229–237.

8. J. B. Priestly, *Man and Time* (New York: Dell, 1968 [1964]), 207.

9. George Steiner, *Real Presences* (Chicago: University of Chicago Press, 1989), 185.

10. Steiner, 188.

11. The conclusion of the opening paragraph of Percy Bysshe Shelley, "The Defence of Poetry" (1821), in *Criticism: The Foundations of Modern Literary Judgment,* ed. Mark Schorer, Josephine Miles; rev. ed. Gordon McKenzie (New York: Harcourt, Brace & World, 1958), 455.

12. See Annemarie Schimmel, *The Mystery of Numbers* (New York: Oxford University Press, 1993).

13. William Blake, *Marriage of Heaven and Hell,* line 34.

14. See Stanley Hauerwas and William H. Willimon, *Resident Aliens: Life in the Christian Colony* (Nashville: Abingdon, 1990).

15. See Belden C. Lane, "The Mountain That Was God," *The Christian Century* 102, no. 20 (June 5–12, 1985): 579–581.

16. *Lutheran Book of Worship,* no. 445.

Chapter Three: Daily Prayer: Hallowing Time

1. See also the powerful and haunting speech by Chief Seattle ceding his ancestral land to the United States. The conclusion is included in Philip H. Pfatteicher, *Festivals and Commemorations* (Minneapolis: Augsburg Publishing House, 1980), 227–228.

2. See the comments of the child psychologist Bruno Bettelheim (*The Uses of Enchantment* [New York: Random House, 1977]) that violent fairy tales are in fact healthful, for they teach children to deal with violent thoughts that already exist in children's minds.

3. Joseph Campbell, *The Masks of God: Primitive Mythology* (New York: Viking, 1970), 62.

4. Campbell, 66.

5. Mircea Eliade, *Rites and Symbols of Initiation: The Mysteries of Birth and Rebirth*, trans. Willard R. Trask (New York: Harper & Row, 1965), 9.

6. See, for example, the prayer composed from phrases drawn from two sermons of John Henry Newman, "O Lord, support us all the day long, until the shadows lengthen..." (*Book of Common Prayer* [New York: The Church Hymnal Corporation and the Seabury Press, 1979], 833; *Lutheran Book of Worship* [Minneapolis: Augsburg Publishing House; Philadelphia: Board of Publication, Lutheran Church in America, 1978], 158); and Robert Bridges's translation of a hymn by Paul Gerhardt, "The duteous day now closeth" (*The Hymnal 1982* [New York: The Church Hymnal Corporation, 1985], no. 46).

7. Campbell, 57.

8. Robert Bridges translation, *Service Book and Hymnal* (Minneapolis: Augsburg Publishing House; Philadelphia: Board of Publication, Lutheran Church in America, 1958), no. 206.

9. William Chatterton Dix, "As with gladness men of old," stanza 5, *The Hymnal 1982* (New York: The Church Hymnal Corp., 1982), no. 119.

10. A.-M. Roguet, commentary on the General Instruction on the Liturgy of the Hours, *The Liturgy of the Hours*, trans. Peter Coughlan and Peter Perdue (London: Geoffrey Chapman, 1971), 23.

11. Second Vatican Council, *Constitution on the Sacred Liturgy*, chapter 4, "The Divine Office," 89a, in ed. Walter M. Abbott, *The Documents of Vatican II* (New York: Guild Press, America Press, Association Press, 1966), 164.

12. Isabel Florence Hapgood, *Service Book of the Orthodox-Catholic Apostolic Church*, 5th ed. (Englewood, N.J.: Antiochian Orthodox Christian Archdiocese, 1975), 592.

13. See David S. Landes, *Revolution in Time: Clocks and the Making of the Modern World* (Cambridge, Mass.: Harvard University Press, 1983).

14. General Instruction on the Liturgy of the Hours 1, *The Liturgy of the Hours,* 17.

15. *Hymnal 1982*, no. 179, "Welcome, happy morning!" stanza 3.

16. In Somerset Lowry's hymn,

> Son of God, eternal Savior,
> Source of life and truth and grace,
> Word made flesh, whose birth among us
> Hallows all our human race....
> (*Lutheran Book of Worship,* no. 364)

The original third line was "Son of Man, whose birth among us."

17. Roguet, 127.

18. Roguet, 132.

19. John Keble, "New Every Morning Is the Love," *The Hymnal 1982*, no. 10; *Service Book and Hymnal*, no. 201.

20. F. P. Harton, *The Elements of the Spiritual Life: A Study in Ascetical Theology* (New York: Macmillan, 1932), 295.

21. Dietrich Bonhöffer, *Life Together*, trans. John W. Doberstein (New York: Harper & Bros., 1954), 4, 46; Louis Bouyer, *Liturgical Piety* (Notre Dame, Ind.: University of Notre Dame Press, 1955), 230.

22. Abraham Joshua Heschel, *Man's Quest for God: Studies in Prayer and Symbolism* (New York: Scribner's, 1954), 46.

23. Bonhöffer, 57–58.

24. Bouyer, 232.

25. Alan Paton, *Too Late the Phalarope* (New York: Scribner's, 1953), 252.

26. C. S. Lewis, *Reflections on the Psalms* (New York: Harcourt, Brace & Co., 1958), 20–33, 136.

27. Bonhöffer, 45.

28. Richard Herbel, *St. Augustine's House Newsletter*, Lent 1991.

29. Herbel. See also Bonhöffer, 47–48.

30. Bonhöffer, 45–46.

31. Bonhöffer, 46–47.

32. Martin Luther, "Preface to the Psalter" 1545 (1528), *Luther's Works* 35:254, 255.

33. Bonhöffer, 47.

34. Bouyer, 229–230.

35. Bonhöffer, 50–51.

36. See the *Rule* of St. Benedict, chapter 48.

37. Bonhöffer, 52.

38. Bonhöffer, 53.

39. Bonhöffer, 53.

40. Bonhöffer, 54.

41. Bonhöffer, 54.

42. Bonhöffer, 54.

43. Massey Hamilton Shepherd Jr., *The Oxford American Prayer Book Commentary* (New York: Oxford, 1950), 92. See also John 5:39; Acts 17:11; 1 Corinthians 10:11; 2 Timothy 3:16–17.

44. Guigo II, *The Ladder of Monks: A Letter on the Contemplative Life*, trans. Edmund Colledge and James Walsh (Kalamazoo, Mich.: Cistercian Publications, 1981), 68–69.

45. Frank Whaling, ed., *John and Charles Wesley: Selected Writings* (New York: Paulist Press, 1981), 88–89.

46. Hierotheus, quoted in William Inge, *Christian Mysticism* (New York: Meridian, 1956 [1899]), 103.

47. Christopher Marlowe, *Hero and Leander*, line 186: "True love is mute."

48. Thomas Carlyle, *Sartor Resartus*, book 3, chapter 3.

49. "It is in the silence after the storm that God reveals himself to man. God is silence." Elie Wiesel, *The Gates of the Forest*, trans. Frances Frenaye (New York: Schocken, 1982), 63. And the reticent hero of George Bernanos's novel, *The Diary of a Country Priest*, trans. Pamela Morris (New York: Carroll & Graf, 1983 [1937]), 259, muses, "Keep silent, what a strange expression! Silence keeps us."

50. Lucy Violet Hodgkin, *The Surrender of Silence*, rev. ed. London: Friends' Bookshop, 1925 [1913]. See also Margaret Guenther, "Embracing the Silence," *The Christian Century* 112, no. 19 (June 7, 1995): 603.

51. Edward Grubb, *What is Quakerism?*, 3d ed. (London: George Allen and Unwin, 1929), 52.

52. William Wistar Comfort, *Just Among Friends: The Quaker Way of Life* (New York: Macmillan, 1941), 35.

53. Comfort, 31.

54. Comfort, 32.

55. Grubb, 50–51.

56. Comfort, 33.

57. Comfort, 40.

58. Grubb, 51

59. In Cyril Hepher, ed., *The Fellowship of Silence* (London: Macmillan, 1915) 175. Quoted in Grubb, 53.

60. Comfort, 31.

61. Cyril Hepher, ed., *The Fruits of Silence* (London: Macmillan, 1915), 18. Quoted in Grubb, 52.

62. Thomas Comber, *A Companion to the Temple, or A Help to Devotion in the Use of the Common Prayer* (1672–76/1684), quoted in J. Robert Wright, ed., *Prayer Book Spirituality* (New York: Church Hymnal Corporation, 1989), 147.

63. Comfort, 35.

64. Rufus M. Jones, *The Trail of Life in the Middle Years* (New York: Macmillan, 1934), 45.

65. *Lutheran Book of Worship*, Ministers Edition (Minneapolis: Augsburg Publishing House; Philadelphia: Board of Publication, Lutheran Church in America, 1978), 221, 257, 293.

66. According to the rites in *Lutheran Book of Worship*, 142 (and Ministers Edition, 16); *Book of Common Worship* (Louisville, Ky.: Westminster John Knox Press, 1993), 505; and *Morning Praise and Evensong*, ed. William G. Storey, Frank C. Quinn, David F. Wright (Notre Dame, Ind.: Fides, 1973), vii-viii, 1, 25; see also "An Order of Worship for the Evening," *Book of Common Prayer*, 108–114.

67. St. Basil the Great (ca. 330–379) said of it, "The people ... still use the ancient formula." *On the Holy Spirit* 29.73. *Nicene and Post-Nicene Fathers*, vol. 8 (Grand Rapids: Eerdmans, 1956 reprint), 46.

68. M. Eleanor Irwin, "PHOS HILARON: The Metamorphoses of a Christian Hymn," *The Hymn: A Journal of Congregational Song* 40 (April 1989): 7–12.

69. See, for example, Bonhöffer, 59–60.

70. In the Liturgy of St. John Chrysostom, the Anaphora concludes with the commemoration of the living: "Grant that we may with one mouth and one heart glorify and praise your sublime and all-powerful name, Father Son, and Holy Spirit, now and always, and unto ages of ages."

71. Gregory Dix, *The Shape of the Liturgy* (Westminster: Dacre, 1945), 87.

72. Translation from *Morning Praise and Evensong,* 26; also in *Lutheran Book of Worship,* 177, and, in a new translation, in the *Book of Common Worship* (1993), 504, no. 4.

73. Translation from *Morning Praise and Evensong,* 2; also in he *Lutheran Book of Worship,* 177.

74. "An Order of Worship for the Evening" in the *Book of Common Prayer* follows this pattern and provides seven prayers for light in the traditional collect form (110–111).

75. *Book of Common Worship,* 508–511.

76. *Lutheran Book of Worship,* 144; the source is *Morning Praise and Evensong,* 73–74.

77. The source is *Morning Praise and Evensong,* 59.

78. See Arthur Carl Piepkorn, "Mary's Place Within the People of God According to Non-Roman-Catholics," *Marian Studies* 18 (1967): 79–81.

79. Martin Luther, "The Magnificat" (1521), *Luther's Works,* 21:321.

80. Luther, 322.

81. Luther, 323. It was apparently this passage that was quoted by Polish Archbishop Josef Gawlina in the second day of debate on the Marian chapter of the schema *De Ecclesia* at the Second Vatican Council, September 17, 1964, ironically in support of a maximalist view of the role of Mary as Mediatrix and Mother of the Church. According to the report in the *New York Times,* September 18, 1964, the passage was said to come from a 1523 exposition of a passage from St. John. It was probably the first time Luther was quoted without censure within the walls of St. Peter's Basilica, and unfortunately he continued to be misunderstood.

82. John Milton in his *sonetto caudato* (a "tailed sonnet"), "On the New Forcers of Conscience Under the Long Parliament," line 20.

83. This translation is by Paul Zeller Strodach in *The Works of Martin Luther,* Philadelphia Edition, vol. 6 (Philadelphia: Muhlenberg Press, 1932), 358. Luther had made a German translation of the prayer.

84. Luther D. Reed, *The Lutheran Liturgy* (Philadelphia: Muhlenberg Press, 1960), 447.

85. Thomas Comber, *A Companion to the Temple, or A Help to Devotion in the Use of the Common Prayer* (1672–76/1684), in *Prayer*

Book Spirituality, ed. J. Robert Wright (New York: Church Hymnal Corporation, 1989), 159–160.

86. Massey Hamilton Shepherd Jr., *The Oxford American Prayer Book Commentary* (New York: Oxford University Press, 1950), 31.

87. Karl Barth, *Prayer,* 2d ed., trans. Sara F. Terrien, ed. Don E. Saliers (Philadelphia: Westminster Press, 1985), 51.

88. Barth, 43–44.

89. Frederick Denison Maurice, *Sermons on the Prayer Book and the Lord's Prayer* (1848–1849) in Wright, 202.

90. Barth, 47.

91. Barth, 37.

92. C. S. Lewis, *The Efficacy of Prayer.* The Advent Papers (Cincinnati: Forward Movement, n.d.), 10. First published in the *Atlantic Monthly,* 1958.

93. Hapgood, 120.

94. See Thomas Secker, *Sermon XXV, in Explanation and Defense of the Liturgy of the Church of England,* in Wright, 173.

95. Comber in Wright, 151–152.

96. Comber in Wright, 152.

97. Comber in Wright, 152.

98. General Instruction on the Liturgy of the Hours 1.1, *The Liturgy of the Hours,* 17.

99. G. B. Caird, *Saint Luke* (Baltimore: Penguin, 1963), 58.

100. See Richard A. Horsley, *The Liberation of Christmas* (New York: Crossroad, 1989), 107–123.

101. Abraham Johannes Muste (1885–1967).

102. *Book of Common Prayer,* p. 100.

103. Shepherd, 17.

104. Martin Luther, *The Small Catechism,* in *The Book of Concord,* ed. Theodore G. Tappert (Philadelphia: Muhlenberg Press, 1959), 347.

Chapter Four: The Easter Vigil: Hallowing Memory

1. *The Collected Poems of Louis MacNeice,* ed. E. R. Dodds (New York: Oxford University Press, 1967), 119.

2. Robert Graves, *The Greek Myths,* vol. 1 (Baltimore: Penguin, 1955), 13–16.

3. See 1 Samuel 20:5; 2 Kings 4:23; 1 Chronicles 2:4; 31:3; Ezra 3:5; Nehemiah 10:33; Isaiah 1:13–14; 66:23; Ezekiel 45:17; 46:1, 3, 6; Amos 8:5; Hosea 2:11; Colossians 2:16.

4. Mircea Eliade, *Cosmos and History: The Myth of the Eternal Return,* trans. Willard R. Trask (New York: Harper & Row, 1959), 86.

5. [Hal Borland,] "The Voice of the Turtle," *New York Times,* April 2, 1972. Note also the "County Diary" and the essays by Ralph Whitlock (1914–1995) in the *Manchester Guardian Weekly.*

6. [Hal Borland,] "A New Tomorrow," *New York Times*, March 30, 1975.

7. Hal Borland, "Spring: A Reiteration," *The Progressive* 36, no. 4 (April 1972): 23.

8. Theodor Gaster, *Festivals of the Jewish Year* (New York: Morrow, 1952), 31.

9. Gaster, 32.

10. Venantius Honorius Fortunatus, " 'Welcome, happy morning!' Age to Age Shall Say," trans. John Ellerton, *Service Book and Hymnal* (Minneapolis: Augsburg Publishing House; Philadelphia: Board of Publication, Lutheran Church in America, 1958), no. 93. See *The Hymnal 1982* (New York: The Church Hymnal Corporation, 1985), no. 179.

11. Byzantine liturgy at the beginning of the Easter Eucharist; see *Book of Common Prayer* (New York: The Church Hymnal Corporation and the Seabury Press, 1979), 483, 500.

12. G. Van der Leeuw, *Nature in Essence and Manifestation*, vol. 2, trans. J. E. Turner (New York: Harper & Row, 1963), 576.

13. *The New Golden Bough*, ed. Theodor H. Gaster (New York: New American Library, 1959), 703–704.

14. Gaster, 602, 604, 605, 608, 610, 614, 618–619, 639.

15. Gaster, 287.

16. Gaster, 399; Eliade, *Cosmos and History*, 62.

17. Gaster, 178.

18. Eliade, *Cosmos and History*, 61.

19. Eliade, *Cosmos and History*, 63–64.

20. Eliade, *The Sacred and Profane*, trans. Willard R. Trask (New York: Harcourt, Brace & World, 1959), 79.

21. Eliade, *Sacred and Profane*, 105.

22. Eliade, *Sacred and Profane*, 147.

23. John Ellerton, "The Day Thou Gavest, Lord, Has Ended," stanza 2, *The Hymnal 1982*, no. 24; *Service Book and Hymnal*, no. 227.

24. *Book of Common Prayer* (1928), 80.

25. When Einstein was travelling to lecture in Spain,
   He questioned a conductor time and again:
   "It may be a while,
   He said with a smile,
   "But when does Madrid reach this train?"
Contributed by A. Anderson to Robert L. Weber, ed., *Science with a Smile: An Anthology* (Philadelphia: Institute of Physics, 1992), 102.

26. Alfred, Lord Tennyson, "Break, break, break."

27. William Faulkner, *Intruder in the Dust* (New York: Random House, 1948), 194.

28. Henri and H. A. Frankfort, John A. Wilson, Thorkild Jacobsen, *Before Philosophy:The Intellectual Adventure of Ancient Man* (Baltimore: Penguin, 1949), 33.

29. Mircea Eliade, *Sacred and the Profane,* 68–69.

30. Eliade, 70.

31. Frankfort, 31.

32. See Paul Tillich, *The Dynamics of Faith,* chapter 3.

33. Frankfort, 34.

34. Lewis Carroll, *The Annotated Alice: Alice's Adventures in Wonderland and Through the Looking Glass,* ed. Martin Gardner (Cleveland and New York: World Publishing Co., 1960), 248.

35. Percy Bysshe Shelley, "To_____," lines 1–2.

36. Walter de la Mare, "Fare Well," i.

37. William Cowper, "O For a Closer Walk with God," *Service Book and Hymnal,* no. 466, stanza 3.

38. Thomas Moore, *National Airs,* "Oft in the Stilly Night."

39. Loren Eisley, *The Immense Journey* (New York: Vintage, 1957), 179–180.

40. See "The Cool Web" by Robert Graves: "Children are dumb to say how hot the day is . . . / But we have speech, to chill the angry day. . . . "

41. See Eliade, *Cosmos and History,* 54.

42. Rudolf Otto, *The Idea of the Holy,* trans. John W. Harvey (New York: Oxford, 1958), 68.

43. Van der Leeuw, *Nature,* vol. 2, 432–433.

44. Van der Leeuw, *Nature,* vol. 1, 61.

45. Faulkner, *Intruder in the Dust,* 95.

46. See Hugh Howard, *The Preservationist's Progress* (New York: Farrar Straus Giroux, 1991), 52.

47. Mircea Eliade, *The Two and the One,* trans. J. M. Cohen (New York: Harper & Row, 1969), 14.

48. Eliade, *Cosmos and History,* 56.

49. Mircea Eliade, *Patterns in Comparative Religion,* trans. Rosemary Sheed (Cleveland and New York: World Publishing Co., 1963), 399.

50. *Beowulf,* trans E. Talbot Donaldson, ed. Joseph F. Tuso (New York: Norton, 1975), 2.

51. Van der Leeuw, *Nature,* vol. 1, 60.

52. Erich Fromm, *The Forgotten Language* (New York: Grove Press, 1957), 16.

53. Van der Leeuw, *Nature,* vol. 1, 62.

54. Van der Leeuw, *Nature,* vol. 1, 63, quoting Livy.

55. The first line of a hymn by Bernhardt Severein Ingemann (1789–1862), translated by Sabine Baring-Gould, *Service Book and Hymnal,* no. 529.

56. A verse sung at the beginning of the Service of Light at the beginning of Evensong (Evening Prayer) in *Morning Praise and Evensong,* ed. William G. Storey, Frank C. Quinn, David F. Wright (Notre Dame, Ind.: Fides, 1973), 1ff; *Lutheran Book of Worship* (Minneapolis: Augsburg Publishing House; Philadelphia: Board of Publication, Lutheran Church

in America, 1978), 142; the *Book of Common Worship* (Louisville, Ky.: Westminster John Knox Press, 1993), 505.

57. For example, Adrian Nocent, *The Liturgical Year*, vol. 3, trans. Matthew J. O'Connell (Collegeville, Minn.: Liturgical Press, 1977), 112–113.

58. "O Christ, Our Hope, Our Heart's Desire," *Service Book and Hymnal*, no. 400, stanza 3.

59. Ernst Cassirer, *An Essay on Man* (New York: Bantam, 1970 [1944]), 191.

60. *Hymnal 1982*, nos. 199, 200.

61. See Cassirer, 68.

62. *Service Book and Hymnal*, no. 93; *Hymnal 1982*, no. 179, stanza 6.

63. "O Paschal Feast, What Joy Is Thine," *Service Book and Hymnal*, no. 102 stanza 3.

64. "Come, Ye Faithful, Raise the Strain," *Hymnal 1982*, nos. 199, 200, stanza 4.

65. *The Heliand. The Saxon Gospel*, trans. G. Ronald Murphy (New York: Oxford, 1992), 191.

66. C. S. Lewis, *English Literature in the Sixteenth Century Excluding Drama* (Oxford: Clarendon Press, 1954), 392.

67. Lewis, 393.

68. Van der Leeuw, *Nature*, vol. 1, xxi.

69. Eliade, *Patterns*, 188.

70. See Philip Larkin's poem "Water," in *Collected Poems*, ed. Anthony Thwaite (New York: Farrar Straus Giroux, 1989), 93. It begins, "If I were called in / To construct a religion / I should make use of water."

71. Fromm, 16–17.

72. See Paul Friedrich, *The Meaning of Aphrodite* (Chicago: University of Chicago Press, 1978), 11, 93, 180–181.

73. Eliade, *Patterns,* 189.

74. Joseph Campbell, *The Masks of God*, vol. 3, *Occidental Mythology* (New York: Viking, 1970), 11.

75. Eliade, *Patterns*, 189.

76. Campbell, 10.

77. Van der Leeuw, *Nature*, vol. 1, 59.

78. Eliade, *Patterns,* 200–201.

79. Tertullian, *On Baptism* 3.

80. Eliade, *Patterns,* 188.

81. Eliade, *Patterns,* 188–189.

82. Eliade, *Patterns,* 193.

83. Eliade, *Patterns,* 194.

84. Eliade, *Patterns,* 212.

85. Eliade, *Patterns,* 212.

86. Eliade, *Patterns,* 197.

87. For an account of the vivid rites in North Africa, see Thomas M. Finn, "It Happened One Saturday Night: Ritual and Conversion in Augustine's North Africa," *Journal of the American Academy of Religion 58*, no. 4 (Winter 1990): 589–616.

88. Eliade, *Cosmos and History,* 68.

89. Prayer of the Day for the Fourth Sunday of Easter, *Lutheran Book of Worship,* 155. The present translation in the Roman rite is simply "reject"; the collect is used on the Fifteenth Sunday of Ordinary Time.

90. *Service Book and Hymnal,* 91. The American *Book of Common Prayer* softened the verb "eschew," replacing it with "avoid"; the present Prayer Book does not use the collect.

91. William Chatterton Dix, "As with Gladness Men of Old," stanza 5 (*Lutheran Book of Worship,* no. 92; *Hymnal 1982,* no. 119).

92. Eliade, *Cosmos and History,* 53, 68.

93. *Esther Rabbah* 3.14.

94. *Eliyahu Rabbah* 1.2.

95. George Wallace Briggs, "Our Father, by whose servants / Our house was built of old," stanza 4 (*Service Book and Hymnal,* no. 248). (The stanza is unfortunately omitted from the *Hymnal 1982,* no. 289.) The whole text of the hymn is given on p. 170.

96. See Kenneth Clark, *The Nude* (Garden City, N.Y.: Doubleday, 1959), 396.

97. *Book of Common Prayer,* 295.

98. Eliade, *Cosmos and History,* 61.

99. Tacitus *Germania* quoted in Campbell, *Occidental Mythology,* 474.

100. George Steiner, *Real Presences* (Chicago: University of Chicago Press, 1989), 231–232.

101. T. S. Eliot, *The Use of Poetry* (1933), chapter 6.

Chapter Five: The Christian Year: Hallowing the Seasons

1. Translated by E. T. Donaldson.

2. Joseph Sittler, in *The Environmental Journal* of the National Parks and Conservation Department (1972), quoted in *Circle,* May 1972, a publication of the Department of Campus Ministry of the Lutheran Council in the USA.

3. Hal Borland, "July: High Noon," *The Progressive* 36, no. 7 (July 1972): 26.

4. [Hal Borland,] "The Big Certainties," *New York Times,* Sunday, December 5, 1971.

5. [Hal Borland,] "The Continuity," *New York Times,* Sunday, December 19, 1971.

6. "The Big Certainties." See also Rachel Carson, *The Sea Around Us,* rev. ed. (New York: New American Library, 1961), 28.

7. See Joseph Campbell, *The Masks of God*, vol. 2, *Oriental Mythology* (New York: Viking, 1962), 115–129. He makes the same point in "On Mythic Shapes of Things To Come — Circular and Linear," *Horizon* 16, no. 3 (Summer 1974): 35–37.

8. Robert Frost, "Two Tramps in Mud Time," lines 17–24.

9. William Pierson Merrill, "Not Alone for Mighty Empire," *Service Book and Hymnal* (Minneapolis: Augsburg Publishing House; Philadelphia: Board of Publication, Lutheran Church in America, 1958), no. 345; *Lutheran Book of Worship* (Minneapolis: Augsburg Publishing House; Philadelphia: Board of Publication, Lutheran Church in America, 1978), no. 437.

10. The phrase is Samuel Noah Kramer's, speaking of Egyptian mythological genealogy, in his *Mythologies of the Ancient World* (Garden City, N.Y.: Doubleday, 1961), 41.

11. Hans Urs von Balthasar, in *Heart of the World,* trans. Errasmo S. Leiva (San Francisco: Ignatius Press, 1979), 219, provocatively reverses Augustine's prayer and suggests that until we are reconciled, there is disquiet even in the heart of God: "Your Heart [,O God,] is restless until it rests in me. Your Heart is restless until we rest in you, once time and eternity become interfused."

12. Quoted in Elizabeth Drew, *Poetry: A Modern Guide to Its Understanding and Enjoyment* (New York: Dell, 1959), 63.

13. Drew, 64.

14. Deuteronomy 32:10; see Thomas Oliver's hymn, "The God of Abraham Praise," *Service Book and Hymnal,* no. 410, stanza 2.

15. Walt Whitman, *I Sing the Body Electric,* no. 6.

16. Northrop Frye, *Anatomy of Criticism* (Princeton, N.J.: Princeton University Press, 1957), 158.

17. [Hal Borland,] "June's Options," *New York Times,* Sunday, June 13, 1971.

18. Robert Frost, "Directive," lines 45–47.

19. Gabriel Marcel, *Homo Viator: Introduction to a Metaphysics of Hope,* trans. Emma Craufurd (Chicago: H. Regnery, 1951).

20. Edward Hopper's painting *The House by the Railroad Tracks* is a striking portrayal of such an insight. The remarkable number of roads, highways, and railroad tracks in Hopper's paintings show his continuing fascination with passage; it is not a comforting message.

21. Samuel Johnson, *Rambler,* no. 5 (Tuesday, April 3, 1750).

22. See especially John Hillaby, *A Walk Through Europe* (Boston: Houghton Mifflin, 1972).

23. See Monica Furlong, *Travelling In* (London: Hodder and Stoupton, 1971).

24. See Richard Barber, *Pilgrimages* (Rochester, N.Y.: Boydell and Brewer, 1992). See also *Parabola* 9, no. 3 (Fall 1984).

25. The Parson's Tale, lines 46–51.

26. See Ernst Cassirer, *Essay on Man* (New York: Bantam, 1970 [1944]), 247.

27. Augustine in his *Enchiridion* identified four stages: Innocence, Misery, Grace, and Glory.

28. Wesley Kort (*Story, Text, Scripture: Literary Interests in Biblical Literature* [University Park, Pa.: Pennsylvania State University Press, 1988], 95) suggests in passing that the Gospel of St. Mark may have served as a surrogate pilgrimage to Jerusalem for those who did not find it possible to make the physical journey to the holy city.

29. Henry David Thoreau, conclusion to *Walden,* in *Walden and Civil Disobedience* (New York: Norton, 1966), 215: "If a man does not keep pace with his companions, perhaps it is because he hears a different drummer."

30. It is the thesis of Philip Carrington, *The Primitive Christian Calendar* (Cambridge, Mass.: Cambridge University Press, 1952) that the chapter divisions in Mark's Gospel in *Codex Vaticanus* correlated with the early Christian Jewish year, from Passover to Passover.

31. See D. J. A. Clines, "The Evidence for an Autumnal New Year in Pre-Exilic Israel Reconsidered," *Journal of Biblical Literature* 93, no. 1 (March 1974): 22–40.

32. The explanation has been offered that Judaism had an "ecclesiastical" year beginning on 1 Nisan, used for festivals and the reigns of Jewish kings, and a civil year, beginning on 1 Tishri, used for secular events and the reigns of foreign kings. G. B. Caird, *Saint Luke* (Baltimore: Penguin, 1963), 71.

33. *Sir Gawain and the Green Knight,* line 502, trans. into modern English by Marie Borroff, part of a remarkable summary of the passage of the seasons from Yule to All Hallows, ll. 500–538.

34. *The Taizé Office* (London: Faith Press, 1966), 12.

35. Some, however, have attempted to make it so. See, for example, Donald Macleod, *Presbyterian Worship: Its Meaning and Method* (Richmond, Va.: John Knox Press, 1966), following A. Alan McArthur, *The Christian Year and Lectionary Reform* (Chicago: Allenson, 1958).

36. Cassirer, *Essay on Man,* 57.

37. "Editors' Preface," *Spacial Form in Narrative.* ed. Jeffrey R. Smitten and Ann Daghistany (Ithaca, N.Y.: Cornell University Press, 1981), 13, 17.

38. Joseph Gelineau, *Voices and Instruments in Christian Worship,* trans. Clifford Howell (Collegeville, Minn.: Liturgical Press, 1964), 31.

39. Gelineau, 31.

40. Cassirer, 57.

41. Cassirer, 58.

42. See Loren R. Fisher, "A New Ritual Calendar from Ugarit," *Harvard Theological Review* 63, no. 4 (October 1970): 496.

43. See S. Vernon McCasland, Grace E. Cairns, David C. Yu, *Religions of the World* (New York: Random House, 1969), 96, for the practice at Rome.

44. See P. Lyle McCarter Jr., *II Samuel*, vol. 8, *Anchor Bible* (Garden City, N.Y.: Doubleday, 1984), 284–285.

45. Jesse L. Weston, *From Ritual to Romance* (Garden City, N.Y.: Doubleday, 1957 [1920]), 93.

46. *Lutheran Book of Worship*, Ministers Edition (Minneapolis: Augsburg Publishing House; Philadelphia: Board of Publication, Lutheran Church in America, 1978), 129.

47. Quoted in George K. Anderson and William E. Buckler, eds., *The Literature of England*, vol. 2, 5th ed. (New York: Scott, Foresman, 1968), 1740.

48. Northrop Frye, *Anatomy of Criticism* (Princeton, N.J.: Princeton University Press, 1971 [1957]), 192.

49. See Michael Hoffmann, "A Complicated Scream: The Unpredictable Dislocations of Exile," review of *The Oxford Book of Exile*, ed. John Simpson, *Times Literary Supplement*, May 26, 1995, 19–20.

50. St. Germanus's hymn, translated by John Mason Neale, "A Great and Mighty Wonder," *Service Book and Hymnal*, no. 18, stanza 6.

51. See Charles Davis, "Liturgy and Doctrine," *Journal of Ecumenical Studies* 6, no. 3 (Summer 1969): 400; and Alexander Schmemann, *Introduction to Liturgical Theology*, trans. Ashleigh E. Moorehouse (Portland, Me.: The American Orthodox Press, 1966), 124: "Easter...was the key to the liturgical year, the beginning and the end, the transition from the old into the new year as a figure of transition from the old into the new life."

52. *Concilium* 39, 95.

53. "Many contemporary liturgists think that the church year should begin with the Septuagesima season rather than Advent. This theory is based upon the fact that the reading of the Scriptures is begun at Septuagesima time, which is also the early spring, the beginning of the natural year. Furthermore they contend that the liturgical texts of the Advent Season are concerned with the end of the world rather than with the beginning." Paul Thiry, Richard M. Bennett, Henry L. Kamphoefner, *Churches and Temples* (New York: Reinhold, 1953), 10c ff.

54. Percy Dearmer, *The Parson's Handbook*, 12th ed. (New York: Oxford, 1932), 450.

55. This is the contemporary form in the *Book of Common Prayer* (New York: The Church Hymnal Corporation and the Seabury Press, 1979), 219; *Lutheran Book of Worship* slightly abbreviates the prayer. The prayer, from the Gelasian sacramentary, is also used in the Roman sacramentary.

56. *Lutheran Book of Worship*, Ministers Edition, 134.

57. Saint Ephrem, deacon, *Sermo de Domino nostro* 3–4.9

58. Ephrem.

59. Translated after John Mason Neale in *The Hymnal 1982* (New York: The Church Hymnal Corporation, 1985), nos. 165, 166; *Service Book and Hymnal*, no. 61; *Lutheran Book of Worship*, no. 118.

60. Translated in the *Hymnal 1982*, no. 162. In the *Inferno*, where everything is distorted and perverted, Dante heard in Latin an infernal parody of Fortunatus's hymn, *Vexilla regis prodeunt inferni*, "the banners of the king of hell advance." *(Inferno* xxxiv.1)

61. Gregorian sacramentary, no. 1837; a modernized translation is used in *Lutheran Book of Worship*, Ministers Edition, 212, 249, 285.

62. *Hymnal 1982*, no. 165, stanzas 4 and 5.

63. Ephrem, in the *Liturgy of the Hours*, vol. 2 (New York: Catholic Book Publishing Co., 1976), 735–736.

64. Theodore the Studite, *Oratio in adorationem crucis*, in the *Liturgy of the Hours*, vol. 2, 677.

65. But see Gerard S. Sloyan, "A Plea for Unadulterated Joy," *Liturgy: Hosanna* 12, no. 4 (1995): 6–9: the day should celebrate the glad reception of Jesus on the pilgrim feast and hold off the emphasis on suffering until Good Friday.

66. *Lutheran Book of Worship*, no. 123, translated by Robert Bridges.

67. In Book IX of *Paradise Lost* John Milton described the fall, first of unsuspecting Eve and then of willing Adam,

> Forth reaching to the Fruit, she pluck'd, she ate:
> Earth felt the wound, and Nature from her seat
> Sighing through all her Works gave signs of woe,
> That all was lost.
>
> (lines 781–784)

> Earth trembled from her entrails, as again
> In pangs, and Nature gave a second groan,
> Sky lour'd and muttering Thunder, some sad drops
> Wept at completing of the mortal Sin
> Original. . . .
>
> (lines 1000–1004)

68. Henry Vaughan, "Corruption," lines 15–16.

69. *Hymnal 1982*, no. 165 stanza 3.

70. Noted by Michael Seidel, *Exile and the Narrative Imagination* (New Haven, Conn.: Yale University Press, 1986), 1.

71. Pius Parsch, *The Church's Year of Grace*, vol. 2, 2d ed. (Collegeville, Minn.: Liturgical Press, 1964), 5.

72. Cyril of Alexandria, commentary on the Gospel of John, in the *Liturgy of the Hours*, vol. 3, 833.

73. Augustine, treatise on John, tractate 65:1–3.

74. Cyril of Jerusalem, Cat. 16, *De Spiritu Sancto* 1, in the *Liturgy of the Hours*, vol. 2, 967.

75. Thus in the (Lutheran) *Church Book* (Philadelphia: Lutheran Book Store, 1868), *Common Service Book* (Philadelphia: Board of Publication of the United Lutheran Church in America, 1918), *Service Book and Hymnal* (1958). *Lutheran Book of Worship*, 21, has put the translation in more modern language. The *Book of Common Prayer* expanded the translation with the addition of the phrase "We humbly beseech thee that, *as by thy special grace preventing us* thou dost put into our minds good desires. . . . "

76. Luther D. Reed, *The Lutheran Liturgy*, rev. ed. (Philadelphia: Fortress Press, 1960), 508, quoting Charles Neill and J. M. Willoughby, *The Tutorial Prayer Book* (London: Harrison Trust, 1913), 173.

77. *Book of Common Prayer*, 222.

78. *O quanta qualia*, translated by John Mason Neale, the *Hymnal 1982*, no. 623, stanza 2.

79. Gaster, 43.

80. Augustine, sermon 34, 5–6, in *The Liturgy of the Hours*, vol. 2, 713.

81. Augustine, treatise on St. John's Gospel, tractate 65, 1–3.

82. Cf. Gaster, 48–49.

83. See the Jerusalem Catecheses, cat. 21, mystagogia 3, 1–3, in *The Liturgy of the Hours*, vol. 2, 608–610.

84. Jerusalem Catecheses, cat. 21, Mystagogia 3, 1–3, *The Liturgy of the Hours*, vol. 2, 597.

85. Sermon 35, 6–9, in *The Liturgy of the Hours*, vol. 2, 583.

86. Basil the Great, *On the Holy Spirit* 15, 35–36, in *The Liturgy of the Hours*, vol. 2, 762.

87. The unity of these three Sundays was preserved in the *Service Book and Hymnal*, "The Propers for the following three Sundays may be used on the last three Sundays after Trinity," 105. The unity was also suggested in the office lectionary, "Psalms and Lessons for the Christian Year," in the 1928 *Book of Common Prayer* amended in 1952: Third Sunday before Advent, Second Sunday before Advent, Sunday Next before Advent (New York: Oxford University Press, 1953), xl–xli.

88. See Job 36:25; Jeremiah 30:10; 46:27; Ezekiel 38:9, 16; Matthew 11:3; Micah 4:7; Psalm 49:2; 80:1; 24:7. Translation from Philip H. Pfatteicher, *The Daily Prayer of the Church* (Delhi, N.Y.: ALPB Books), 1997.

89. Richard Hoggart, *Speaking to Each Other*, vol. 2. "Why I Value Literature," *About Literature* (New York: Oxford University Press, 1970), makes similar observations about literature.

90. See Cleanth Brooks, *The Well-Wrought Urn: Studies in the Structure of Poetry* (New York: Harcourt, Brace & World, 1947), 255–256.

91. Arnold Stein, preface to *New Essays on Paradise Lost*, ed. Thomas Kranidas (Berkeley, Calif.: University of California Press, 1970).

92. Prudentius's hymn *O sola magnarum urbium*, in the *Hymnal 1982*, no. 127, "Earth Has Many a Noble City," stanza 4.

Chapter Six: Architecture: Hallowing Space

1. Mircea Eliade, *The Sacred and the Profane*, trans. Willard R. Trask (New York: Harcourt, Brace & World, 1959), 20.

2. Frank Kermode, "John," in *The Literary Guide to the Bible*, ed. Robert Alter and Frank Kermode (Cambridge, Mass.: Belknap Press of Harvard University Press, 1987), 450.

3. Eliade, *The Sacred and the Profane*, 25.

4. Eliade, *The Sacred and the Profane*, 36–47.

5. Eliade, *The Sacred and the Profane*, 57.

6. G. Van der Leeuw, *Religion in Essence and Manifestation*, trans. J. E. Turner (New York: Harper and Row, 1963), 393–394.

7. Eliade, *The Sacred and the Profane*, 26.

8. Eliade, *The Sacred and the Profane*, 27.

9. Eliade, *The Sacred and the Profane*, 21.

10. See the conclusion of chapter 2 above, 28–31.

11. *Lutheran Book of Worship* (Minneapolis: Augsburg Publishing House; Philadelphia: Board of Publication, Lutheran Church in America), no. 499. *The Hymnal 1982* (New York: The Church Hymnal Corporation, 1985), no. 486, alters the first line to "Here I find my greatest treasure."

12. Johannes Pedersen, *Israel: Its Life and Culture*, vols. 3–4 (London: Oxford University Press, 1940), 218.

13. Archibald MacLeish, "Chartres," *The Collected Poems of Archibald MacLeish* (Boston: Houghton Mifflin, 1962), 37–38.

14. Mircea Eliade, *Patterns in Comparative Religion*, trans. Rosemary Sheed (Cleveland and New York: World, 1963), 370.

15. Eliade, *Patterns*, 371.

16. Eliade, *The Sacred and the Profane*, 49.

17. Plutarch, "Romulus," *Plutarch's Lives of Illustrious Men*, vol. 1, trans. John Dryden and others (Boston: Dana Estes and Co., n.d.), 42–43.

18. Plutarch, 41. Some have attempted to reconcile the contradiction by suggesting that *quadrata* is to be understood as "quadripartite"; that is, the circular city was divided into four parts by the two main streets, one running north and south and the other east and west.

19. Aniela Jaffe, "Symbolism in the Visual Arts," in *Man and His Symbols*, ed. Carl G. Jung (New York: Dell, 1968), 272.

20. Eliade, *The Sacred and the Profane*, 61–62.

21. Ananda K. Coomaraswamy, "An Indian Temple: The Kandarya Mahadeo," *Parabola* 3, no. 1 (1978): 5.

22. Will Durant, *The Age of Faith*, part 4 of *The Story of Civilization* (New York: Simon and Schuster, 1950), 856, 880.

23. Durant, 893.

24. A classic appreciation is Henry Adams, *Mont-Saint-Michel and Chartres* (Boston and New York: Houghton Mifflin, 1933 [1905]).

25. Durant, 894.

26. John James, *Chartres: The Masons Who Built a Legend* (Boston: Routledge and Kegan Paul, 1980), 190.

27. See the detailed study by John James.

28. James, 147.

29. Vincent Scully, *Architecture: The Natural and the Manmade* (New York: St. Martin's Press, 1991), 171.

30. Scully, 171.

31. James, 5, 7.

32. Nikolaus Pevsner, *Outline of European Architecture,* 5th ed. (Baltimore: Penguin, 1957), 75.

33. James, 178.

34. James, 43.

35. James, 190.

36. Scully, 171.

37. James, 127.

38. Dante in his *Divine Comedy* saw empty places in the mystic rose of heaven (*Paradiso,* canto 32, lines 23–27). The spaces are not yet all occupied.

39. Augustine, *Sermon* 336, 1.6. The passage is an alternative reading in the Office of Readings in the Common of the Dedication of a Church in the *Liturgy of the Hours* (London: Geoffrey Chapman, 1971).

40. James D. Van Trump, *Life and Architecture in Pittsburgh* (Pittsburgh: Pittsburgh History and Landmarks Foundation, 1983), 93. (See 193–200.) The other church, also by Notman, is St. Mark's, Locust Street, Philadelphia (1847–48).

41. See John Ruskin, *The Stones of Venice,* particularly vol. 2, chap. 6, "The Nature of Gothic." Ruskin said (*The Crown of Wild Olive,* Lecture II) that he wrote *The Seven Lamps of Architecture* "to show that certain right states of temper and moral feeling were the magic powers by which all good architecture, without exception, had been produced."

42. The integrated view of aesthetics and morality derived from Kenelm Digby, *Broadstone of Honour* (1822). The Gothic Revival was promoted by Augustus Welby Northmere Pugin (1812–1852). For the situation in Germany, see Michael J. Lewis, *The Politics of the German Gothic Revival: August Reichensperger* (Cambridge, Mass.: MIT Press, 1994).

43. See the *Book of Common Prayer* (1928), 577.

44. See Edgar S. Brown Jr., "Sicut Erat III. Sacred Space," *The Bride of Christ* 18, no. 1 (Advent 1993): 22–24.

45. See Penelope Reed Doob, *The Idea of the Labyrinth from Classical Antiquity Through the Middle Ages* (Ithaca, N.Y.: Cornell University Press, 1990), 117–133. See also W. R. Matthews, *Mazes and Labyrinths: Their History and Development* (New York: Dover Books, 1970 [1922]); Janet Bord, *Mazes and Labyrinths of the World* (London: Latimer New Dimensions, 1976), 88–103; and Eliade, *Patterns,* 380–382.

46. Eliade, *Patterns*, 381.

47. Doob, 123–124.

48. The hymn, translated as "Christians to the paschal victim," is no. 137 in *Lutheran Book of Worship* and no. 183 in *The Hymnal 1982.*

49. Doob, 125.

50. John Leyerle, *University of Toronto Quarterly* 46 (1977), 303, quoted in Doob, 129.

51. Doob, 132. See also Keith Critchlow, Jane Carroll, and Llewylyn Vaughan Lee, "Chartres' Maze: A Model of the Universe?" *Architectural Association Quarterly* 5, no. 2 (1973): 11–20; Painton Cowen, *Rose Windows* (San Francisco: Chronicle Books, 1979), 98–99; and John G. Demaray, *Dante and the Book of the Cosmos.* Transactions of the American Philosophical Society 77, pt. 5 (1987), 22–24.

52. See *Holy Week Offices,* ed. Massey H, Shepherd Jr. (Greenwich, Conn.: Seabury Press, 1958), 7–26. The nine biblical stations are given (1, 2, 5, 8, 10, 11, 12, 13, 14). See "The Way of the Cross," *The Living Church* 144, no. 11 (March 18, 1962). Some Lutherans have devised a devotion consisting of ten stations, the nine biblical incidents plus number 3, Jesus falls.

53. "Christ Is Made the Sure Foundation," the *Hymnal 1982,* no. 518, trans. *Hymns Ancient and Modern* (London: Novello, 1861), after John Mason Neale. The Latin hymn is part of the longer hymn *Urbs beata Ierusalem.*

54. *Service Book and Hymnal* (Minneapolis: Augsburg Publishing House; Philadelphia: Board of Publication, Lutheran Church in America, 1958), no. 246.

55. *Lutheran Book of Worship,* no. 365 stanza 2. The translation adapts the work of Carl Doving revised by Fred C. M. Hansen.

56. *The Book of Common Prayer* (New York: The Church Hymnal Corporation and the Seabury Press, 1979), 305.

57. *Parabola* 3, no. 1 (1978): 12–19.

58. *Service Book and Hymnal,* no. 245; see the *Hymnal 1982,* nos. 519, 520.

59. Durandus, *Rationale* 1.1.

60. Peter Abelard in his hymn *O quanta qualia* sings of heaven, "Truly Jerusalem name we that shore, / Vision of peace, that brings joy evermore." *Service Book and Hymnal,* no. 596, stanza 2. The translation is by John Mason Neale.

61. *Service Book and Hymnal* no. 240.

62. *The Hymnal 1940* (New York: Church Pension Fund, 1940), no. 227; *Service Book and Hymnal,* no. 244.

63. Robert Furneaux Jordan, *Le Corbusier* (New York: Lawrence Hill, 1972), 133.

64. See Francis Thompson's poem *The Hound of Heaven* (1893).

65. *Service Book and Hymnal,* no. 248; the *Hymnal 1982,* no. 289 (minus the final stanza).

66. Marcel Proust, *Swann's Way,* trans. C. K. Scott Moncrieff (New York: Modern Library, 1956 [1928]), 75.

67. D. H. Lawrence, *Etruscan Places,* in *The Norton Anthology of English Literature,* vol. 2, ed. M. H. Abrams, et al., 6th ed. (New York: Norton, 1993), 2110. Percy Dearmer suggested oak grave markers for the churchyards rather than stone monuments, "but doubtless the ideal is to have no monuments at all." See his *Parson's Handbook,* 12th ed. (New York: Oxford University Press, 1932), 42.

68. See above, 28.

69. T. S. Eliot, *The Criterion* (1932), 74–75.

70. Michel de Montaigne, *Essays,* trans. J. M. Cohen (Baltimore: Penguin, 1958), 114.

71. Pliny, *Natural History,* vol. 2, 7.

72. Montaigne, *Apology for Raimond Sebond,* book 2, chapter 12.

73. See Frank Kermode, *The Classic: Literary Images of Permanence and Change* (New York: Viking Press, 1975), 43.

Chapter Seven: The Holy Eucharist: Hallowing Sustenance

1. This helpful distinction between East and West was suggested by a reading of Nicholas Arsen'ev, *We Beheld His Glory* (New York and Milwaukee: Morehouse, 1936). See also Kallistos Ware, *The Orthodox Way* (Crestwood, N.Y.: St. Vladimir's Seminary Press, 1993). Also two books by Roman Catholic scholars are useful: Robert Taft, *The Byzantine Rite: A Short History* (Collegeville, Minn.: Liturgical Press, 1993); and Hans-Joachim Schulz, *The Byzantine Liturgy,* trans. Matthew J. O'Connell (New York: Pueblo, 1986).

2. From Isaac Watts's hymn "When I Survey the Wondrous Cross," in *The Hymnal 1982* (New York: The Church Hymnal Corporation, 1985), no. 474.

3. Martin Luther, *Liturgy and Hymns, Luther's Works* 53:137.

4. "Lo, He Comes with Clouds Descending," *The Hymnal 1982,* nos. 57, 58.

5. *Book of Common Prayer* (New York: The Church Hymnal Corporation, 1979), 334, 341.

6. For a delightful and suggestive study of the importance of learning to behave properly at meals, with consideration of the moral dimensions of such behavior, see Margaret Visser, *The Rituals of Dinner: The Origins, Evolution, Eccentricities, and Meaning of Table Manners* (New York: Penguin Books, 1991). For an exploration of the role of the arts in expressing the mystery at the heart of religion (*mysterium tremendum et fascinans*), see Edward Robinson, *The Language of Mystery* (Philadelphia: Trinity Press International, 1987).

7. Antiphon (*O sacrum convivium*) to the Magnificat in second Vespers of Corpus Christi, attributed to Thomas Aquinas.

8. In the Lutheran Common Service of 1888 and its use in the *Common Service Book* (Philadelphia: Board of the United Lutheran Church in America, 1918) and the *Service Book and Hymnal* (Minneapolis: Augsburg Publishing House; Philadelphia: Board of Publication, Lutheran Church in America, 1958), the Confession of Sins at the beginning of the service was introduced with an invitation echoing this passage from Hebrews (in the Authorized and in the Revised Standard Version), "Beloved in the Lord! Let us draw near with a true heart, and confess our sins unto God our Father, beseeching him, in the Name of our Lord Jesus Christ, to grant us forgiveness."

9. Martin Luther, Explanation of the Third Article of the Apostles' Creed, *The Small Catechism*, in *The Book of Concord*, ed. Theodore G. Tappert (Philadelphia: Muhlenberg Press, 1959).

10. In recognition of this fact, the general rubrics in older Lutheran books (*Common Service Book, Service Book and Hymnal*) suggested, "A Hymn of Invocation of the Holy Ghost may be sung at the beginning of all Services."

11. See Georg Roppen and Richard Sommer, *Strangers and Pilgrims: An Essay on the Metaphor of Journey* (Oslo: Norwegian Universities Press, 1964), 18, 75.

12. Translation of "Savior of the Nations, Come," in *Lutheran Book of Worship* (Minneapolis: Augsburg Publishing House; Philadelphia: Board of Publication, Lutheran Church in America, 1978), no. 28, stanza 5.

13. *Book of Common Prayer*, 123. See Revelation 21.

14. Martin Luther, *The Blessed Sacrament of the Holy and True Body of Christ*, in *Luther's Works* 35:53, 67.

15. John Ruskin, *Praeterita*, vol. 3, chapter 1.

16. Romano Guardini in *The Spirit of the Liturgy* (London: Sheed and Ward, 1930) calls a chapter "The Playfulness of the Liturgy"; J.-J. von Almen (*Studia Liturgica* 2 [1963]: 124–135) speaks of worship as "an eschatological game"; Johan Huizinga (*Homo Ludens: A Study of the Play-Element in Culture*, [Boston: Beacon Press, 1955]) has suggested that play is not simply wasting time but is an important element in the development of human culture. See also Josef Pieper, *Leisure: The Basis of Culture* (New York: Pantheon, 1952).

17. Gregorian sacramentary, no. 383. The translation is that of *Lutheran Book of Worship*. The Roman rite and the *Book of Common Prayer* replace the petition in the Gregorian collect with the conclusion of the collect in the Missale Gallicanum vetus and the Gelasian sacramentary (no. 463):

Almighty God, who through your only-begotten Son Jesus Christ overcame death and opened to us the gate of everlasting life: Grant that we, who celebrate with joy the day of the Lord's resurrection, may be raised from the death of sin by your life-giving Spirit.

18. Massey H. Shepherd Jr., *The Oxford American Prayer Book Commentary* (New York: Oxford University Press, 1950), 163.

19. Paul Zeller Strodach, *The Church Year* (Philadelphia: United Lutheran Publication House, 1924), 151–152.

20. Thomas Aquinas, *Pange, lingua, gloriosi corporis,* stanza 3, translation from *The Hymnal 1982,* no. 329.

21. Donald Hall and Sven Birkerts, *Writing Well,* 7th ed. (New York: HarperCollins, 1991), 4. The reference to greeting cards was deleted in the 8th ed. (1994), p. 3.

22. Dante, *The Divine Comedy: The Inferno* XXI, 80–81, trans. John Ciardi.

23. The actual text of these two brief acclamations varies slightly in Roman, Episcopal, and Lutheran use, but the forms are similar and the meaning is the same.

24. *Apostolic Constitutions* 2.7.57.

25. Lancelot Andrewes, *Preces Privatae,* beginning of the Intercession for Morning Prayers for a Week, I. Sunday, abbreviated.

26. *Book of Common Prayer,* 372.

27. Martin Luther, *Treatise on the New Testament, that is the Holy Mass,* in *Luther's Works* 35:98.

28. Augustine, *The City of God,* Book X. Noted by Frank C. Senn, *Protestant Spiritual Traditions* (Mahwah, N.J.: Paulist Press, 1986), 27.

29. Luther, 35:99.

30. Donald Attwater, *Eastern Catholic Worship* (New York: Devin-Adair, 1945), 164.

31. Translation by August W. Kjellstrand, revised in *Lutheran Book of Worship,* no. 247.

32. *Service Book and Hymnal,* no. 162, translated by John Wesley.

33. *The Book of Common Worship* of the Church of South India (New York: Oxford University Press, 1963), 16.

34. *Formula of Concord,* Solid Declaration VII, in *The Book of Concord,* ed. Theodore G. Tappert, et al. (Philadelphia: Muhlenberg Press, 1959), 575.

35. Augustine, *Confessions* 7.10.

36. William Harry Turton, "Thou who at thy first Eucharist didst pray / That all thy church might be forever one," *The Hymnal 1982,* no. 315.

37. *Didache* 9.4.

38. Magnus Landstad's hymn "A multitude comes from the east and the west / To sit at the feast of salvation," *Lutheran Book of Worship,* no. 313, has made the image familiar to Scandinavians. See also Luke 13:29.

39. John Chrysostom, homily 24.4.

40. Augustine, *Sermon* 272.
41. Augustine, *Sermon* 227.
42. Liturgy of St. Basil.
43. *The Hymnal 1982,* no. 312.
44. See Luther, *The Large Catechism* IV.85, in *The Book of Concord,* 446.

Chapter Eight: Hymns: Hallowing Song

1. The Lutheran *Common Service Book* (Philadelphia: Board of Publication of the United Lutheran Church in America, 1918) provided in an index the denominational affiliation of each author represented in the collection of hymns, but subsequent books have not continued the practice. To learn, for example, that James Montgomery was a Moravian is interesting but largely irrelevant to appreciating his hymn "Angels from the Realms of Glory." To find Sarah Doudney identified not by denomination but as "novelist" is even less helpful.

2. *Lutheran Book of Worship* (Minneapolis: Augsburg Publishing House; Philadelphia: Board of Publication, Lutheran Church in America, 1978), no. 144; originally "Good Christian Men, Rejoice and Sing," as in *Service Book and Hymnal* (Minneapolis: Augsburg Publishing House; Philadelphia: Board of Publication, Lutheran Church in America, 1958), no. 109. In *The Hymnal 1982* (New York: The Church Hymnal Corporation, 1982), and *The Presbyterian Hymnal* (Louisville, Ky.: Westminster John Knox Press, 1990) the first line is "Good Christians All, Rejoice and Sing."

3. *The Hymnal 1982,* no. 596.
4. *The Hymnal 1982,* no. 525, stanza 3.
5. *Book of Common Prayer* (New York: The Church Hymnal Corporation, 1979), 59, 71–72.
6. *The Hymnal 1940* (New York: Church Pension Fund, 1940), no. 297, stanza 2.
7. *Lutheran Book of Worship,* no. 560.
8. *The Hymnal 1940,* no. 95 (ii); *Service Book and Hymnal,* no. 99; *The Presbyterian Hymnal,* no. 113.
9. *Lutheran Book of Worship,* no. 552, stanza 2.
10. Hosmer's hymn, written in 1888, is deeply dependent upon John Ellerton's hymn "God of the living, in whose eyes / Unveiled thy whole creation lies," written in 1859 and revised and enlarged in 1867.
11. *Pilgrim Hymnal* (Boston: Pilgrim Press, 1958), no. 469; *Service Book and Hymnal,* no. 600.
12. *Dryden's Poems,* ed. Bonamy Dobree (New York: Dutton, 1954), 17.
13. *The Hymnal 1982,* no. 657; *The Presbyterian Hymnal,* no. 376; *Lutheran Book of Worship,* no. 376.

14. *Lutheran Book of Worship*, no. 321.

15. *Common Service Book*, no. 515; *The Hymnal 1940*, no. 468.

16. *Common Service Book*, no. 517.

17. Sir Philip Sidney, *The Defense of Poesy*, in Robert Kimborough, ed., *Sir Philip Sidney: Selected Prose and Poetry*, 2d ed. (Madison, Wis.: University of Wisconsin Press, 1983), 102–158, particularly 110.

18. Samuel Johnson, *Lives of the Poets: Milton*, in *The Norton Anthology of English Literature*, vol. 1, ed. M. H. Abrams, et al. 6th ed. (New York: Norton, 1993), 2408.

19. Augustine, *Confessions* IX.6.

20. Friedrich Schleiermacher, *Die Weinachtsfeier*, quoted in *The Oxford American Hymnal*, ed. Carl F. Pfatteicher (New York: Oxford University Press, 1930), iii.

21. *The Hymnal 1940*, no. 179, stanza 4; *Service Book and Hymnal*, no. 227. *The Presbyterian Hymnal*, no. 576 revises the second line, "Thy children 'neath the western sky"; further revised in *Lutheran Book of Worship*, no. 274. The stanza is omitted in *The Hymnal 1982*.

22. *The Hymnal 1940*, no. 265, stanza 4; *Service Book and Hymnal*, no. 322.

23. *The Presbyterian Hymnal*, no. 151, stanzas 3–4; *Lutheran Book of Worship*, no. 170, stanzas 5–6.

24. *The Hymnal 1982*, no. 360, stanza 2.

25. *Lutheran Book of Worship*, no. 375, stanza 4.

26. *The Hymnal 1982*, no. 360, stanza 4.

27. *Lutheran Book of Worship*, no. 515.

28. In the *Common Service Book* (1918), no. 47; and in the *Hymnal of the Moravian Church* (1969), no. 100. In *Lutheran Book of Worship*, the hymn appears in a composite translation, "O Christ, Our Light, O Radiance True," no. 380.

29. *Lutheran Book of Worship*, no. 37.

30. *The Hymnal 1982*, no. 59; *Service Book and Hymnal*, no. 1.

31. Augustine, *Confessions* IX.12.

32. *Common Service Book*, no. 72, stanza 4; *Service Book and Hymnal*, no. 517.

33. *The Hymnbook* (Richmond, Va.: Presbyterian Church in the United States, The United Presbyterian Church in the U.S.A., Reformed Church in America, 1955), no. 81; *Common Service Book*, no. 492. *Service Book and Hymnal*, no. 161, and *Pilgrim Hymnal*, nos. 9, 10, spell the troublesome word "aweful."

34. *Service Book and Hymnal*, no. 206, stanza 6.

35. *The Hymnal 1982*, no. 199; *The Presbyterian Hymnal*, nos. 114, 115; *Lutheran Book of Worship*, no. 132.

36. *Lutheran Book of Worship*, no. 347, stanza 2.

37. *The Presbyterian Hymnal*, no. 76; *The Hymnal 1982*, no. 458.

38. *The Hymnal 1982*, no. 623.

39. *The Hymnal 1982,* no. 424.

40. *Lutheran Book of Worship,* no. 76.

41. *The Hymnal 1940,* no. 262, stanza 2; *Service Book and Hymnal,* no. 317.

42. *The Hymnal 1982,* no. 293, stanza 3.

43. *Lutheran Book of Worship,* no. 228.

44. *The Hymnal 1982,* no. 681, stanza 3.

45. Augustine, *Confessions* IX.7.

46. Preface to *The English Hymnal* (London: Oxford University Press, 1975).

47. See Robert W. Jenson, *America's Theologian: A Recommendation of Jonathan Edwards* (New York: Oxford University Press, 1988), 182.

Chapter Nine: Baptism: Hallowing Life and Death

1. See, for example, *In Memoriam,* especially sections 35 and 123, also "Break, Break, Break," "The Kraken." See also Algernon Charles Swinburne, *The Triumph of Time,* lines 257–304 (stanzas 33–38); John Ruskin, *Modern Painters,* vol. 1, part 2, section 5 ("of Truth of Water"), chap. 3, especially the concluding two paragraphs; Dante Gabriel Rossetti, "The Sea-Limits."

2. James Hamilton-Patterson, *The Great Deep: The Sea and Its Thresholds* (New York: Random House, 1992), 165. See also W. H. Auden, *The Enchafed Flood or, The Romantic Iconography of the Sea* (New York: Vintage Books, 1967 [1950]).

3. See William Beebe, *Half Mile Down* (New York: Harcourt, Brace and Co., 1934), 175.

4. Hamilton-Patterson, 10.

5. Louis Bouyer, *Liturgical Piety* (Notre Dame, Ind.: University of Notre Dame Press, 1955), 161.

6. Bouyer, 181.

7. Gregorian sacramentary, no. 1837.

8. Bouyer, 175.

9. Hamilton-Patterson, 149, 150.

10. Hamilton-Patterson, 151.

11. Hamilton-Patterson, 151.

12. Hamilton-Patterson, 286.

13. Bouyer, 179.

14. *The Hymnal 1940* (New York: Church Pension Fund, 1940), no. 395; *Service Book and Hymnal* (Minneapolis: Augsburg Publishing House; Philadelphia: Board of Publication, Lutheran Church in America, 1958), no. 157.

15. *Book of Common Prayer* (New York: The Church Hymnal Corporation and the Seabury Press, 1979), 306–307. For a comparative discussion of this prayer in its Roman, Episcopal, and Lutheran forms, see

Philip H. Pfatteicher, *Commentary on the Lutheran Book of Worship: Lutheran Liturgy in Its Ecumenical Setting* (Minneapolis: Augsburg Fortress, 1990).

16. See above, pp. 89, 132, 150, 186.

17. See Richard Crashaw's poem "I am the Doore," no. 25 of his *Divine Epigrams.*

18. The list that follows is from *Baptism, Eucharist and Ministry,* Faith and Order Paper No. 111 (Geneva: World Council of Churches, 1982), 2–3.

19. Martin Luther, *The Babylonian Captivity of the Church* (1520), *Luther's Works* 36:68.

20. Luther, *Luther's Works* 36:58.

21. Luther, *Luther's Works* 36:58.

22. Luther, *Luther's Works* 36:63.

23. Martin Luther, *The Large Catechism,* in *The Book of Concord,* ed. Theodore G. Tappert, et al. (Philadelphia: Muhlenberg Press, 1959), 441.

24. Luther, *Luther's Works* 36:68.

25. Henry E. Jacobs, in *Works of Martin Luther,* vol. 1 (Philadelphia: Muhlenberg Press, 1943), 51–55.

26. Gustav Aulen, *The Faith of the Christian Church,* trans. Eric H. Wahlstrom and G. Everett Arden (Philadelphia: Muhlenberg Press, 1948), 380.

27. *Book of Common Prayer,* 322.

28. Luther, *Luther's Works* 36:68.

29. Luther, *Luther's Works* 36:59.

30. Luther, *Luther's Works* 36:69.

31. Luther, *The Large Catechism,* 442.

32. Jerome, *Letter,* 130.

33. Luther, *Luther's Works* 36:58, 61.

34. Luther, *Luther's Works* 36:60.

35. Richard G. Herbel, *Saint Augustine's House Newsletter,* Lent 1994.

36. Alternative Prayer of the Day for the First Sunday in Lent, *Lutheran Book of Worship* (Minneapolis: Augsburg Publishing House; Philadelphia: Board of Publication, Lutheran Church in America, 1978), 18.

37. John Donne, *Devotions upon Emergent Occasions,* Meditation XVII, in *John Donne: Poetry and Prose,* ed. Frank J. Warnke (New York: Modern Library, 1967), 338–339.

38. Donne, 339.

39. Martin Luther, *The Holy and Blessed Sacrament of Baptism,* in *Luther's Works* 35:39.

40. Luther, *Luther's Works* 35:30.

41. Luther, *Luther's Works* 35:31.

42. Luther, *Luther's Works* 35:31.

43. Athanasius, *On the Incarnation,* 54.

44. *Book of Common Prayer,* 214; *Lutheran Book of Worship,* 14.

45. John Athelstan Laurie Riley, "Ye Watchers and Ye Holy Ones," *The Hymnal 1982* (New York: The Church Hymnal Corporation, 1985), no. 618, stanza 2.

46. For a splendid expression of the unity of the family of God, see George Wallace Briggs's hymn "Our Father, by whose servants / Our house was built of old," above, p. 170, and in *Service Book and Hymnal,* no. 248; *The Hymnal 1982* unfortunately omits the final stanza.

47. *Book of Common Prayer,* 245. The Lutheran rite since 1868 has used this same prayer.

48. Luther, *Luther's Work's* 36:60.

49. Martin Luther, "A Sermon on Preparing To Die," *Luther's Works,* 42:112.

Chapter Ten: The Source of Renewal

1. *Daily Prayer,* comp. Eric Milner-White and George W. Briggs (Oxford: Oxford University Press; London: Humphrey Milford, 1941), 4.

2. Dante, *Inferno* III.53 (lines 55–57 in the Italian), trans. John Ciardi. See T. S. Eliot, *The Waste Land,* line 63.

3. Henry Francis Lyte, "Abide with me, fast falls the eventide," in *The Presbyterian Hymnal* (Louisville, Ky.: Westminster John Knox Press, 1990), no. 542, stanza 2; also in *The United Methodist Hymnal* (Nashville: The United Methodist Publishing House, 1989), no. 700, stanza 2; also the *Service Book and Hymnal* (Minneapolis: Augsburg Publishing House; Philadelphia: Board of Publication, Lutheran Church in America, 1958), no. 576, stanza 2. In *Lutheran Book of Worship* (Minneapolis: Augsburg Publishing House; Philadelphia: Board of Publication, Lutheran Church in America, 1978), no. 272, this stanza curiously becomes stanza 3; *The Hymnal 1982* (New York: The Church Hymnal Corporation, 1985) inexplicably omits this stanza altogether.

4. G. K. Chesterton, *Orthodoxy* (London: Allen Lane, 1908), 150–152.

5. Augustine, *Confessions* I.1.

6. T. S. Eliot, *Little Gidding,* lines 239–242.

7. *Book of Common Prayer* (New York: The Church Hymnal Corporation and the Seabury Press, 1979), 375, the conclusion of Eucharistic Prayer D, the ecumenical Great Thanksgiving.

8. *Book of Common Prayer,* 101.

Index